Bampton Lectures

CHRISTIANITY & THE STATE IN THE LIGHT OF HISTORY

BY

T. M. PARKER

FELLOW AND CHAPLAIN OF UNIVERSITY COLLEGE
OXFORD

LONDON
ADAM AND CHARLES BLACK
1955

FIRST PUBLISHED 1955

A. AND C. BLACK LIMITED
4, 5 AND 6 SOHO SQUARE, LONDON W.1

MADE IN GREAT BRITAIN
PRINTED BY R. & R. CLARK, LTD., EDINBURGH

TH Gripper

July 1956.

⁰/₆ £3

CHRISTIANITY AND THE STATE IN THE LIGHT OF HISTORY

EXTRACT FROM THE LAST WILL
AND TESTAMENT OF
THE REV. JOHN BAMPTON
CANON OF SALISBURY

'. . . I give and bequeath my Lands and Estates to the Chancellor, Masters, and Scholars of the University of Oxford for ever, to have and to hold all and singular the said Lands or Estates upon trust, and to the intents and purposes hereinafter mentioned; that is to say, I will and appoint that the Vice-Chancellor of the University of Oxford for the time being shall take and receive all the rents, issues, and profits thereof, and (after all taxes, reparations, and necessary deductions made) that he pay all the remainder to the endowment of eight Divinity Lecture Sermons, to be established for ever in the said University, and to be performed in the manner following:

'I direct and appoint, that, upon the first Tuesday in Easter Term, a Lecturer may be yearly chosen by the Heads of Colleges only, and by no others, in the room adjoining to the Printing-House, between the hours of ten in the morning and two in the afternoon, to preach eight Divinity Lecture Sermons, the year following, at St. Mary's in Oxford, between the commencement of the last month in Lent Term, and the end of the third week in Act Term.

'Also I direct and appoint, that the eight Divinity Lecture Sermons shall be preached upon either of the following subjects—to confirm and establish the Christian Faith, and to confute all heretics and schismatics— upon the divine authority of the holy Scriptures—upon the authority of the writings of the primitive Fathers, as to the faith and practice of the primitive Church—upon the Divinity of our Lord and Saviour Jesus Christ—upon the Divinity of the Holy Ghost—upon the Articles of the Christian Faith, as comprehended in the Apostles' and Nicene Creed.'

CONTENTS

CHAP.   PAGE

I. BIBLICAL CONCEPTIONS OF CHURCH AND STATE   I

II. THE PRE-CONSTANTINIAN CHURCH   22

III. THE CONSTANTINIAN REVOLUTION AND THE CHRISTIAN
     ROMAN EMPIRE   43

IV. BYZANTINE THEOCRACY   65

V. THE WESTERN CHURCH AND THE POST-ROMAN WORLD   81

VI. THE MEDIEVAL ATTEMPT AT PAPAL THEOCRACY   99

VII. THE BREAK-UP OF THE MEDIEVAL WORLD   120

VIII. REFORMATION ECCLESIOLOGY AND THE STATE   143

     EPILOGUE   171

     INDEX   173

CHAPTER I

BIBLICAL CONCEPTIONS OF CHURCH AND STATE

A study of the historical relations of Christianity with the political State may well begin with the enunciation of a truism—one which, nevertheless, is fundamental to the subject. The truism is this: there cannot be a relationship unless there are at least two terms to be related. The title chosen for these lectures implies the existence of the Christian religion, organised in the Church, side by side with the political organisation of the State. But we have not far back to go in history to reach a time in which the notion of relationship between Church and State would have been incomprehensible. In ancient times, as in primitive society to-day, there existed no problem of Church and State, for the very good reason that no church, in the modern sense of the word, existed. In Western Europe, at least, it requires some imagination to visualise such a state of affairs; yet we must do so in order to approach the subject fruitfully.

When first human society emerges from the darkness of its origins we can discern in it only one pattern, not the interlacing series of human associations now found in those societies which claim with the best right the title of civilised communities. Instead we find a unified society, within the framework of which all human life is conducted, of which the separate parts, kindreds, families and the like, are subdivisions only, and in no sense competitors. In particular is this true of man on his religious side. Religion in early times, and for very many centuries, was a matter not for the individual or group, but for the community as a whole. Man's church was his state, his state his church.[1]

Two reasons especially may be singled out for this phenomenon:

(1) To primitive man the distinction between natural and supernatural is unreal, for to him the whole universe is an object of

[1] The very term *ecclesia*, derived from the word used for Greek assemblies of citizens, illustrates the point. Ancient language had no word for a *religious* grouping distinct from the political organisation.

I

wonder and he sees no difference between nature and that which seems to transcend it. The changes of the weather, the growth of plants and animals, human birth, life and death are neither more nor less miraculous than events we now should consider outside the order of nature. Still less has primitive man any idea that his relationship to deity is essentially different from his relationship to his fellow man, or, indeed, to what we call inanimate nature. His whole life is full of mystery and it does not occur to him to divide it into compartments. He draws no sharp line between a realm of nature in which all is predictable and ultimately comprehensible and another world in which his reason is transcended by realities he can neither fully comprehend nor clarify. All is possible in every aspect of existence and at best he can draw a distinction only between the probable and the impossible: he does not even distinguish between the animate and the inanimate. Two recent American authors, Professor and Mrs. Henri Frankfort, have thus described primitive man's attitude to the universe: 'The ancients, like the modern savages, saw man always as part of society, and society is imbedded in nature and dependent upon cosmic forces. For them nature and man did not stand in opposition and did not, therefore, have to be apprehended by different modes of cognition. . . . Natural phenomena were regularly conceived in terms of human experience . . . and human experience was conceived in terms of cosmic events. . . . The fundamental difference between the attitudes of modern and ancient man as regards the surrounding world is this: for modern, scientific man the phenomenal world is primarily an "It"; for ancient—and also for primitive—man it is a "Thou".' The meaning of this last phrase is explained thus: '"Thou" has the unprecedented, unparalleled, and unpredictable character of an individual, a presence known only in so far as it reveals itself.'[1]

With such a *Weltanschauung* ancient man cannot think of what we are accustomed to regard as the 'spiritual' side of life as in conflict with, or even separable from, the material or the secular.

[1] H. and H. A. Frankfort, John A. Wilson, Thorkild Jacobsen, *Before Philosophy: The Intellectual Adventure of Ancient Man* (Pelican Books, London, 1949), pp. 12-13.

So, just as we cannot accurately discriminate between primitive natural science and primitive religion, neither can we between sacred and secular, other-worldly and this-worldly, aspects of primitive society. In this way there is reconciled into unity both the Philistine empiricism unsympathetic observers find in primitive religion and Cato's observation, *Maiores nostri, religiosissimi mortales*.

(2) This merging of religion in secular life becomes even more apparent when we consider that the personnel of Church and State (if we can use those terms at all) is identical in early times. One of the achievements of anthropology has been to bring to light the original relationship of kingship and priesthood. An early king is normally the supreme priest of his nation: so much are the two functions tied up together that the abolition of kingship at Athens and Rome necessitated the retention of the *title* for religious purposes. At Athens the ἄρχων βασιλεύς, at Rome the *rex sacrorum* kept, without the secular authority that had once gone with it, the hated title, so that sacrifices which only a king could make pleasing to the gods might still be offered.[1] Indeed that is putting the matter far too low. A primitive king is a priest, because he is a god. Grotesque as the idea of kingly divinity may appear today to us whose idea of godhead is coloured by centuries of monotheism, it was very real to our ancestors, who believed in 'gods many, and lords many'.[2] To a polytheist godhead means, necessarily, not something *ex hypothesi* unique, but little more than a nature superior to ordinary manhood, which a king can well be conceived to possess. So, in the words of Sir James Frazer, 'in early society the divinity that doth hedge a king is no mere figure of speech'.[3] Not merely is the king descended from the race of the gods, as, for example, every Pharaoh of Egypt was believed to be born through the agency of Rē, the sun-god, who assumed temporarily the form of the earthly father and impregnated the queen.[4] He is himself a great god. Pharaoh was Horus and, in accordance

---

[1] Sir J. G. Frazer, *The Golden Bough: A Study in Magic and Religion* (2nd edit., London, 1900), i. 7 and reff. there cited. [2] I Cor. viii. 5.

[3] Sir J. G. Frazer, *Lectures on the Early History of Kingship* (London, 1905), pp. 131-132.

[4] *Before Philosophy*, pp. 81-82. Cf. Frazer, *Kingship*, pp. 171-173.

with the habit of primitive thought not to regard personality as quite exclusive, would also be identified, at least as a figure of speech, with other gods.[1] As a god, the king is responsible for natural phenomena and provides for his people. 'He', it is said of Pharaoh, 'is one who makes the Two Lands brighter than [does] the sun-disc. He is one who makes the land greener than [does] a high Nile. [Thus] he has filled the Two Lands with strength and life. Nostrils are chilled if he inclines towards rage, so that he is peaceful in order that the air may be breathed. He gives food to those who follow him and supplies provisions to him who treads his path.'

This same text goes on to identify the king with the *ka*, the 'double' of each man, which acted as the sustaining and creative 'form' of his body throughout life.[2] 'The ruler was thus seen as the constructive vital force of Egypt, creating and sustaining.'[3]

Such exalted functions are irksome: divinity to some African kings today involves a life of incredible ceremonial complexity and restraint, as it did to the Pharaoh, of whom Diodorus Siculus said: 'The hours of both the day and the night were laid out according to a plan, and at the specified hours it was absolutely required of the King that he should do what the laws stipulated and not what he thought best.'[4] *Il faut souffrir pour être dieu.* We read of kings who can never leave their palaces, of one who may never even rise from his chair.[5] In some cases such taboos are due to the idea that the king's person is dangerous: his 'sacred organism', as Frazer puts it, 'is . . . electrically charged with a powerful spiritual force which may discharge itself with fatal effects on whatever comes in

---

[1] *Before Philosophy*, p. 84; Frazer, *Kingship*, p. 148. Cf. the text quoted, *Before Philosophy*, p. 96, cf. p. 74. 'He is (the fashioning god) Khnum for all bodies, the begetter who brings people into being. He is (the kingly goddess) Bastet, who protects the Two Lands. . . . He is (the punishing goddess) Sekhmet against him who transgresses his command. . . .'
[2] Quoted, *Before Philosophy*, p. 95.
[3] *Before Philosophy*, p. 96.
[4] πρῶτον μὲν τοίνυν οἱ βασιλεῖς αὐτῶν βίον εἶχον οὐχ ὅμοιον τοῖς ἄλλοις τοῖς ἐν μοναρχικαῖς ἐξουσίαις οὖσι καὶ πάντα πράττουσι κατὰ τὴν ἑαυτῶν προαίρεσιν ἀνυπευθύνως, ἀλλ' ἦν ἅπαντα τεταγμένα νόμων ἐπιταγαῖς, οὐ μόνον τὰ περὶ τοὺς χρηματισμούς, ἀλλὰ καὶ τὰ περὶ τὴν καθ' ἡμέραν διαγωγὴν καὶ δίαιταν. . . . διατεταγμέναι δ' ἦσαν αἵ τε τῆς ἡμέρας καὶ τῆς νυκτὸς ὧραι, καθ' ἃς ἐκ παντὸς τρόπου καθῆκον ἦν τὸν βασιλέα πράττειν τὸ συντεταγμένον, οὐ τὸ δεδογμένον ἑαυτῷ (I. 70).
[5] Frazer, *The Golden Bough*, i. 313 *sqq.*; cf. i. 238-239. *Kingship*, pp. 117-118 (i. 70).

contact with it'.[1] In others, they depend upon the belief that contact with the outside world might harm the king and lose the people the benefit of his divine magical powers. 'If I were to go outside this compound,' said a chief of Etatin (in Nigeria) to an English Commissioner, 'I should fall down dead on returning to this hut.' Clearly, in societies which think like this, there cannot be even a rudimentary separation of Church and State, for the head of the State is himself an incarnate deity and so necessarily also the priest, the intermediary between his people and heaven. Professor Evans-Pritchard, in his interesting Frazer Lecture for 1948, has re-examined the notion of divine kingship by means of a study of the polity of the Shilluk in the Sudan, and has suggested certain modifications of ideas earlier held. He sums up the matter thus: 'In my view kingship everywhere and at all times has been in some degree a sacred office. *Rex est mixta persona cum sacerdote.* This is because a king symbolises a whole society and must not be identified with any part of it. He must be in the society and yet stand outside it and this is only possible if his office is raised to a mystical plane. It is the kingship and not the king who is divine.'[2] One could hardly state in a more striking way the absolute unity of primitive society on (to use misleading modern terminology) both religious and secular levels. In the light of it we can appreciate the full force of the expression used,[3] Professor Evans-Pritchard tells us, by the Shilluk when their king dies—*piny bugon*, 'there is no land'. As he puts it, 'The centre of the Shilluks' world has fallen out'. With the death of the god-priest-king, society collapses until the link with heaven is restored by the installation of a new king, at once religious and political head of the community.

The Old Testament

It is, I am sure, with such a background in mind that we ought to approach Biblical conceptions of the relationship between the human community in its religious aspects and the human com-

[1] *The Golden Bough*, i. 319.
[2] E. E. Evans-Pritchard, *The Divine Kingship of the Shilluk of the Nilotic Sudan* (Cambridge, 1948), p. 36. [3] *Op. cit.* p. 19.

munity as what we should call a State. Especially, of course, is this approach necessary to the Old Testament. It is not now seriously questioned that the Old Testament books emerged from a society steeped in folk-lore and sharing the common experiences of mankind in its development from earliest times. So the ideas of the inseparability of religion and politics and of the sacred character of kingship must have been familiar to the Hebrews as the common assumptions of all their neighbours, if not as their own.

Yet it is a remarkable fact that those assumptions in their crudest form are by no means characteristic of Israel. This is especially the case with the notion of the divinity of rulers. It is true that in Semitic usage the name 'king' (*melek*) was applied both to the tribal deity and to the human ruler. It is also no doubt true, as Dr. A. Lukyn Williams says, that: 'the fact of the identity of titles tended to strengthen enormously the king's position'.[1] A fact no less important in Israel than elsewhere, since Yahweh, like other gods, was described as King. Yet, of any formal ascription of deity to Israelite kings little trace remains. Ps. 87 twice (vv. 2 and 6) describes the princes of Israel as *Elohim*: yet it goes on immediately to insist that, if they are unjust, they will die like men and fall like one of the princes. In Ps. 45 the king is called unequivocally 'God' (*Elohim*) and yet, almost immediately afterwards Yahweh is spoken of as the king's *Elohim*. No doubt the underlying idea is not far from the ethnic notion of the king as an incarnation of deity (as among the Shilluk the king is the incarnation of Nyikang, the national god).[2] Yet of divine honours given to the ruler there is little sign. C. F. Burney's interpretation of the evidence seems a fair one: 'the titles *Elim*, *Elohim* are used in some few cases of *men*, as possessors of God-like power or rank'.[3] An older commentator, Dr. Alfred Barry, puts the matter well when he says: 'In Ps. viii. 5 man is but "a little lower than God". They who are exalted by Him above their fellows catch by that exaltation some brighter reflection of the Divine majesty.'[4] Something of this kind is no

---

[1] H.D.B., ii. 840. Art. 'King'.   [2] Evans-Pritchard, *op. cit.* p. 17.
[3] C. F. Burney, *Old Testament Theology* (London, 3rd edit., 1923), p. 15.
[4] A. Barry, *The Teacher's Prayer Book* (London, 16th edit.), n.d. p. 220b.

doubt meant when the king is described as God's son or as an 'angel of God'.[1] In other words, the tradition of monotheism, the strength of which, even in very early times, has probably been underestimated by many expositors dominated by nineteenth-century presuppositions of gradual and inevitable progress, was sufficient to clip and restrain the old tendency to political apotheosis. Of no King of Israel could it be said as of a Pharaoh of Egypt that he was the cause of natural phenomena.[2]

Matters stand otherwise when we consider the idea of the ruler as priest. The facts can perhaps best be brought out by a rapid survey of the chief phases of Israel's chequered constitutional

[1] Cf. II Sam. vii. 14, xiv. 17-20. Cf. Ps. cx. 2.

[2] Of recent years much attention has been paid to the possible connection between Jewish pre-exilic ritual and a presumed Near-Eastern cult pattern in which the king plays a part in securing the polity of the land. The matter is still under discussion by scholars, but it seems clear that, whatever the truth about it, any magical efficacy attributed to the Israelite king's person fell short of strictly divine power. *Vide* Norman H. Smith, *The Jewish New Year Festival* (London, 1947), who refers to the earlier literature and scouts the notion of a close connection between Hebrew and Babylonian polity rites involving the participation of the divine king. 'We should hold it to be very unlikely that the Hebrew-Israelitish kings ever took the part of the god in any ritual ceremony, but that they were regarded as being possessors of *mana* is beyond question' (p. 218). This view is reinforced by one of the latest writers on the subject, Professor Henri Frankfort, in his *Kingship and the Gods: A Study of Ancient Near Eastern Religion as the Integration of Society and Nature* (Chicago, 1948). 'The Hebrews, though in the Near East, were only partly of it. Much is made nowadays of Canaanite and other Near Eastern elements in Hebrew culture, and a phenomenon like Solomon's kingship conforms indeed to the type of glorified native chieftainship which we have characterised in the preceding paragraph. But it should be plain that the borrowed features in Hebrew culture, and those which have foreign analogies, are least significant. In the case of kingship they are externalities, the less important since they did not affect the basic oddness of the Hebrew institution. If kingship counted in Egypt as a function of the gods, and in Mesopotamia as a divinely ordained political order, the Hebrews knew that they had introduced it on their own initiative, in imitation of others, and under the strain of an emergency' (pp. 338-339).'The Hebrew king normally functioned in the profane sphere, not in the sacred sphere. He was the arbiter in disputes and the leader in war. He was emphatically not the leader in the cult. The king created the conditions which made a given form of worship possible. . . . But the king played little part in the cult. He did not, as a rule, sacrifice; that was the task of the priests. He did not interpret the divine will; that again was the task of the priests, who cast lots for an oracle. Moreover, the divine intentions were sometimes made known in a more dramatic way when prophets—men possessed—cried, "Thus saith the Lord." These prophets were often in open conflict with the king precisely because the secular character of the king entitled them to censor him' (p. 342). The whole discussion in Professor Frankfort's 'Epilogue' (pp. 337-344) is illuminating. He regards the Israelitish king as a 'third type of King' in the ancient Near East, distinct alike from the Egyptian and Mesopotamian types. 'The relation between the Hebrew monarch and his people was as nearly secular as is possible in a society wherein religion is a living force' (p. 341).

history. For kingship was but one episode in the story of a nation as variable in its forms of polity as modern France. We need not here consider the many and complicated problems connected with the exact historicity of the picture of each period presented in the Old Testament as we have it. Our concern is with ideas rather than with facts, for it is the ideas, as presented by the completed Old Testament books, which were to be formative for the Christian Church, the historic relations of which with political society form our theme. Only occasionally will critical problems demand attention.

As the narrative stands, then, we find a period of nomadic, pastoral society at the dawn of Israelite history, a type of life under patriarchal rule which exists to this day in Arabia and Central Asia. As one might expect, in such conditions the unity of the religious and the social community is absolute. There is no professional priesthood, not even of the inchoate form to be found in Central Asian Shamanism. The head of the tribe is its priest, ruler and intermediary with heaven all at once. Some aura of quasi-divinity may attach to this position, but such notions, if any there were, are too vague and shadowy seriously to affect the tradition. It is an idyllic age, in which the minuteness and close unity of the Chosen People make any notion of a problem in the relation between religion and mundane life out of the question.

In the Mosaic Age, however, we find a new and slightly more complicated picture. It was for the polity he attributed to Moses that Josephus coined the now famous expression 'theocracy'. 'Some legislators', he says, 'committed political authority to monarchies, some to oligarchies, others to the people. But our legislator had no regard to any of these forms, but he ordained our government to be what, by doing violence to words, may be termed a "theocracy", by ascribing the authority and the power to God.' [1] His interpretation of his phrase is coloured by later ideas and by his aim of presenting Judaism in a favourable light to

[1] οἱ μὲν γὰρ μοναρχίαις, οἱ δὲ ταῖς ὀλίγων δυναστείαις, ἄλλοι δὲ τοῖς πλήθεσιν ἐπέτρεψαν τὴν ἐξουσίαν τῶν πολιτευμάτων. ὁ δ' ἡμέτερος νομοθέτης εἰς μὲν τούτων οὐδοτιοῦν ἀπεῖδεν, ὡς δ' ἄν τις εἴποι βιασάμενος τὸν λόγον, θεοκρατίαν ἀπέδειξε τὸ πολίτευμα, θεῷ τὴν ἀρχὴν καὶ τὸ κράτος ἀναθείς (Cont. Apion. ii. 16).

Gentiles, but the word he invents does convey well the spirit of the Mosaic system. Moses himself is the appointed prophet, to whom God reveals His will, and as such both the religious and the political leader of the people. So far there is no breaking of the identity of religious and political society, for, as Josephus well expresses it: 'Moses did not make religion a part of virtue, but he saw and ordained other virtues to be parts of religion; I mean justice, and fortitude, and temperance, and a universal agreement of the members of the community with one another.'[1]

Nevertheless we can see in the arrangements stated to have been made by Moses something else, namely the germ of a distinction between the religious and the more secular sides of a polity. For, though Moses himself led and controlled worship, Aaron is represented as being appointed by Divine command what might be called Moses' 'Vicar General in Spirituals', and later Judaism regarded him and his descendants as the only lawful possessors of the priesthood—a position which carried with it, besides the conduct of worship, the interpretation of the religious law. The historicity of this incipient dualism is, as is well known, doubtful, for the origins of the Jewish priesthood are a disputed problem. What matters, however, is that the idea was to be formative in later times.

The times of the Judges, which followed, were regarded later as a warning and stood to other periods of Jewish history in much the same relation as do Stephen's reign or the period of the Commonwealth to the main tradition of English history. They were an age of expedients, of personalities setting up *ad hoc* régimes, thought of as without positive example for the future. Yet it is of interest to us that we see in them once again the idea of dualism in a new form, in the cases in which political heroes are guided by independent prophets, Barak by Deborah or, at the end of the period, Saul, the first king, by Samuel, who had himself originally combined the twin functions of Moses.

---

[1] οὐ γὰρ μέρος τῆς ἀρετῆς ἐποίησε τὴν εὐσέβειαν, ἀλλὰ ταύτης τὰ μέρη τἆλλα συνεῖδε καὶ κατέστησε, λέγω δὲ τὴν δικαιοσύνην, τὴν κατεργίαν, τὴν σωφροσύνην, τὴν τῶν πολιτῶν πρὸς ἀλλήλους ἐν ἅπασι συμφωνίαν (*ibid.*).

The mention of Samuel introduces us to a period of notable change, with the establishment of Israelite monarchy. Students need hardly to be reminded that the Bible preserves two discordant streams of tradition about its origin. One, assumed to be the older, regards kingship as God's gracious gift to his people. The other treats it as the result of wilful apostasy from the true divinely authorised polity of Israel, effected by an unimaginative people in the interests of unintelligent imitation of surrounding nations. To an age which found monarchy oppressive this latter historian would have said: *Vous l'avez voulu, George Dandin.*[1] We may suppose the earlier narrative to come from the Augustan Age of David and Solomon, the later from the time of Solomon's oppressive rule, or the epoch in which monarchy, undermined by bad kings and revolutions, was tottering to its fall.

But even more interesting for our purpose is the relation of the Israelitish kings to the national religion, though, despite the reverence felt for the Lord's Anointed, there is little trace of divinity attributed to the king;[2] yet, at least in the early days of kingship, the king fulfilled sacrificial functions—a practice abhorrent to later Jewish orthodoxy. Saul offered sacrifice,[3] as did David,[4] who also, like Solomon, blessed the people.[5] David, too, on at least one occasion, wore the linen ephod, the garment of priesthood.[6] The king was also the controller of the national religion, appointing chief priests,[7] and dismissing them.[8] He could, within

[1] Molière, *George Dandin*, Act I, sc. 9.

[2] 'There are no such traces of taboos around Hebrew royalty as are found among other primitive nations' (Joseph Jacobs, art. 'King' in *The Jewish Encyclopaedia*, vol. vii (New York and London, 1904), p. 501. This is perhaps too strong, but substantially true. It has been suggested that anointing was considered necessary only when a new *dynasty* began (as in the case of Saul, David, Joshua or Joash), the four instances mentioned in the Old Testament, but this seems unlikely. *Vide* Jacobs, *ibid.*) If, as some think, Ps. 110 is pre exilic, the title priest may have been given him officially. 'Thou art a priest for ever, after the order of Melchizedek' (Ps. cx. 4). *Vide* W. O. E. Oesterley, *The Psalms* (London, 1939), ii, 461, 463.

[3] I Sam. xiii. 1-14. His offence seems to have lain rather in refusing to wait for Samuel than in performing the liturgical act himself. In the case of Uzziah the Chronicler (writing from the standpoint of a later age) regards his burning of incense in the Temple as a serious usurpation of priestly function (II Chron. xxvi. 16-21. But cf. II Kings xvi. 12).

[4] II Sam. vi. 13 and 17.

[5] II Sam. vi. 18, I Kings viii. 14, II Kings iii. 4.

[6] II Sam. vi. 14.   [7] II Sam. viii. 17.   [8] I Kings ii. 27 and 35.

limits, control worship.[1] Indeed, so effective was royal control over religion, that the two great cult reforms of this period are represented as wholly the work of Hezekiah and Josiah,[2] just as the great apostasies were due to royal precept or example.[3] In view of all this it is a relatively minor point to find that the economic side of the cultus was under royal control: *e.g.* the building and repair of the Temple.[4]

Monarchy in Israel was both sacred in itself and closely concerned with sacred matters. Indeed, there appears no very effective rival to it in the sphere of religion. For, if prophets and priests rebuke erring kings, theirs is but a temporary and informal assertion of the spiritual power against the temporal. In the days of the monarchy, the Israelite Church was emphatically a state-church or, better, a unified 'nation-church'.

In the nature of things the Exile, which destroyed the monarchy, enhanced the power of the professional priesthood, which was the only authority left to lead the nation. Difficult as it is, from the fragmentary nature of the sources, to disentangle the history of the Return, it would seem that there was at least one abortive attempt to restore kingship, probably upon the basis of a close alliance between king and priesthood, which was crushed by the Persian overlords. The mysterious disappearance of Zerubbabel,[5] the original civil governor, who seems to have been of Davidic descent, may indicate this. It would seem as if those who worked for restoration could not envisage Israel without a king. Ezekiel's Utopian scheme for a new polity (Ezek. xl-xlviii) makes provision, albeit a somewhat grudging one, for a 'prince' (*nasi*)[6] as leader of the Israelite people in their attendance at worship, supplier of the means of sacrifice and bearer of civil power. But he is a very limited monarch and it is severely chastened monarchy which is envisaged. The prince is warned to avoid the land-grabbing and oppressive customs of the old kings,[7] whilst even the administra-

[1] II Kings xvi. 10-16.   [2] II Kings xviii. 3-6, xxii, xxxiii. 1-25.
[3] *E.g.* Jeroboam I (I Kings xii. 26-33), Ahab (I Kings xvi. 30-33), Manasseh (II Kings xxi. 109).   [4] I Kings v-vi, II Kings xii. 4-16, xxii. 3-7.
[5] Ezra ii. 2, Haggai i. 1, ii. 2, Zech. iii. 8-10, iv, vi. 9-15.
[6] Ezek. xlvi, cf. xliv. 3, xlv. 17.   [7] Ezek. xlv. 8-22, xlvi. 16-18.

tion of judgement belongs to the priesthood and not to him.[1] He is little more than the clerically controlled churchwarden of the Temple.

Under Persian rule such schemes could be no more than chimerical. The continuance and strength of the Messianic hope—a vast subject not to be entered upon here—shows the latent strength of the monarchical and legitimist principles in Judaism, for the increasing power and prestige of the priesthood and of the professional expounders of the Pentateuchal Law never wholly removed from Jewish minds the idea that kingship was a divinely instituted and therefore permanent institution. Israel became an ecclesiastically organised nation, a Church in modern phrase, far more from force of circumstances than from conviction.[2]

The Maccabean revolt led, almost by accident, to a period of High Priestly rule, when Israel from 160 to 37 B.C. was ruled rather in the manner of the Papal States. The leadership of the revolt against Antiochus Epiphanes's attempt to suppress Judaism as a religion fell into the hands of Mattathias, the head of the Hasmonean priestly family, and his famous sons. Judas, the original leader after Mattathias's death, seems never to have assumed the High Priesthood,[3] but Jonathan, his brother, was made High Priest by

---

[1] Ezek. xliv. 24.

[2] W. O. E. Oesterley holds that from the days of Hosea there had been a current of thought opposed to the very idea of monarchy (cf. Hos. x. 9, 'O Israel, thou has sinned from the days of Gibeah'—i.e. from the time of the election of Saul, whose home was at Gibeah. Cf. Hos. ix. 9). This would be connected with the anti-monarchical narrative in I Sam. and the very cautious approval of monarchy in Deut. xvii. 14-20, coupled with warnings against the characteristic vices of the Israelite monarchy. Oesterley associates this with Ezekiel's plan for a *principate* instead of a monarchy (Ezek. xxxiv. 23-24) and thinks that the absence of any reference to a king in Deutero-Isaiah, together with the application of the name there to Yahweh, shows the anti-monarchic sentiments of the prophets (cf. 20. xli. 21, xliv. 6). On this view Haggai and Zechariah are neo-royalists, opposed by a 'theocratic' party, whose views have not survived to the same extent. But all this seems to overlook the fact that, as Deuteronomy shows, the ideas of monarchy and theocracy are not incompatible. Nor does the application of the term 'king' (*melek*) to God, prevent its application to anyone else. Indeed it has been suggested that it was first applied to man as God's representatives since MLK is such a usual Semitic term for a god (*vide* A. Lukyn Williams in H.D.B., ii, 840 *sqq.*). If the anti-monarchical 'theocratic' idea was so influential it is difficult to explain the survival of Messianism. On the use and misuse of Josephus's coined term 'theocracy' *vide* Kautzsch in H.D.B., extra vol., pp. 629-630. W. O. E. Oesterley and T. H. Robinson, *A History of Israel*, vol. ii (Oxford, 1932), pp. 99-103. [3] Oesterley and Robinson, *op. cit.* p. 241.

Alexander Balas, the pretender to the Seleucid throne, in 152 B.C.,
though it would seem that he was not recognised as such by the
more religious element in Judaism. But in 140 B.C. a third brother,
Simon, was formally elected by the people as both 'High Priest'
and 'Captain and Governor' (ethnarch) of the Jews and priests.[1]
But it is interesting to find in the record of this event the evidence
that the more religiously minded Jews thought this a *pis aller*. 'The
Jews and priests were well pleased that Simon should be their
governor and high priest for ever, *until there should be a faithful
prophet*.' The verbal contradiction implies the notion that the plan
lacks direct divine sanction and that even priestly rule without
prophetic guidance was thought a bad thing.

Indeed, the actual record of the Hasmonean priest-kings, most
of them anything but edifying models either of priesthood or of
kingship, amply justified this diffidence. To religious Jews there
was always something incongruous in a High Priest who was also
a warrior. Bloodily suppressed revolts on the part of the *Chasidim*,
or pietist party, against the priest-kings showed the depth of this
feeling. There are few more terrible pictures of degraded priesthood in history than that given by Josephus of Alexander Jannaeus
(102–76 B.C.) feasting with his concubines whilst watching the
dying agonies of eight hundred crucified Jewish rebels, before
whose eyes, as they hung on their crosses, he had already mas-
sacred their wives and children.[2] Few lamented when the family of
priestly liberators, as they had originally been, was swept away,
even though their lay successors, the flamboyant Idumean Herods,
whose history approaches authentic Hollywood standards of
spectacular vice and crime, were no less unpopular. Herod the
Great, indeed, posed as a Jewish king of the old type, and, by
sumptuously rebuilding the Temple, deliberately recalled the
memory of Solomon. But he never succeeded in winning recognition as the Lord's Anointed. Henceforward Judaism fell more and
more deeply under the foreign yoke, until the wild theocratic
revolts of A.D. 66 and 132 ended in the destruction of the Jews as a
nation.

[1] I Macc. xiv. 41.   [2] *Antiq.* xiii. 380.

To sum up what can be gleaned of Old Testament attitudes to Church and State relations from our copious, but not very precise, evidence:

(1) Israel, like all other early peoples, had no idea of Church and State as separate communities. Nation and 'Church' were one, even though a distinction can be drawn by the outside observer between secular and religious activities and, at least to some degree, between religious and secular leaders.

(2) The ideal of government is at all times conceived as (to borrow Josephus's useful term) 'Theocracy'. Yahweh is the ultimate and only true King of Israel, who communicates His will to national leaders, whether prophets, kings or priests.

(3) Formal kingship was a development of the eleventh century B.C. in Israel. Probably regarded originally by all Israelites as a good development, a gift by Yahweh of a personal representative of Himself to His people, it came, in the light of events, to be viewed by an increasing minority as a mistake, even as an apostasy from the rule of God mediated by prophets. But the older idea survived and took eventually the form of the Messianic hope, the expectation of an ideal king to be given to Israel when the nation proved worthy of him.

(4) The experiment of priestly monarchy, arising almost by chance in the Maccabean rebellion, was in the nature of things received in mixed fashion. The pious always suspected it: they were shocked at the spectacle of warrior-priests and doubtful of the motives of the Hasmoneans. As time justified their suspicions, the majority of the Jews were content to see the Levitical monarchy supplanted even by foreign rule. Sir Edwyn Bevan has well summed up the matter: 'It appears to be a question whether it was not at great spiritual cost that the Jewish people allowed itself to be launched by the sons of Hashmon upon a career of carnal strife. For the Jewish community could not be amenable to the same laws as ordinary nations; it was, as we said, more like a church; and the laws of a church's life were in that degree the true laws of its being. . . . Just as, according to the Mosaic law, Levi had to renounce many of the things possessed by his brethren

because of his pre-eminent and sacred vocation, so perhaps, the peculiar vocation of the Jewish community entailed inevitably the deprivation of certain rights belonging to men whose kingdoms are only kingdoms of this world. . . . And when we judge this struggle by its fruits, the same doubts are suggested. The war of the Greeks with the Persians, the wars of independence in modern Europe, resulted in the enriching and ennobling of national life; but what was the issue of the battling of Judas and his brethren? The establishment of a dynasty by whose dominion the national life was poisoned, and whose presence at the altar the religious denounced as a pollution. Perhaps this explains why the general conscience of Judaism so soon allowed the memory of Judas and his brethren to fade, why it ultimately abstained from putting any book of *Maccabees* in its sacred canon. The Israelite has a history which at too many points rises to catch the radiance of heaven for him to make much account of such titles to fame as he would, after all, have in common with the Mahdists of the Sudan.'[1]

(5) Nevertheless, the nationalistic fervour aroused by the Maccabees, survived in another form to be the basis of Zealotry. This, by the time Christianity appeared, divided the allegiance of Jewry with the quietist attitude which, whether in its Sadducean realist or opportunist form, or in the more positive world-renouncing ethic of some forms of Pharisaism, adopted the view that Israel's destiny was to be a church rather than a nation, a religion rather than a political state, at least until it should please God to restore again the kingdom to Israel.[2]

The New Testament

Passing now into New Testament times, we must enquire what new idea or changed conception of religious and political society and their relations were added as a result of the revelation of Jesus Christ to those accumulated in the Church of the Old Covenant. We may recall first of all the well-known fact that the time of

[1] Edwyn Bevan, *Jerusalem under the High Priests* (London, 1904), p. 99.
[2] Acts i. 6.

Christ's ministry and the greater part of the following Apostolic Age fell in a period of intense political crisis for all Jews. It was the incubation phase of the nationalistic revolt which finally broke out in A.D. 66. The Gospels give many indications of the tension between those on the one hand who believed, by conviction or from expediency, in acquiescence in foreign rule and those on the other who were becoming committed to violent revolution. Inasmuch as Judaism was primarily a religious fraternity this cleavage of opinion produced what would now be called a problem of Church and State. For it was upon religious grounds that the revolutionaries aspired to political freedom. We can understand something of the feelings involved if we recollect the part played by the notion of Pakistan in recent Indian history.

Hence, the primary question of the hour was that of the right of heathen rulers to obedience, and it was a question which no religious movement of the time could avoid answering. It is, therefore, remarkable that comparatively little is said, in our Lord's recorded teaching, upon this burning topic. Clearly He was exposed to much pressure. His ministry raised hopes among the theocratic nationalists that He might prove to be their awaited leader, and such expectations, the Gospels make clear, were shared even in the circle of His immediate disciples. St. John's Gospel represents Him as withdrawing once, lest His hearers should actually 'come and take him by force, to make him a king'.[1] For no doubt, as in the case of John the Baptist, 'all men mused in their hearts whether he were the Christ or not'.[2] The immediacy of the matter is indicated also by its prominence in the Passion narratives, where one can see the opposed pressure, that of the disciples urging Him to use force[3] and that of His enemies, who likewise connect Him with Messianism but only to the extent of fearing Him as a reformer and potential revolutionary. Indeed the poignancy of the Passion story consists largely in the fact that Jesus had to play the difficult role of claiming Messiahship, either by implication or explicitly, whilst at the same time showing that His claim involved a radically different interpretation of the Messiah's office from that

[1] John vi. 15. [2] Luke iii. 15. [3] E.g. Luke xxii. 49-50.

16

current among the Jews. His immediate followers persisted to the end in seeing Him as a militaristic conqueror: 'Lord, shall we smite with the sword?'[1] was their question at the crisis of the arrest. Even after the Resurrection they are preoccupied with the thought of the restoration of Israel's kingdom, presumably in material form.[2] On the other hand, His enemies equally regarded Him as a potential revolutionary.

Dr. Wilfred Knox has drawn attention to the divided state of opinion among the Jews about allegiance to the Roman Empire in the first century A.D., showing that it was not a clear-cut issue between Pharisees and Sadducees, as a superficial reader of the Gospel evidence might assume.[3] Some of the Pharisaic party were opposed to militant nationalism,[4] no less than the Sadducees. Christ's ministry, we must realise, took place in a land distracted by confused political arrests and cross-currents.

It is in the light of these facts that we must consider our Lord's attitude to civil government, as represented in those records which constitute our only evidence for it.[5] What can be gathered about this? On the one hand it seems clear that Christ rated civil government as a thing of secondary importance compared with the great issues of religion which it was His primary purpose to impress upon men.[6] He spoke deprecatingly of the whole system of enforced political obedience, as it existed in His world. One cannot miss the irony in the sentence: 'The kings of the Gentiles exercise

[1] John xxii. 49.   [2] Acts i. 6.

[3] 'Church and State in the New Testament', *J.R.S.*, vol. xxxix (1949), pp. 23-30.

[4] Cf. Dr. W. O. E. Oesterley. 'The Pharisees thought that Roman overlordship was to be regarded as a just retribution for national sin, and was therefore to be submitted to in resigned humility until it should please God to remove the yoke' (Oesterley and Robinson, *History of Israel*, ii. 366). He quotes as typical of the attitude Gamaliel's reported advice about early Christianity in Acts v. 35-39.

[5] No attempt is made here to consider the problem of how far the experiences and problems of the early Church have coloured the transmission of Jesus's recorded teaching. Such a task is highly specialised and can hardly fail to be subjective in its findings; from the historian's point of view it is almost hopeless. So the Gospels must, for our purpose, be taken as they stand. And it is worth while remembering that what was formative for the future was what Jesus was *believed* to have taught.

[6] We may suppose, too, that, especially with His knowledge of the disaster in which the political ferment of the time would end, He knew that, not merely to take sides, but even to give political issues prominence in His teaching, would divert attention from His redemptive mission.

lordship over them: and they that exercise authority upon them are called benefactors. But ye shall not be so.'[1]—a passage which may shed further light upon the famous declaration: 'My kingdom is not of this world'.[2] He declined on one occasion even to enter into a question of rights of property, as irrelevant to His office. 'And one of the company said unto him, Master, speak to my brother, that he divide the inheritance with me. And he said unto him, Man, who made me a judge or a divider over you? And he said unto them, take heed and beware of covetousness: for a man's life consisteth not in the abundance of the things which he possesseth.'[3]

But, despite this, it would be rash to conclude that Jesus considered civil government a matter wholly beneath His notice or totally irrelevant to faith. For there remains, general considerations apart, the famous and classic injunction to render to Caesar the things that are Caesar's and to God the things that are God's. We may take it in its traditional sense, despite the late Dr. Loewe's ingenious attempt to make the question which provoked it—that of the lawfulness of paying tribute to Caesar—refer rather to the morality of 'gazing upon' idolatrous symbols on Roman coins.[4] If so, the saying is a simple but far-reaching ruling that Christians are to obey established civil authority in all matters which do not trench upon God's prior rights. It is certainly in this sense that the Christian Church understood it, from the beginning.

[1] Luke xxii. 25-26.   [2] John xviii. 36.   [3] Luke xii. 13-15.

[4] For this *vide* Herbert Loewe, '*Render unto Caesar': Religious and Political Loyalty in Palestine* (Cambridge, 1940). No doubt Dr. Loewe is right in calling attention to the fact that more was involved in the problem of tribute than those not familiar (as Dr. Loewe was) with contemporary Jewish disputes would realise. Though the Emperor's picture was not thought of as abhorrent, since, though forbidden to Jews, image-making was not regarded as wrong for Gentiles, yet the coin symbols associated with heathen deities or those which appeared to extend imperial authority to the whole universe, were objectionable. So Dr. Loewe thinks that the question put to Christ concerned primarily this matter of the occasion of idolatry which the use of Roman coins might provide and ingeniously suggests that the phrase attributed to the questioners in their flattering of Christ (οὐ γὰρ βλέπεις εἰς πρόσωπον ἀνθρώπων (Matt. and Mark), οὐ λαμβάνεις πρόσωπον (Luke)) has been misunderstood and in its original Aramaic form referred to what was technically known as 'gazing upon' coins (pp. 104-106). But it is difficult to believe that the whole incident (which fits too well into the political background of the period) can have been so completely distorted in transmission and the obvious preoccupation of Dr. Loewe's book —the date of which is significant—with the desire to demonstrate historic Jewish loyalty to *de facto* civil authority makes one regard his argument with reserve.

Here the connection between our Lord's teaching and that of the Apostolic Age is clear. Two familiar passages from St. Paul's Epistle to the Romans and the First Epistle of St. Peter enforce in the strongest terms the conscientious duty of obedience to the civil power and have become *loci classici* in all later Christian theology dealing with this subject.[1] But one aspect of them has perhaps not received the notice which it should be paid. The most obvious feature of these injunctions and their insistence that secular power has not merely the *conditio possidentis* in its claim upon us, but is instituted by God and so, by divine sanction, its claims weigh upon conscience.[2] But it is no less true that the Apostolic attitude seems to echo something of that depreciation of secular power as such which we have seemed to see in the teaching of Jesus. The ruler's function is seen chiefly as the maintenance of order and the punishment of the wicked—a negative duty—even though 'the praise of them that do well' is also mentioned.[3] In the whole New Testament, indeed, there is nothing of the Hellenic conception of the State as existing for the good life or as being the chief or only educative influence upon human nature. At most one can trace a conviction in St. Paul that the civilisation of the Roman Empire and its ordered unity has made a useful vehicle for the spread of the Gospel; and this is to be inferred from his policy, as described in Acts, of cultivating the sympathy of the Roman authorities, rather than from any words of his.[4] Of any Christian duty to contribute actively to that civilisation nothing is said. Moreover, if we adopt the exegesis favoured by St. Augustine,[5] which sees in the mysterious entity, mentioned in I Thess. ii. 7, which 'now letteth' the coming of Antichrist, the Roman Empire, the Apostle would appear to think of the civil power he knew as

[1] Rom. xiii, I Pet.

[2] 'Wherefore ye must needs be subject, not only for wrath, but also for conscience sake.' (Rom. xiii. 5).

[3] This attitude seems to derive partly from Jewish tradition. 'R. Hanina the Prefect of the Priests said: Pray for the peace of the ruling power, since but for fear of it men would have swallowed up each other alive' (*The Mishnah*, tr. Herbert Danby (Oxford, 1933), *Pirqe Aboth*, 3.2, p. 450). For the later influence of this idea upon Reformation divines *vide infra*.

[4] It has been suggested that St. Luke heightened the picture of St. Paul's loyalty to Rome for apologetic purposes, Acts being partly an apology for Christianity as a law-abiding religion. [5] *De Civ. Dei*, xx. 9.

CHRISTIANITY AND THE STATE

serving no higher function than that of delaying the appearance of a nakedly blasphemous régime. We shall see a not dissimilar view held by Tertullian.

The thought leads on naturally to the consideration of another and different strand of New Testament teaching, the apocalyptic notion of earthly power as essentially and always opposed to the Kingdom of God and as therefore destined to be destroyed when God at the climax of history—shortly to be expected, as most Christians probably thought—lays bare His arm. Without entering into the complex problems surrounding the Book of Revelation, we cannot fail to recognise this as one of its leading ideas, especially when we compare it with earlier apocalyptic literature. In this aspect the Christian Church appears in the last resort to be hostile to the powers that be. No call to active rebellion is necessarily implied. But the attitude, taken by itself, negatives the very idea of any permanent or close co-operation of Church and State. We must pay due attention to this aspect of New Testament thought if we are to gain a balanced idea of New Testament teaching as a whole, which is not simple or uniform. For the apocalyptic outlook is deeply embedded in it, as all recent theological research has demonstrated, and cannot be ignored. It is to be seen, for example, even in one of the least militant of New Testament books, St. John's First Epistle, which roundly declares that 'the whole world lieth in the evil one', whilst 'we' (the Christians) alone are 'of God'.[1] It would be a bold man who asserted that the New Testament, taken as a whole, supports an immanentist view of human society.

Indeed, the New Testament appears to lend far more countenance to the less 'social' type of thought to be found in the Old, than to the conception of Israel as a closely knit nation-church-state which had prevailed in pre-exilic days. The one element taken from this façon de penser, that of Davidic monarchy, is swallowed up and transformed by a Messianism which transfers the Messiah's primary sphere of activity from earth to heaven. That is not surprising in a Church which had come to assert the

---

[1] I John v. 18-19, R.V.

Messiah's Deity. But, besides this, we must remember, as said above, that even the reverence for civil authority, inculcated by apostolic *dicta*, is much modified upon analysis by the low view taken of the function of Caesar, and still more by the complementary current of apocalyptic thought, which was accepted as basic by those same authors. Later we shall see the working out of these apparent antinomies in the earlier centuries of the Church's life. Though the principle is often disregarded or disputed, the historic Church's understanding of the New Testament is by no means the least useful commentary upon the meaning of its contents. Indeed it may be that the study of the whole of Church history is necessary to a full understanding of the Bible and of its seminal ideas. 'What I do thou knowest not how; but thou shalt know hereafter.'[1] It is in that conviction partly that these lectures have been conceived.

[1] John xiii. 7.

CHAPTER II

THE PRE-CONSTANTINIAN CHURCH

It is in one sense unfortunate that the period in the history of the Christian Church for which our evidence is slightest, its first three centuries, should also be its heroic age. For inevitably tradition, in the vague form in which it reaches the man in the street, has painted far too highly coloured a picture of this epoch. The cult of its martyrs, which began contemporaneously with the persecutions (as documents such as the *Martyrdom of Polycarp* show) and reached its climax later, in the fourth century, led inevitably to a dramatisation of the martyrs' age—one which has lasted ever since. To the average man the idea of the age of persecution still conjures up a picture of a continuous, unrelieved reign of terror, with death in its most horrible forms a daily occurrence and the Church living permanently in catacombs in the manner of partisans during a war. The various attempts to represent the period in novel, play or film show more clearly than anything else the popular conception.

Serious students have long understood that the reality was far less dramatic. Indeed a school of minimisers, of whom Merrill [1] is the best representative, would have us believe that most Christian accounts of persecution are legendary, and that to be a member of the Church in the first three centuries was an easy and almost enjoyable experience. It is an unhappy thing that historical study should so often proceed, by a kind of Hegelian dialectic, from one exaggeration to its opposite, and it must be confessed that ecclesiastical history has suffered more from this process than other branches of the science. For oscillation between opposed misconceptions, whether caused by prejudice or by simple inability to weigh evidence, prevents the building up of that imaginative picture of the past, as accurate as critical study can make it, which also enables us to evaluate and distinguish the thoughts of our ancestors.

Let us, then, begin our discussion of the first phase of Chris-

[1] Elmer Truesdell Merrill, *Essays in Early Christian History* (London, 1924).

tianity's relationship to the State by trying to imagine what professing the faith involved in everyday life. It meant, of course, abstention from pagan worship in the first place. To absent oneself from conventional religious observance nowadays is not very difficult in most countries with which we are familiar; the hold of religion is slight and few people interest themselves in observing whether their neighbours go to church or not. Moreover, city populations are so vast that, even if State religion were more popular than it is, a recusant minority could easily mislead even the curious. Places of worship are numerous and the parish as such has ceased to meet for worship, except in the countryside. In early Christian times conditions were far different. The chief cause of this was the intimate association of religion with secular life mentioned in the last chapter—or rather the lack of any distinction between them. Religion was not conceived as a private matter or as the affair of any organisation other than the State itself. Sacrifice, the characteristic activity of ancient religion, was carried out at State expense and by State officials: the city, the real unit of the ancient world, even under the Roman Empire, worshipped as a whole.[1] Thus Ephesus, in St. Paul's day, was, as its town clerk said, corporately the 'temple-sweeper', the devotee of Great Artemis.[2] Indeed, an attentive reading of that tumultuous scene in the Ephesian amphitheatre, described in Acts xix, gives a vivid picture of corporate civic religion in classical days. The mob which filled it, bawling for two hours without pause, 'Great Artemis of the Ephesians',[3] was (as the town clerk showed by his formal dismissal of them after his pacificatory speech) nothing less than a highly irregular and informal assembly of the *ecclesia*, the citizen parliament, meeting in its ordinary place.[4] It would seem as if some

[1] See Fustel de Coulanges, *La Cité antique* (3e édit., Paris, 1870), the classic statement of the place of religion in classical civilisation, esp. Libre III, chaps. vi-viii: 'L'État et la religion étaient si complètement confondue ensemble qu'il était impossible non seulement d'avoir l'idée d'un conflit entre eux, mais même de les distinguer l'un de l'autre'.

[2] νεωκόρον τῆς μεγάλης Ἀρτέμιδος (Acts xix. 35).

[3] Μεγάλη ἡ Ἄρτεμις Ἐφεσίων (Acts xix. 34).

[4] The fact that the same word ἐκκλησία in Christian parlance meant the assembly of the Christian brotherhood for worship brings home even more forcibly the identity of politics and religion among the contemporary pagans. For the association of religion with popular assemblies *vide* Fustel de Coulanges, *op. cit.* pp. 192-193.

at least of the crowd mistook the riot for a kind of pagan re-
vivalist service, since 'the more part knew not wherefore they
were come together'[1] and yet joined lustily in the frenzied invoca-
tions of the municipal goddess without cognisance of the economic
motives which had caused Demetrius the silversmith and his associates to begin this mass protest against Christian propaganda.

So, to stand aside from the prevailing cultures in the first century meant virtually to boycott political life, since public functions
were inextricably mixed up with religious observances and public
office involved a duty of leading worship. It involved also social
difficulties, since to avoid some degree of participation in such
domestic ceremonies as libations to the gods at meals was as
difficult as absenting oneself from pre-breakfast family prayers or
from grace before meals when visiting friends in Victorian days.
Indeed, as the space St. Paul devotes to the casuistic problems
aroused thereby reminds us, the very *pièce de résistance* at a friend's
dinner might well be meat from the carcase of a sacrificed animal
—polluted food to anyone who regarded the gods as demons in
the way most Christians did.[2] Anyone familiar with Jewish life today will realise the awkward social situations brought about by
religion in daily intercourse.[3]

If religious dissidence involved of necessity what seemed anti-
social behaviour, the positive obligations imposed upon Christians
by their own system of worship and by a moral code which seemed
to pagans impossibly puritanical, made it impossible for a Christian
to escape notice in contemporary society. He was bound to be a
marked man. The idea of the Church as a successful Fifth Column,
or underground movement, in a pagan *milieu* vanishes into thin air
as an historical myth. Indeed, a Christianity completely concealed
is almost bound to be to some extent a conforming and com-

---

[1] Acts xix. 32.

[2] I Cor. x. 19-33. Cf. Acts xv. 20 and 29, xxi. 25, Rev. ii. 14 and 20.

[3] The importance of religion within the family circle cannot be underestimated and
must have increased acutely the difficulties of Christians. 'A man's foes shall be they of his
own household' was a text with special force among early Christians (Matt. x. 36). For
family religion in classical civilisation, *vide* Fustel de Coulanges, *op. cit.* Livres I and III,
'La famille antique est une association religieuse plus encore qu'une association de nature',
p. 40.

promised Christianity.[1] In fact, therefore, contemporaries usually knew fairly well who were the Christians among them, and even who were their leaders. When the Smyrnean mob in A.D. 155 clamoured for official punishment of the Christian bishop, Polycarp, no one had any doubt about his identity.[2] The cry of *Christianos ad leonem*[3] was rarely directed against nameless suspects.

Why then was the new religion not quietly stamped out? It seems clear that a determined and sustained persecution, for which the Roman Empire was not without the necessary resources, could have effected its destruction within the borders of the Empire within a comparatively short time. No doubt, as Tertullian said, the blood of Christians was a seed,[4] and the martyr's fortitude gained recruits for the Church. Nevertheless really ruthless and intelligent witch-hunting could have reduced the Church to a tiny knot of lucky escapees at best, and certainly could have checked the steady growth which in fact went on up to the time of Constantine.

How then must we envisage the character of the persecution which undoubtedly took place? We are perhaps in a better position to understand its incompleteness and illogicalities than were our grandparents: we live ourselves in an age of extensive persecution, sometimes religious, though more often political or racial, and can observe the unsavoury phenomenon at first—or in this country, so far—at second hand. And, even though the persecutors of today enjoy the use of techniques unknown to Rome, and are for the most part more practical than the imperial Romans, yet there are frequently gaps in their comb. So we notice exceptions made for special reasons. (Goering is alleged to have said that it was he who decided who was a Jew and who was not.) We find

[1] The one apparently successful historical example of underground Christianity, in Japan between the seventeenth-century persecutions and the reopening of the country in the nineteenth century, shows this. Whilst some Christians had retained enough of their faith to make their reintegration into the Christian Church possible, others had to some extent distorted it. See Otis Cary, *A History of Christianity in Japan* (New York, 1909), i. 258 *sq.*, 336 *sq.*, cf. pp. 229, 294. A fuller account is given in I. Marnas, *La Religion de Jésus ressuscitée au Japon*, 2 vols. (Paris, 1896).

[2] *Martyrium Polycarpi*, §3, cf. §5.   [3] Tertullian, *Apologeticus*, 40.

[4] 'Plures efficimur quotiens metimur a vobis; semen est sanguis Christianorum' (*Apol.* 50).

areas where for some reason the ordinary policy cannot be applied, as when in Finland, though allied to Germany, Jews were left alone. We find fluctuations of outlook on the part of governments, as when foreign and domestic policy caused a change in the U.S.S.R.'s attitude to the Orthodox Church. We note degrees of proscription. (It is a fact that the profession of Christianity has never been illegal *ipso facto* in Russia.) There are, too, the innumerable cases of men under persecution finding means to bribe or to arouse the pity of individual officials. All of these hindrances to a policy of 'thorough' we find operating *mutatis mutandis* in the Roman Empire.

If we wish to make a true picture of the position of the Church in these centuries there is an historical analogy with several points of resemblance in the history of our own country. In England, from the sixteenth to the eighteenth century, Roman Catholicism was a proscribed religion. The profession of it was not illegal, but the faithful practice of it inevitably made one obnoxious to the law in several ways, for it was an offence to attend Papist rites and equally an offence *not* to frequent those of the Established Church. Priests of the Roman Church were officially outlaws and the active propagation of Roman Catholicism a crime, punishable in some cases by death. All Papists were subject to severe civil disabilities. Yet Roman Catholicism was by no means a wholly concealed religion. Its worship was for long periods carried on in secret conventicles, yet, especially towards the end of the times of persecution, Roman Catholic services took place, sometimes without concealment, and nearly always were well known to take place. The government knew with some exactitude the numbers and names of the recusants, of whom official returns were made by the parishes. Priests were frequently known as such, and yet not hunted down. It was only occasionally, when foreign dangers or political crises stirred and roused public opinion, that real intensive hunting down of Papist priests and large-scale imprisonments and executions were indulged in. The religious laws themselves varied from time to time with changes in legislation and the degree of their application far more. At times the forbidden faith was openly tolerated or even enjoyed high influence. It was the professed religion of the King of England for three years and that of three Queens Consort.[1] Even at times when the law was more strictly applied one finds extraordinary anomalies, for example: the Papist musicians, Byrd and Tallis, maintained in Elizabeth's Chapel Royal,[2] or the aid offered by Archbishop Bancroft to the Appellant secular priests in their suit against the Jesuits.[3] There could hardly be a better example of the differences there can be between the letter of the law and officially proclaimed policy on the one hand and actual historical fact on the other than the history of the penal laws against English Roman Catholicism.

An existence not unlike that of the English Papists was led by the Christian body in the Roman Empire. Officially, by the second century at least, the policy of Rome towards Christians was embodied in Tertullian's famous phrase, *non licet esse vos*.[4] In practice this benevolent intention to exterminate was implemented only at intervals and then rarely with utter resolution. It has become a commonplace to say that before Decius's edict in the middle of the third century no persecution was universal or continuous. Outbreaks recurred here and there and went on for periods of weeks or months. There were trials, imprisonments, tortures, executions, then peace, in the phrase of the time, returned to the Church of this

---

[1] James II, Henrietta Maria (wife of Charles I), Catherine of Braganza (wife of Charles II), Mary of Modena (wife of James II). I do not include the death-bed conversion (following a long period of half-hearted adherence) of Charles II, nor the reputed conversion of Anne of Denmark, Consort of James I.

[2] See art. 'Byrd' in *Grove's Dictionary of Music and Musicians*, 4th edit., by H. C. Colles (London, 1940), i. 509–514, and 'Tallis', v. 256–260. A passage from the former well describes some of the complex anomalies of these times:
'It is a curious fact that while Byrd was actually in the possession, under a Crown lease, of lands confiscated from a Catholic recusant, and was a member of the Chapel Royal on the accession of James I, both he and his family were not only regularly presented in the Archidiaconal Court of Essex from 1605–12, and probably later, but since the year 1598 had been excommunicated by the same ecclesiastical body. A *modus vivendi* under these circumstances must have been rather difficult, and Byrd can only have remained secure from more serious consequences by the protection of powerful friends.' Cf. *D.N.B.* vol. iii (London, 1908), p. 577: 'From 1605 until 1612, and probably later, it was regularly recorded that the Byrd family were "papisticall recusants". Mrs. Byrd in particular, if the reports of the minister and churchwardens of Stondon are to be believed, seems to have been very zealous in making converts.'

[3] See Roland G. Usher, *The Reconstruction of the English Church* (New York and London, 1910), vol. i, chaps. 7 and 8.   [4] *Apol.* 4.

or that province or city, so rapidly sometimes that the martyred Bishop of Antioch, Ignatius, in the early second century, could hear of the cessation of persecution in his own city before he had been taken further from it than Asia Minor on his way to Rome for trial.[1] As time went on, such intervals became longer and more widespread, so that the third century is the story of two long 'Peaces of the Church', separated by a comparatively short, if fierce, series of attacks in the middle of the century.

Moreover, Christian writers could and did address memorials to the imperial authorities defending the harmlessness of their creed and asking for toleration. Christian propaganda, though rarely public, was widespread: the pagan pamphleteer, Celsus, complains of its frequency in pagan households.[2] The army itself was invaded by the new religion, which also made its appearance on more than one occasion in Caesar's household. Marcia, the Christian favourite of Commodus, could obtain an amnesty for those with whom she sympathised.[3] It is noteworthy that the Catechetical School of Alexandria, the lectures of which seem to have been open to pagan enquirers, flourished almost without a break at a time when the religion it existed to elucidate was unlawful.

The Church, then, was no hidden hand, however much excited pagans may have liked to consider it such. Its mysteries, it is true, were not open to the world, but this was due as much to the desire to close them to the profane as to fear of discovery by the authorities. The Church was a self-contained, exclusive body, but not one which concealed its existence. So, in studying its relation to the State, we must not imagine a struggle between an invisible conspiracy and a government trying without much success to bring it to light. Rather it was a fight between the State on the one hand and, on the other, an organisation which defended itself by endurance, by apologetic, by open challenge or by other public means short of armed resistance, going partially underground only when no other course was possible and never for long. If it was a conspiracy, it was one of the most open in mankind's history.

---

[1] *Ad Philadelph.* §10.   [2] Origen, *Cont. Celsum*, iii. 55.
[3] Hippolytus, *Philosophumena*, ix. 12.

Having tried thus to set the scene, let us go on to study the plot of the drama. Why did Rome persecute the Church? How did the Church regard Rome in consequence? To take the first question first. It is clear that up to the time of Nero there was no thought of Christianity's being unlawful as such. The Acts of the Apostles is at great pains to make this clear. Possibly, as has been suggested, that book is partly a *Tendenzschrift*, designed to demonstrate the law-abiding nature of the new religion whose first days it describes —the first Christian apology in fact: it may therefore lay undue stress upon the repeated refusals of Roman officials to convict St. Paul as a disturber of the imperial peace. But it cannot be painting a wholly unreal picture: to do so would defeat its supposed object. We can reach the same conclusion by observing the shock which the Neronian persecution undoubtedly gave the Church: it was, in the words of I Peter, ξένον,[1] a 'strange thing', to those who had not previously come into collision with the law of the Empire.[2] From the other side Tacitus confirms this by implying quite clearly that no attempt had been made by the authorities to crush Christianity since its Founder's crucifixion, which he seems (rather oddly) to regard as a piece of religious persecution on the part of Pilate.[3] The same writer asserts, no less clearly, that Nero's savage attack was a device to overcome the immediate difficulties caused to the Emperor by the rumours of his responsibility for the Fire of Rome.[4] Nevertheless, as so often happens, an isolated *coup de*

[1] I Peter iii. 12.
[2] This argument, of course, assumes the early dating of this document; it has not yet conclusively been put later than Neronian times.   [3] Tacitus, *Annals*, xv. 44.
[4] There has been of late a tendency to discredit Tacitus's apparent suggestion—his language is universally agreed to be vague—that the Christians were actually charged with incendiarism. A. Momigliano writes: 'The testimony of sources generally leaves no doubt that persecution was directed against the Christians as Christians, and we must suppose that Nero, in unloosing the attack, aimed rather at directing the fury of the people upon a section that was notoriously hated, and so winning back the favour of the mob, than at attributing the charge of firing Rome specifically to the Christians.' But he goes back upon this by writing elsewhere: 'it is likely that among the charges that were levelled at them [the Christians] was that of having set fire to Rome' (*Cambridge Ancient History*, x. 725 and 885). He argues in favour of a double tradition, one version of which made the Christians responsible for the fire, the other one making Nero's victims suffer merely as Christians, pointing out that Suetonius does not speak of any connection between the persecution of the Christians and the Fire of Rome. (*De Vita Caesarum*, Nero 16.) [Indeed Suetonius seems to classify the persecution among Nero's better deeds.] He thinks that the

théâtre becomes the origin of a policy and, by the early second century the suppression of the Christian faith is quite clearly an axiomatic—though perhaps not urgent—principle of imperial government.

The date and legal basis of this New—and very raw—Deal has become a classic problem of Roman and of Church history. No one believes, as once was thought, that Nero followed up his sensational devilries with a formal law against Christians. Tertullian's famous reference to an *institutum Neronianum*[1] as the basis of persecution can, especially in the mouth of a trained lawyer, mean only precedent, not a written enactment. It is inconceivable that, had there been a written law against the Church in the reign of Trajan (98–117), Pliny, his *Legatus* in Bithynia, should not know of it. Yet, it is quite clear from his much canvassed letter asking for directions that he does not.[2] He is, nevertheless, quite aware that Christianity is a religion under the ban of the Empire: he knows that trials of Christians take place, even though the accidents of his service have never afforded him an opportunity of hearing one, so that he is ignorant both of the procedure and the charges to be investigated. He could not conceivably write like this if any precise law existed: if he had done so Trajan's answer[3] would have been a sharp rebuke for wasting the Emperor's time rather than a commendation of Pliny's extempore decisions.

How are we to explain this anomaly, the absence of any statutory enactment side by side by a policy, already established, of persecution? The answer seems to be in our failure to remember one principle of Roman law. We are so well accustomed to the English constitutional principle that what the law does not specifically forbid it allows, that we forget that not all legal

admitted ambiguities of Tacitus's language (notably as to *what* he believes the Christians to be guilty of, or to have confessed to) result from an unconscious mixing of these two stories.

Professor I. W. Clayton has recently argued that the real cause of confusion is Tacitus's desire both to blacken Nero's character as a murderer of the innocent and at the same time to express his agreement with the popular estimate of Christians as dangerous criminals. ('Tacitus and Nero's Persecution of the Christians', *The Classical Quarterly*, xli. 81-85, July–Oct. 1947.) Views like this imply, of course, that Christianity could have been punished as such even before Nero's day: but they do not prove that it had been so punished.   [1] *Ad Nat.* i. 7.   [2] *Epp.* x. 96.   [3] x. 97.

systems work this way. An English citizen has a right to do anything he wishes, unless a specific law forbidding it can be produced.[1] Roman law, it is almost true to say, proceeded from the opposite assumption. To prove an absolute right the citizen must produce a law authorising it: failing this, the State can punish him for any activities it considers undesirable or anti-social. So, under their legal power of *coërcitio*, the right to compel obedience to what they considered proper, Roman magistrates possessed a very wide measure of discretion. 'This *coërcitio*', says E. G. Hardy, '. . . was for the state an extraordinary means of self-defence: it was not restricted to the regular rule of procedure: the offences or misdemeanours with which it interfered were not defined by any technical nomenclature, and the punishments which it inflicted were, if not arbitrary, at least not specified with any undeviating precision.'[2] It was Mommsen who first drew attention to the nonspecific nature of much Roman criminal law as the probable explanation of persecution of Christians going on without any specific anti-Christian legislation,[3] and subsequent study has done nothing to shake his view.

The conclusion is of importance. For, to quote Mommsen himself, it follows that 'the current notions of the so-called Christian persecutions suffer from the defective idea of the legal norms and legal practice prevailing in the Roman Empire: in fact the persecution of Christians was permanent like that of brigands and it was only that the regulations were sometimes applied more mildly or carelessly, sometimes more severely, whilst every now and then particularly enforced from above.'[4] This would leave the field

---

[1] 'Englishmen are ruled by the law, and by the law alone; a man may with us be punished for a breach of law, but he can be punished for nothing else.' (A. V. Dicey, *Introduction to the Study of the Law of the Constitution* (9th edit., London, 1939), p. 202.)

[2] E. G. Hardy, *Studies in Roman History*: First Series (London, 1906), p. 57.

[3] Theodor Mommsen, 'Der Religionsfrevel nach römischem Recht' in *Historische Zeitschrift*, Band 64 (1890), pp. 389-429.

[4] 'Die gangbaren Vorstellungen von den sogenannten Christenverfolgungen leiden unter der mangelhaften Anschauung der im römischen Reich bestehenden Rechtsnorm und Rechtspraxis; in der That war die Verfolgung der Christen stehend wie die der Räuber, und kamen nur diese Bestimmungen bald milder oder auch nachlässiger, bald schärfer zur Anwendung, wurden auch wohl einmal von oben herab besonders eingeschärft' Theodor Mommsen, *Römische Geschichte*, Band V (Berlin, 1885), p. 523, n. 2).

open for just such desultory and localised persecution as in fact we find, as well as for elasticity of method. Trajan's reply to Pliny illustrates this last point, in its ruling that Christians are not to be sought out, but merely punished if properly accused. Only when the attention of the executive is forcibly directed to the existence of Christians need they, for form's sake, be proceeded against. Apart from this the State can attack them or leave them alone as seems best. (For one need not suppose that the Roman Empire was wholly blind to the effect of persecution in sometimes stimulating a stagnating creed.)

If one can speak of a relationship between the Church and a hostile State, the relationship between Christianity and the Roman Empire in the first three centuries was, then, curiously undefined, even in enmity. But the more important question for us is, not under what precise formula Christians were persecuted, but why it was thought necessary to persecute them at all. Rome, it has often been pointed out, was not given to religious coercion. The Empire did not discourage the cults of local gods. The worship of the Emperor became universal by spontaneous popular action rather than by enforcement from above: it was in origin a genuine expression of loyalty in pagan form of the subjects, not a test of it.[1] In the case of the Jews, exemption from official polytheism and from Emperor worship was allowed, provided only that they sacrificed to Jehovah on behalf of the public authorities. Why then was Christianity singled out for attack? Several reasons may be seen:

(1) It is not strictly true that it *was* singled out. Other cults thought harmful were from time to time repressed and certain orgiastic forms of worship controlled. Magic rites thought dangerous to society were prohibited. When Manichaeism appeared in the third century it was persecuted as a public danger. Christianity is the most obvious, though not quite the only case of a religion thought not to merit the toleration Rome gave to most cults. Professor Last, indeed, has argued powerfully that 'the view that before the third century A.D. apostasy from the national gods was

---

[1] On the Emperor-cult see E. Beurlier, *Le Culte impérial: son histoire et organisation depuis Auguste jusqu'à Justinien* (Paris, 1891).

accounted in itself a crime should be examined with special care',[1] and in his view Christianity was at first persecuted as an immoral rather than as a dissident religion. If this view is correct Christianity stood in no different position from the other religions which felt the weight of Rome's arm.

(2) But Rome, being a community soaked through and through (like every state of its day) with polytheistic assumptions, had no understanding of a monotheistic religion. Once you have assumed a multiplicity of gods there is no logical objection to adding to the number: the more, in one sense, the merrier. Variety of cults is interesting and stimulating. So the spread of the Empire meant a glad incorporation of new deities, as, for example, the many Roman inscriptions in Britain to oddly named Celtic gods show. There was some amount of syncretistic identification of new gods with old, but this, on polytheistic principles, was not essential. Even those who were evolving the idea of a single Deity, worshipped under many names and manifestations, still supported, as in the parallel case of Hinduism today, the popular polytheism. Such an attitude meets a religion preaching a 'jealous God' with incomprehension. Why should men, even if they have a devotional preference, refuse to worship any gods but their own? Narrowmindedness—*obstinatio* is Pliny's word for it—and poverty of spirit seems the most natural answer. Such qualities ought to be stamped out of a world-state, with membership of which they are incompatible.

(3) The Jews could be allowed their irritating exclusiveness because tolerance here had proved to make for peace and order; the Romans no doubt knew of the Maccabean outbreak caused by Antiochus Epiphanes's intolerance. Judaism was a national religion and did not spread widely outside the Jewish race. But Christianity freely admitted all men willing to accept its faith and yet refused to let them practise the established religion. It looked, therefore, like a conspiracy of withdrawal from society, aiming at setting up a kingdom of its own. Thus the chronic fear of *imperia in*

[1] Hugh Last, 'The Study of the "Persecutions"' in *Journal of Roman Studies*, vol. xxvii (1937), p. 92.

imperio common to all authoritarian states made it seem an enemy of Rome: persecution followed by instinct.

(4) The populace reacted to Christianity even more instinctively than the government. Here were an odd, priggish and anti-social kind of men withdrawing from the vague, lighthearted, but very real comradeship of pagan worship and festivity. They must be bad citizens, who no doubt practised abominable rites in their own secret assemblies and perhaps plotted against the common weal, the *respublica*. In any case they were 'atheists', who neglected the gods whom all other men except Jews, whatever their private religious predilections, acknowledged. Such neglect would draw down the wrath of the gods upon the whole community. Hence arose a popular clamour which from time to time prodded the authorities to active persecution. For their part they were no doubt glad, like all rulers, to have scapegoats on whom could be laid the responsibility for public calamities, to their own exoneration. As late as Augustine's day it was a proverb in Africa: *Pluvia defit; causa Christiani sunt.*[1]

It may be noted that it is not true, as some have thought, that refusal to worship the Emperor was the prime reason for outlawing Christians. True, such a refusal, to the polytheistic mind which could appreciate no other reasons, suggested a *prima facie* suspicion of treason. But it is to be noted that not merely acknowledgement of the Emperor's deity, but also worship of 'the gods', the great, universally recognised deities, was demanded from Christians.[2] In addition they were normally required formally to reject Christ. It was not merely civic religion in the narrowest sense which Rome required of her subjects: paganism as such was

---

[1] *De Civitate Dei*, ii. 3. For other examples of the popular attitude see Tertullian, *Apol.* 40: 'Praetexentes sane ad odii defensionem illam quoque vanitatem, quod existiment omnis publicae cladis, omnis popularis incommodi Christianos esse in causam. Si Tiberis ascendit in moenia, si Nilus non ascendit in arva, si caelum stetit, si terra movit, si fames, si lues, statim Christianos ad leonem! adclamatur.' Cf. *Martyrium Polycarpi*, 3: τὸ πλῆθος . . . ἐπεβόησαν· Αἶρε τοὺς ἀθέους· ζητείσθω Πολύκαρπος. And 12: οὗτός ἐστιν ὁ τῆς ἀσεβείας διδάσκαλος, ὁ πατὴρ τῶν Χριστιανῶν, ὁ τῶν ἡμετέρων θεῶν καθαιρέτης, ὁ πολλοὺς διδάσκων μὴ θύειν, μηδὲ προσκυνεῖν τοῖς θεοῖς.

[2] '. . . aucun texte, avant le IIIᵉ siècle, n'établit que le motif propre de la poursuite contre les Chrétiens soit le refus qui les fait coupables de lèse-majesté. On les accuse plutôt, auparavant de manquer aux dieux de l'empire en général. . . .' (J. Zeiller in *Histoire de l'Église*, edd. A. Fliche and V. Martin, vol. i (Paris, 1946), p. 293.)

the established cult. And it is a great mistake to imagine that it was a dead, or even a dying faith. There had been much scepticism in the later days of the Republic, when Epicureanism was fashionable. But Augustus had set himself to revive traditional religion, and with considerable success: it was part of his plan for reinstating conscious *Romanitas* as the mainspring of political loyalty. Even the philosophers were not disbelievers in the gods, however much they thought themselves beyond the crude ideas of the vulgar. The gods could as well be fitted into their *Weltanschauung* as popular Hinduism into Hindu philosophy today. We must do the pagans the credit of attributing to them a belief in their own religion, and understand that the Christian refusal to worship the Olympian gods hurt them as deeply as their 'idolatry' did the Christians: 'But to us they *are* gods' was, according to Tertullian, their almost pathetic reply to the Christian denial of the divine status of the traditional objects of worship.[1]

The Christian Reaction

What effect upon Christian opinion had condemnation by the State under whose authority Christians lived and the hostility of the society of which that State was the embodiment? Two different attitudes can be traced, not always sharply distinguished and sometimes, indeed, mingling together in a curious way.

On the one hand there is the disposition one would expect, to accept fully the Apostolic doctrine that the powers that be are ordained of God and, in the light of it, to regard persecution as a hideous mistake on the part of the providentially ordained authority. (In a similar way the first Christians had accepted without doubt the authority of the Jewish Church and assumed that its crucifixion of the Messiah was a tragic error, soon to be rectified by the opening of the eyes of the leaders of Israel.) The early Apologists all seem to adopt the view that the Roman State, if only it could look at the matter reasonably, would see that the Christians are its best citizens, not disloyal or treacherous persons,

[1] *Sed nobis dei sunt.* Tertullian, *Apol.* 10 and 13.

so that it is in its own interests to tolerate them. This implies, of course, that the Roman Empire is a force for good and that alliance between it and the Christian Church is the ideal. The Apologists assert that, though Christians cannot worship him, they pray regularly for the Emperor and wish well to the State. Persecution does not, it would seem, embitter them: their one thought is to endure it with as much resignation as possible, looking forward to the conversion of their opponents, whom they regard as well-meaning but deluded men, rather than as limbs of the Devil. The attitude seems to spring directly from what we found to be the common teaching of the Apostolic Age, which in turn reflects Christ's precept about duty to Caesar. Their attitude might well be summed up in the well-known passage of the *Epistle to Diognetus* which compares the Christian community to the soul of the world. Indeed this attractive document, of unknown authorship, might well be regarded as the classic expression of the 'world affirming' or co-operative Christian tradition in respect of human society. Its author insists upon the conformity of Christians to the natural life around them and seems to regard their primary duty as the preservation of natural morality—though he thinks of them as surpassing it and as obeying a higher standard.[1] He recognises that Christianity is supernatural: 'Christians have their abode in the world, and yet they are not of the world'.[2] But he regards the influence they are called upon to exercise upon the natural order as in a sense constituting their highest vocation. 'So great is the office for which God hath appointed them, and which it is not lawful for them to decline.'[3]

On the other hand there was not wanting a different outlook, which we may attribute to the apocalyptic current of thought to be seen so plainly in the New Testament. This regards the Empire as a hostile force, under the influence of demonic deities and opposed necessarily to the Kingdom of God. It is to be expected that this

---

[1] πείθονται τοῖς ὡρισμένοις νόμοις, καὶ τοῖς ἰδίοις βίοις νικῶσι τοὺς νόμους (*Ep. ad Diog.* 5).

[2] καὶ Χριστιανοὶ ἐν κόσμῳ οἰκοῦσιν, οὐκ εἰσὶ δὲ ἐκ τοῦ κόσμου (*Ep. ad Diog.* 6).

[3] εἰς τοσαύτην αὐτοὺς τάξιν ἔθετο ὁ θέος, ἣν οὐ θεμιτὸν αὐτοῖς παραιτήσασθαι (*Ep. ad Diog.* 6).

idea continued, especially among the poorer and less educated Christians, drawn from what Arnold Toynbee calls the 'internal proletariat'[1] of the classical world, disinherited people who looked forward to the ultimate destruction of the Empire which kept them in poverty and often in slavery. It is to be expected also that this point of view should be represented sparingly in extant Christian literature; for the Apologists and others who committed their views to writing belonged to the better educated and more philosophical elements in the Church, whereas apocalyptic resentment against the government came more naturally from the poorer, less literate, hot-gospelling Christians. Yet the attitude is not absent in literature. The simple Hermas, who belonged to the depressed classes, has it in his gentle way. The Lady of his Fourth Vision, who represents the Church, explains to him the colours of the strange beast he had seen upon the Campanian Way. 'The black is this world in which ye dwell; and the fire and blood colour showeth that this world must perish by blood and fire; and the golden part are ye that have escaped from this world. . . . But the white portion is the coming age, in which the elect of God shall dwell.'[2] The contrast between Christianity and the world is here absolute and the whole of the present world order seems to be condemned.

But in fierceness of criticism of pagan society the more educated Christians fell sometimes little behind the mass of the faithful, those unkindly described by Tertullian as *simplices . . . ne dixerim imprudentes et idiotae, quae maior semper credentium pars est.*[3] The ordinarily calm, and perhaps unduly immanentist Clement of Alexandria can be as biting about what he calls the 'mysteries of the atheists',[4] as Tertullian, whose alleged *Apology* deserves the phrase Newman applied to Pusey's *Eirenicon*—'an olive branch as

---

[1] Arnold J. Toynbee, *A Study of History*, 2nd edit., vol. i (London, 1935), pp. 40-41 and elsewhere.

[2] τὸ μὲν μέλαν οὗτος ὁ κόσμος ἐστίν, ἐν ᾧ κατοικεῖτε· τὸ δὲ πυροειδὲς καὶ αἱματῶδες, ὅτι δεῖ τὸν κόσμον τοῦτον δι᾽ αἵματος καὶ πυρὸς ἀπόλλυσθαι· τὸ δὲ χρυσοῦν μέρος ὑμεῖς ἐστε οἱ ἐκφυγόντες τὸν κόσμον τοῦτον . . . τὸ δὲ λευκὸν μέρος ὁ αἰὼν ὁ ἐρχόμενός ἐστιν, ἐν ᾧ κατοικήσουσιν οἱ ἐκλεκτοὶ τοῦ θεοῦ εἰς ζωὴν αἰώνιον (Shepherd, Vis. iv. 3).

[3] *Adv. Prax.* iii.

[4] ταῦτα τῶν ἀθέων τὰ μυστήρια (Protrept. ii).

if from a catapult'.[1] The Christian contempt, shared by lettered and unlettered alike, for popular paganism was one of the sources of their dislike for an Empire necessarily, in the conditions of the ancient world, bound up with it. That feeling went, indeed, beyond contempt; for it must always be remembered that most early Christians regarded the pagan deities not as mere empty names, but as devils who, under borrowed plumes, had tricked men into worshipping them.[2] Pagan rites, therefore, were not mere foolishness, but dangerous black magic. An Empire that acknowledged gods of this kind and practised such rites could not but be the enemy of God.

Not all, however, pushed the logic of the matter to extremes. Tertullian, who blusters loudly against paganism, is yet not anti-imperialist. He protests, as much as any apologetic Apologist, that Christians pray for the safety of the Emperors to the God who has really given them empire.[3] But the reasons he gives for the practice are not those which would have satisfied a Jingoistic Roman. We are told, he says, to pray for our enemies, and there-fore for our persecutors.[4] Moreover, if the Empire suffers, its Christian citizens suffer with it, so that it is in their own interests to pray for it.[5] The final reason given is the most curious of all. 'There is another reason, a greater one, for our praying for the Emperors, and for the whole estate of the Empire and the interests of Rome. We know that the great force which threatens the whole world, the end of the age itself with its menace of hideous

---

[1] Quoted in H. P. Liddon, *Life of Edward Bouverie Pusey*, vol. iv (London, 1897), p. 136. 'There was one of old time who wreathed his sword in myrtle; excuse me—you discharge your olive branch as if from a catapult.'

[2] See, for classic statements of this attitude, St. Athanasius, *De Incarnatione*, 11, Tertullian, *Apol.* 22-23.

[3] 'Nos enim pro salute imperatorum deum invocamus aeternum, deum verum, deum vivum, quem et ipsi imperatores propitium sibi praeter ceteros malunt. Sciunt quis illis dederit imperium, sciunt, qua homines, quis et animam, sentiunt eum esse deum solum in cuius solius potestate sunt, a quo sunt secundi, post quem primi, ante omnes et super omnes deos' (*Apol.* 30). Cf. *Ad Scapulam*, 2.

[4] 'Scitote exillis [sc. Scripturis] praeceptum esse nobis ad redundantiam benignitatis etiam pro inimicis deum orare et persecutoribus nostris bona precari. Qui magis inimici et persecutores Christianorum quam de quorum maiestate convenimur in crimen' (*Apol.* 31).

[5] 'Cum enim concutitur imperium concussis etiam ceteris membris eius utique et nos, licet extranei a turbis aestimemur, in aliquo loco casus invenimur' (*Apol.* 31).

suffering, is delayed by the respite which the Roman Empire means for us. We do not want to experience all that; and when we pray for its postponement are helping forward the continuance of Rome.'[1]

Whether this series of reasons for State prayers really justifies Tertullian's claim that there is a genuine *religio atque pietas Christiana in imperatore*[2] may be left to the reader to judge. One can imagine a sceptical smile stealing over the face of any Roman official who may have read Tertullian's aggressive claim to toleration, despite (or perhaps because of) the assurance: 'We must needs respect the Emperor as the chosen of the Lord, so that I might say Caesar is more ours than yours, appointed as he is by our God'.[3]

Indeed, we find meeting in Tertullian, in curious juxtaposition, both the idea of obedience to the State for conscience sake and the opposing current of apocalyptic, both of which we have noticed in Christian tradition. In his *Ad Scapulam*, Tertullian can point, though without quite the gusto of Lactantius, to the deaths of persecutors and speak of the wrath of God which is surely coming in the pagan Empire.[4] Nevertheless, he is prepared to give to the *pax Romana* at least that limited and partial value we have already noted. Once again we seem to see the depreciation of civil power as being of small significance, and appointed for very mun-

[1] 'Est et alia maior necessitas nobis orandi pro imperatoribus, etiam pro omni statu imperii rebusque Romanis, qui vim maximam universo orbi imminentem ipsamque clausulam saeculi acerbitates horrendas comminantem Romani imperii commeatu scimus retardari. Itaque nolumus experiri, et dum precamur differri, Romanae diuturnitati favemus' (*Apol.* 32). [2] *Apol.* 33.

[3] 'Quem necesse est suspiciamus ut eum quem dominus noster elegit, ut merito dixerim: Noster est magis Caesar, a nostro deo constitutus' (*Apol.* 33).

[4] 'Possumus aeque et exitus quorundam praesidum tibi proponere, qui in fine vitae suae recordati sunt deliquisse, quod vexassest Christianos. Vigillius Saturninus qui primus hic gladium in nos egit, lumina amisit. Claudius Lucius Herminianus in Cappadocia, cum indigne ferens uxorem suam ad hanc sectam transisse, Christianos crudeliter tractasset, solusque in praetorio suo vastatus peste, cum vivus vermibus ebullisset: Nemo sciat, aiebat, ne gaudeant Christiani. Postea cognito errore suo, quod tormentis quosdam a proposito suo excidere fecisset, pene christianus decessit. Caesilius Capella in illo exitu byzantino *Christiani gaudete*, exclamavit. Sed et qui videntur sibi impune tulisse, venient in diem divini iudicii' (*Ad Scap.* 3).

'Omnia haec signa sunt imminentes irae Dei, quam necesse est, quoquo modo possumus, ut et annuntiemus, et praedicemus, et deprecemur interim localem esse: universalem enim et supremam suo tempore sentient, qui exempla eius aliter interpretantur' (*ibid.*).

dane ends, to which attention was drawn in the last lecture in considering the New Testament.

Perhaps Tertullian is best revealed in this summing up of the matter: 'A Christian is the enemy of no man, least of all the Emperor: knowing that he is set up by his own God, he must needs love him, reverence, honour and wish him well, together with the whole Roman Empire, *as long as this age endures*. For so long shall it endure.'[1] The Roman Empire has no eternal or transcendental value: even if one applies to it Byron's resounding lines, still its value is temporary *sub specie aeternitatis*.

> 'While stands the Coliseum, Rome shall stand;
> When falls the Coliseum, Rome shall fall;
> And when Rome falls—the World.'[2]

To Tertullian, as to most Christians of his time, Rome was but, so to say, an expedient of the Almighty—a mere stop-gap to hold the universe together until the final catastrophe. 'Take heed then', says he to the pagans, 'lest it prove that He dispenses the kingdoms, whose is both the world that is reigned over and the man who reigns; lest it be he that has ordained the progressions of empires each at its own time in the world's story, He who was ere time was, who made the world's story compact of times and seasons; lest it be He who raises up cities or brings them low, He under whom mankind once stood without cities at all.'[3] There speaks the voice of authentic Christian apocalypticism, which, however much it tries to reconcile itself with civic loyalty, yet cannot ultimately but think of all kingdoms as no more than bubbles on the stream of time.

Yet, despite all this, Tertullian and others could and did boast

---

[1] 'Christianus nullius est hostis, nedum Imperatoris: quem sciens a Deo suo constitui, necesse est ut et ipsum diligat, et revereatur, et honoret, et salvum velit, cum toto romano imperio, quousque saeculum stabit. Tamdiu enim stabit' (*Ad Scap.* 2).

[2] *Childe Harold*, canto iv. 145.

[3] 'Videte igitur, ne ille regna dispenset cuius est et orbis qui regnatur et homo ipse qui regnat, ne ille vices dominationum ipsis temporibus in saeculo ordinarit qui ante omne tempus fuit et saeculum corpus temporum fecit, ne ille civitates extollat aut deprimat sub quo fuit sine civitatibus aliquando gens hominum' (*Apol.* 26).

THE PRE-CONSTANTINIAN CHURCH

with truth of the steady infiltration and conquest of the Empire by Christianity.[1] The warfare between the Christian Church and the State was one which the State was steadily losing. Moreover it was a battle with an increasing number of truces. The two great persecutions of the third century, Decius's witch-hunt and the subtle attempt to disrupt the Christian organisation miscalled Diocletian's persecution, both came as surprises to generations of Christians accustomed to *de facto* toleration and accustomed even to that social *modus vivendi* which, as in India today, so often softens communal rivalry in practice. Before the age of persecution ended Christians were worshipping in buildings owned by the Church with a title that the Emperor himself would sometimes uphold.[2] Their leaders were in some cases well-known men of influence in the Roman world. By the time of the last attempt to hold it up the Church was well entrenched in the life of the world around it.

In such an atmosphere a purely hostile attitude to the State could not easily flourish. Even in the second and third centuries, when Christians had less freedom and less influence, hostility, as we have seen, was but one ingredient in the Christian outlook. Though stimulated by further persecution, it had by the time of Constantine even less of a place in the Church. Ferdinand Lot, speaking as a secular historian, has described the Roman Empire as suffering for two and a half centuries from *une maladie interne, le christianisme*.[3] To pagan statesmen it must have seemed very much like that. But what they could not see, and what was perhaps

---

[1] 'Hesterni sumus, et vestra omnia implevimus, urbes, insulas, castella, municipia, conciliabula, castra ipsa, tribus, decurias, palatium, senatum, forum; sola vobis reliquimus templa' (*Apol.* 37).

[2] Cf. the story of the οἶκος τῆς ἐκκλησίας, the church at Antioch occupied by Paul of Samosata, and Aurelian's decision. ἀλλὰ γὰρ μηδαμῶς ἐκστῆναι τοῦ Παύλου τοῦ τῆς ἐκκλησίας οἶκου θέλοντος, βασιλεὺς ἐντευχθεὶς Αὐρηλιανὸς αἰσιώτατα περὶ τοῦ πρακτέου διείληφε, τούτοις νεῖμαι προστάττων τὸν οἶκον, οἷς ἂν οἱ κατὰ τὴν Ἰταλίαν καὶ τὴν Ῥωμαίων τοῦ δόγματος ἐπιστείλαιεν (Euseb. *H.E.* vii. 30).

[3] *La Fin du monde antique et le début du moyen-âge* (Paris, 1927), pp. 25-26.

Additional note. For a recent survey of the historical problems presented by the persecutions of the Church, see Henri Grégoire (avec la collaboration de P. Orgels, J. Moreau et A. Maricq), *Les Persécutions dans l'empire romain* (Académie Royale de Belgique. Mémoires, Classe de lettres, tome xlvi, Brussels, 1950).

4   41

hidden from the Christians themselves, was that this disease was more and more acclimatising itself to the constitution of the body in which it dwelt. If a violent simile may be allowed, it was like a tumour which, beginning as a disfigurement, was now so much a part of the patient as to be able to remould his body into its own likeness. Even before Constantine the pattern of the Christian Roman Empire was latent in that of its pagan predecessor.

CHAPTER III

THE CONSTANTINIAN REVOLUTION AND
THE CHRISTIAN ROMAN EMPIRE

This country is not usually reckoned over-modest about the part it has played in world history. It is strange, therefore, that it has made little of its most substantial claim to have been the starting-place of a European revolution. Yet it was at York in the year 306 that an event leading to such a result took place. For there died in that year, at the northern headquarters of the Roman army of Britain, Constantius Chlorus, the Augustus, or chief Emperor, in the West (according to the new system of collegiate imperial rule established by Diocletian). No sooner had he died than his troops acclaimed as his successor his son Constantine. We need not recall in detail Lactantius's dramatic story of that son's escape from the close surveillance of the jealous Galerius, Augustus of the East, at Nicomedia, and of his swift journey across Europe to his dying father's side. It was alleged (though the story is open to serious doubt) that, as he went, he had the post-horses he left behind him hamstrung, to shake off possible pursuit: the drama of that tale, whether true or false, is at least worthy of the exciting events which followed.[1] For within eighteen years Constantine, by successive strokes of policy, made himself sole master of the Roman world and was free, like another Octavian, to remodel it according to his will.

The stages of his rise to sole power were twofold. By 312 he had defeated his rival Maxentius, and was master of the West. Twelve more years were to elapse before he added the East to his sphere of authority. During that time he had to share power with Licinius, Augustus in the East, who in 313 had defeated Maximin Daia, last of the bitter persecutors of Christianity. A war between Licinius and Constantine in 314 won for the latter Licinius's European provinces and stabilised the balance between them. In 324 a final quarrel between them ended in the utter defeat of Licinius at

[1] Lactantius (*De morte persecutorum*, 24) merely says that he took them away. The more picturesque story is given by Zosimus (*Hist. nov.* ii. 8).

43

Chrysopolis and in Constantine's seizure of sole power. It was, however, this period of uneasy partnership which saw no less than a *bouleversement* of the relations between the Roman Empire and the Christian Church.

What was the nature of this? As we have seen, these relations had never heretofore reached a higher degree of friendliness than a precarious and surreptitious toleration of the Church by the Empire. But by the time of Constantine's death in 337 Christianity had become, not only the personal religion of the Emperor, but, in consequence, one of the two official religions of the Empire, in many respects privileged even more than the old paganism which still remained established. Moreover, the internal affairs of the Church, including its doctrinal and disciplinary disputes and the appointment of its bishops, had come to be matters of active interest at the imperial court.

How did this transformation come about and what was its motive? We touch here upon one of the most controverted historical questions of recent decades, though there seem to be signs that opinion is becoming crystallised in a more uniform pattern. The facts themselves are not seriously in dispute, though some details are obscure. Constantine, on the eve of the decisive battle of the Milvian Bridge in 312, at which he routed Maxentius, his last opponent in the West, adopted Christian insignia for his army. Thus he entered Rome as the confessed champion of Christianity. All this was done, so he claimed, in response to a celestial vision which had promised him success if he fought under the auspices of Christ. Eusebius, indeed, the Emperor's panegyrical biographer, represents the vision as appearing during the early stages of the campaign against Maxentius.[1] It seems likely, however, that the earlier and more sober account of Lactantius is to be preferred, according to which the adoption of a Christian emblem was a last-minute decision at the Milvian Bridge, somewhat like the painting of Liberation signs upon the Allied aircraft which accompanied the invasion of Normandy in 1944, though, as in that case, the plan may have been meditated long in advance.[2]

[1] Eusebius, *Vita Constantini*, i. 28.   [2] Lactantius, *De morte persecutorum*, 44.

However this may be, it is clear that from 312 onwards Constantine claimed to be a Christian ruler.

What was his motive? Was the change of religion a mere pose? From at least the time of Gibbon,[1] a succession of historians, including such great names as those of Burckhardt,[2] Harnack,[3] Schwartz[4] and Caspar[5] have attributed Constantine's conduct to a mere weighing of policy. Christianity, it is said, had proved indestructible. Hence it had to be accepted as a permanent factor in the Roman world, and, by a stroke of genius, Constantine decided to make it the mainspring of a new imperial policy. He would use its proved strength and influence as a support, instead of a menace, to the State. Such a view is intelligible as a reaction from the naïve conception of Constantine as a saint in purple, anointed by the Lord and predestined to assure the Church's triumph—a notion begun by Eusebius and continued by tradition.[6] A revulsion of opinion of this kind was almost inevitable in an age familiar with many examples of conversion for reasons of state, or of political reorganisation of religion. Henry IV of France deemed Paris worth a Mass, Napoleon I stabilised the French Revolution upon a Gallican Catholicism, Frederick William III of Prussia strengthened the solidarity of his kingdom by a forced reunion of Lutherans and Calvinists. According to Gibbon, all religions were regarded by Roman magistrates as 'equally useful'[7] and it is natural to a sceptical age to suppose that no ruler looked beyond utilitarian considerations. Yet Gibbon himself gave his successors

[1] 'But the counsels of princes are more frequently influenced by views of temporal advantage than by considerations of abstract and speculative truth' (*Decline and Fall of the Roman Empire*, chap. xx (ed. J. B. Bury, vol. ii, London, 1897), p. 293). But Gibbon allows that Constantine may have genuinely believed in Christianity; see the whole chapter.

[2] Jacob Burckhardt, *The Age of Constantine the Great* (E.T. by Moses Hadas, London, 1949), chap. ix, pp. 292 *sqq*.

[3] Adolf Harnack, *The Mission and Expansion of Christianity* (E.T., vol. ii, London, 1908), pp. 334-335.

[4] Eduard Schwartz, *Kaiser Constantin und die christliche Kirche* (Leipzig, 1913).

[5] Erich Caspar, *Geschichte des Papsttums*, vol. i (Tübingen, 1930), pp. 107-108.

[6] This apotheosis has reached its climax in the Eastern Church, where Constantine has been raised to the altars as 'Equal to the Apostles'.

[7] 'The various modes of worship which prevailed in the Roman world were all considered by the people as equally true; by the philosopher as equally false; and by the magistrate as equally useful' (*Decline and Fall*, vol. i, chap. ii, p. 28).

a warning they might have been wise to lay to heart. 'The protestant and philosophic readers of the present age will incline to believe that, in the account of his own conversion, Constantine attested a wilful falsehood by a solemn and deliberate perjury. They may not hesitate to pronounce that, in the choice of a religion, his mind was determined only by a sense of interest; and that (according to the expression of a profane poet) he used the altars of the Church as a convenient footstool to the throne of the empire. A conclusion so harsh and so absolute is not, however, warranted by our knowledge of human nature, of Constantine, or of Christianity. In an age of religious fervour, the most artful statesmen are observed to feel some part of the enthusiasm which they inspire; and the most orthodox saints assume the dangerous privilege of defending the cause of truth by the arms of deceit and falsehood. Personal interest is often the standard of our belief, as well as of our practice; and the same motives of temporal advantage which might influence the public conduct and professions of Constantine would insensibly dispose his mind to embrace a religion so propitious to his fame and fortunes. His vanity was gratified by the flattering assurance that *he* has been chosen by Heaven to reign over the earth; success had justified his divine title to the throne, and that title was founded on the truth of the Christian revelation.'[1]

Indeed, the human mind is not quite so logical or so sceptical as the eighteenth and nineteenth centuries were apt to suppose. It may well be that neither Henry IV, Napoleon nor Frederick William were so wholly devoid of religion as we sometimes think. In any case it is grossly anachronistic to look in the fourth century for such cold, calculating sceptics as this theory requires. The besetting sin of that age was credulity rather than indifferentism or blank unbelief. We must remember that paganism was a religion which received genuine acceptance down to its death. Untheological it may have been: a pagan priest or layman would have been hard put to it to write out a logical statement of his creed. But it was practised with fervour by many and with at least

---

[1] *Decline and Fall*, vol. ii, chap. xx, pp. 305-306.

conventional piety by nearly all. It is therefore unlikely that Constantine, at any stage of his career, was not at least a *bien pensant*.

Moreover, the alleged advantages of harnessing Christianity to a new imperial policy can easily be over-estimated. The Church may have been a strong force: it was a third-century Emperor, Decius, who was alleged to have said that he would rather hear of a rival to the throne than of the election of a new Bishop of Rome.[1] But in 312 it did not so obviously command the future, especially in the Western regions in which Constantine began his rule, where it was far weaker than in the East.[2] During his sojourn as a quasi-hostage to Galerius at Nicomedia the young Constantine might have meditated upon the obvious breakdown of that ruler's policy of suppressing the Galilean faith. But when he was acclaimed at York, if he knew at all of the pitifully small group of Christians (perhaps already presided over by that Eborius who later attended the Council of Arles), he cannot have been impressed by their potentialities as a political force. When in 312 he entered Rome it was the inveterate paganism of the senatorial families, rather than the strength of Christianity, which must have struck him. As Alföldi has shown, there is good reason to believe that he had to move very cautiously against their hostility to his new cult. For he was to a great extent dependent upon senatorial support. Maxentius had neglected the Senate. 'Not once in his six years of power', says Alföldi, 'did he confer the distinction of the ordinary consulship on its members, not once did he praise them on his coins.'[3] Indeed the same writer, following Schwartz, suggests that Maxentius may have 'sought in his favours to the Christian masses of the lower orders a counterpoise to the aristocracy' and so even have anticipated the pro-Christian policy associated with Constantine.[4] Constantine on the other hand at first

[1] Cyprian, *Ep.* lv. 9.
[2] See Harnack, *Mission and Expansion* (E.T., vol. ii, London, 1908), pp. 324 *sqq.* 'The radical difference between the eastern and the western sections of the empire is particularly striking' (p. 331). Harnack, who thinks that Constantine acted from political motives, ingeniously argues that he had been impressed by the strength of Christianity during his residence at Nicomedia before his father's death (p. 334).
[3] Andrew Alföldi, *The Conversion of Constantine and Pagan Rome* (E.T., Oxford, 1948), p. 61. [4] Alföldi, *ibid.*

47

posed as the restorer of old Roman traditions, as the *liberator urbis* and *restitutor libertatis publicae* from the innovations of Maxentius: the triumphal arch erected in 315 to celebrate his victory shows him in senatorial dress in the midst of the conscript fathers. Small wonder that he did not dare at once to overthrow the official edifice of established paganism. As *pontifex maximus* he still nominated priests, most of senatorial rank; his legislation expressly (though contemptuously) permits the continuance of public *haruspicina*.[1] To integrate Christianity with the State in the fullest sense would have been an unjustifiable risk, for, since the Christian God was a jealous one, that could have been done only by stigmatising all non-Christian rites as idolatrous.

Nor was it a Church flushed with victory that he was patronising. The persecution had indeed failed: Galerius recognised as much on his death-bed, when he allowed toleration.[2] Nevertheless it had dealt severe blows to the structure of the Church. Of this fact Constantine may not have been fully aware, for it was (as before in the Decian storm) by internal fractures rather than by external that the State had almost unwittingly achieved part of its object of weakening the Christian body. The correspondence of Constantine suggests that the Donatist schism, the greatest of the quarrels produced by persecution, took him by surprise.[3] Nor did he appreciate the doctrinal crisis which was to lead to the appearance of Arianism. Nevertheless such a lack of knowledge of the internal stresses of the Church scarcely suggests such a profound investigation of the state of that body as might be supposed to precede a projected alliance, if that alliance was motivated by political considerations. A calculator would have made closer enquiries before he committed himself to a hazardous policy.

Why then did Constantine embrace Christianity? The answer seems upon examination to be so simple that it has been over-

---

[1] *Cod. Theod.* IX. xvi. 2. Cf. IX. xvi. 1, XVI. x. 1.

[2] Eusebius, *H.E.* viii. 17.

[3] 'Cum perlatum fuisset ad scientiam meam apud Africam nostram plures vesano furore vanis criminationibus contra se invicem super observantiam sanctissimae legis catholicae discedere coepisse' (Appendix to Optatus, *De schismate Donatistarum* (ed. Ziwsa, C.S.E.L., vol. xxvi, Vienna, 1893), no. iii, p. 204).

looked by all who think of an Emperor as necessarily a superman, whose thoughts move on the plane of deeply meditated policy or of exalted theological reflection. Despite Oxenstierna's dictum, we seldom remember with how little wisdom the world is commonly governed. Constantine was a soldier and the military life is not normally associated with such abstract considerations. Indeed the religion of a professional warrior is often marked by a naïve and disarming simplicity, as is witnessed to, for example, by the imposing number of military names to be found in any list of British-Israel supporters. No one doubts why Clovis, that *novus Constantinus*, as Gregory of Tours sapiently calls him, embraced Christianity some hundred and eighty years later.[1] It was a simple case of *do quia dedisti*. He had called upon his wife's God in the heat of battle and gained victory. But what else had Constantine done before the Milvian Bridge? His Christian panegyrists proclaimed the fact without shame and even his pagan adulators had to recognise it, even though their beliefs impelled them to wrap up the details in a conventional vagueness. *Quisnam te deus*, said one in 313, *quae tam praesens hortata est maiestas? . . . Habes profecto aliquod cum illa mente divina, Constantine, secretum, quae delegata nostri diis minoribus cura uni se tibi dignatur ostendere.*[2] The triumphal arch already mentioned says, with the same ambiguity, the same thing, in telling the world that the conquest of Rome was accomplished *instinctu divinitatis.* How true is Boissier's remark: 'When we have to deal with great personalities, who play the chief parts in history, when we try to study their lives and explain their conduct, we are not content to hold to the most natural explanations. Because they have the reputation of being extraordinary men, we will never believe that they have done what everybody else would. We search for hidden reasons for their simplest actions; we attribute to them plots, depths, perfidies of which they were entirely unaware. So it has been with Constantine.'[3]

---

[1] *Hist. Francorum*, II. xxii (31). 'Procedit novus Constantinus ad lavacrum.'

[2] *Panegyrici Romani*, ix. 2.

[3] 'Par malheur, quand nous avons affaire à ces grands personnages, qui jouent les premiers rôles de l'histoire, et que nous essayons d'étudier leur vie et de nous rendre compte de leur conduite, nous avons peine à nous contenter des explications les plus naturelles.

Nor can this explanation of Constantine's motives be overthrown by the fact that he was baptised only on his death-bed. To those familiar with the severity with which the Church of his day treated post-baptismal sin the moral weaknesses shown by Constantine during his life[1] will seem a sufficient reason for his following a prevalent custom of deferring baptism[2] and the delay is not incompatible with a genuine acceptance of the Christian faith. If an Ambrose, brought up in Christianity, could reach the status of a provincial governor without being baptised[3] and receive the sacrament only when called to the episcopate, much more could a new convert of an earlier period defer the mystic bath, which indeed washed away sin but brought with it terrifying responsibilities for future conduct. Later pagan scandal-mongers held that the Emperor's conversion was due to a longing for cleansing from sin which only Christianity, a religion without respectability, could offer:[4] in actual fact that motive can have played little part. But even if outside the sphere of grace, Constantine showed from the first much of the *zèle du converti*—perhaps all the more so because his life did not always correspond with Christian standards. However diplomatically he had to treat paganism, he took no pains to conceal his own convictions and did all he could first to make the status of the Church tolerable and then to give it privileges. Whilst still the colleague of Licinius he persuaded the latter to adopt, in the so-called Edict of Milan,[5] a policy not merely of toleration for

Parce qu'ils ont la réputation d'être des hommes extraordinaires, nous ne voulons jamais croire qu'ils aient agi comme tout le monde. Nous cherchons des raisons cachées à leurs actions les plus simples; nous leur prêtons des finesses, des combinaisons, des profondeurs, des perfidies dont ils ne se sont avisés' (Gaston Boissier, *La Fin du paganisme* (4ᵉ édit., Paris, 1903), i. 24).

[1] 'Constantine was, in any case, only a catechumen till his death-bed, and then an Arian. He persecuted the Catholic bishops, and had a weakness for murdering his near relations. None of these things can be held up as examples of heroic sanctity' (Adrian Fortescue, *The Greek Fathers* (London, 1908), p. 25, n. 2).

[2] Compare the attitude of St. Augustine's parents to the question of his baptism, which he implies was shared by other Christians. (*Conf.* i. 11.) He quotes as a common saying: *Sine illum, faciat; nondum enim baptizatus est.*

[3] Paulinus, *Vita Ambrosii*, iii.   [4] Zosimus, *Hist. nova*, ii. 29.

[5] On the difficulties connected with this document see N. H. Baynes, *Constantine and the Christian Church* (Raleigh Lecture for 1929, *Proc. of the British Academy*, vol. xi), p. 11. 'The Edict of Milan may be a fiction, but the fact for which the term stood remains untouched.' Cf. pp. 69 *sqq.* no. 42.

Christians but of full legal equality for the Church. The Emperor's official correspondence (the genuineness of the extant fragments of which seems to be more and more widely accepted),[1] proclaims in rhetorical terms his belief in Christianity and contempt for paganism.[2] His legislation restored the Church's property and his munificence added to it, both in lands and buildings. 'In this mighty creation of art that reflected the sanctity of the Christian Empire,' writes Alföldi of the Lateran Basilica, 'the omnipotent Emperor set a worthy rival by the side of the Capitol.'[3] The powers and privileges of the Church were steadily increased. As early as 321 emancipation of slaves carried out in church had the same legal effect as the older pagan method.[4] Bishops obtained a jurisdiction parallel in many respects to that of civil magistrates,[5] the clergy gained exemption from civil duties—a very great concession in an age when the State required more and more of every citizen[6]—Sunday observance was made compulsory, though the Christian significance of the requirement was disguised by a reference to the pagan 'Day of the Sun'.[7] Nor was paganism itself left intact. Soldiers were made by compulsory prayers to recognise the monotheism which had been gaining currency even in pagan thought.[8] Certain of the pagan rites most offensive to Christianity were forbidden and there was a fair amount of despoiling of temples—though this last may have been dictated more by fiscal than religious motives.[9]

We seem thus forced to the conclusion that Constantine's action in 312 was something deeper than a feigned, politic conversion

---

[1] Baynes, op. cit. pp. 40 sqq. n. 18.
[2] See, e.g., Eusebius, Vita Constantini, ii. 24-42 and 48-60.
[3] Alföldi, op. cit. p. 52.   [4] Cod. Theod. IV. vii. 1.
[5] Cod. Theod. I. xxvii. 1. Constitutiones Sirmondianae, 1. The authenticity of this legislation has been contested, but the modern tendency is to regard it as genuine. See A. Piganiol, L'Empire chrétien (Histoire générale fondée par Gustave Glotz, Histoire romaine, vol. iv (ii), Paris, 1947), p. 369 and reff. there cited. Cf. Otto Seeck, Geschichte des Untergangs der antiken Welt (edit. 2, Stuttgart, 1921), ii. 181 sqq.
[6] Cod. Theod. XVI. ii. 1 and 2. Constantine himself, however, began to hedge these exemptions with restrictions (Cod. Theod. XVI. ii. 3) and later emperors continued the process.   [7] Cod. Theod. II. viii. 1. Eusebius, Vita Constantini, iv. 18.
[8] Eusebius, Vita Constantini, iv. 19-20.
[9] See A. Piganiol, L'Empereur Constantin (Paris, 1932), pp. 183 sqq.

determined by secular motives. It was, indeed, a gamble on the political side, since the Emperor risked the hostility of a large section of the governing class. Though Christians had penetrated into the civil service before Constantine's time, Diocletian's proscriptions must have removed many. And, at the same time, Constantine was relying upon an ally yet to be proved and believed to be traditionally hostile to the Roman Empire or indifferent to its welfare. Political calculation would have looked longer before it leaped. Constantine was a Christian, not because he thought it would pay politically to be so, but because he had come to believe in Christ firmly, not to say fanatically.

How, then, did he view his new religion, and what was his idea of his own function in the Church? His personal piety was, no doubt, crude. We have only to remember Gregory of Tours's picture of the naïve theology and odd morals of professedly Catholic Merovingian kings[1] to understand that, for Roman civilisation did not necessarily make Emperors greater theologians or potential saints than were barbarian convert monarchs. Neglect of this consideration has led to strange errors about Constantine's ecclesiastical policy. Pierre Batiffol argues against the authenticity of the Emperor's notorious letter to Alexander of Alexandria, which treats the Arian controversy as a dispute about mere trifles,[2] on the sole ground that it shows theological incomprehension, and is, in his words, *un enfantillage.*[3] So it must seem, no doubt, to theologians of Batiffol's eminence. But it is just what we should expect from a man of Constantine's background and it is difficult to believe that anyone else could have the ingenuity to forge such a naïvely revealing document. An intellect at least as penetrating as Constantine's, that of Edward Gibbon, could write of Trinitarian theology: 'These speculations, instead of being treated as the amusement of a vacant hour, became the serious business of the present, and the most useful preparation for a future life'[4]—and Gibbon, unlike Constantine, had read much

---

[1] *e.g. Hist. Francorum*, V. xxxii (44) and VI. xxxiii (46) on Chilperic.
[2] Eusebius, *Vita Constantini*, ii. 64–72.
[3] Pierre Batiffol, *La Paix constantinienne* (4e édit., Paris, 1929), pp. 309 *sqq.* It is referred to as 'cette lettre inconsidérée'.   [4] *Decline and Fall*, chap. xxi, vol. ii, p. 341.

about the subject. Like Constantine, the historian simply was not a theologian and wrote of theology as a theologian might write of mechanics.

How, then, did Constantine see Christianity? To judge by his letters, primarily as a 'law'—a favourite phrase of his[1]—and as a cult. The former word may mean a *Weltanschauung*, a way of looking at the universe, rather than a mere code of behaviour.[2] But the notion of Christianity as a cultus appears to be another form of the old Roman religious principle, *do ut des*. The Emperor attached the greatest importance to the performance of Christian rites, because he thought the safety of the Empire to be bound up with them. It is these twin notions which seem to determine Constantine's idea of his role as Christian Emperor. With Christianity as a revealed philosophy of life he did not directly concern himself: he was not an expert in that field. So he left it to those whose business it was, the bishops. It seems clear that the prelates he assembled in general council at Nicaea did not have to accept an imperial *Diktat* upon the theological questions at issue there and were left fairly free to discuss and decide them. Eusebius, indeed, makes Constantine play the part of James I at the Hampton Court Conference,[3] but Eusebius was a hero-worshipper and Athanasius, who had experience of later Emperors' interference in the doctrinal field, does not suggest that Constantine unduly pushed his own point of view.[4] The most that can be said is that he was apt to listen to personal advisers among the bishops, such as Hosius, and later Eusebius of Nicomedia, and to enforce decisions arrived at by their advice.

In matters of discipline it was different. Here we must retrace our steps and watch Constantine dealing with the first ecclesiastical

---

[1] νόμος. See, *e.g.*, Eusebius, *Vita Constantini*, ii. 69 and 70, *H.E.* x. 5. Constantine was not unique in using this expression; cf. *Acta purgationis Felicis* in Appendix to Optatus (ed. Ziwsa, C.S.E.L., vol. xxvi, Vienna, 1893), p. 198. 'Maximus dixit: loquor nomine seniorum christiani populi catholicae legis'.

[2] I owe this suggestion to Mr. C. E. Stevens of Magdalen College.

[3] *Vita Constantini*, iii. 13.

[4] οὐκ ἀνάγκη δὲ τοὺς κρίναντας ἦγεν ἐπὶ τοῦτο, ἀλλὰ πάντες προαιρέσει τὴν ἀλήθειαν ἐξεδίκουν (*Ep. ad episcopos Aegypti et Libyae*, 13). Athanasius admittedly had an interest in asserting this.

crisis, that concerning Donatism, when he was Western Emperor only. Here the point at issue was largely one of fact. Was Caecilian, the new Bishop of Carthage, consecrated by a *traditor*, a man who had yielded up the Scriptures to persecutors, or not? A doctrinal issue was involved, in the sense that the Donatist claim that the alleged moral defect of Felix of Aptunga, the chief consecrator, invalidated his sacramental act, was a doctrinal assertion. But that question does not seem to have figured prominently in the first stages of the controversy. The Donatists themselves evidently thought that Constantine had a right to intervene in the dispute. It would appear that it became an issue for the Emperor when in 313 the Proconsul of Africa, Anulinus, conveyed to Caecilian and his clergy the tidings of the new privileges offered by the Christian Emperor to the Church, and was faced by the Donatist opposition, who alleged that they, and not Caecilian's supporters, were the true Christian body in Africa and brought accusations against Caecilian. They appealed to Constantine and asked for their case to be tried by Gallic bishops.[1] The Emperor acceded to their request and seems to have ordered the Pope, Miltiades, to act as a kind of imperial commissioner, to arrange the trial. Schwartz sees here a presage of the idea of imperially summoned synods as the highest authority in Church affairs,[2] whilst Seeck thinks that Constantine recognised his own inability to deal with the issue and remitted it to papal authority.[3] Neither view seems correct. The Donatists had not asked for a synod: they wanted the Emperor to appoint arbitrators, *iudices*, according to the ordinary methods of Roman law. That was precisely what Constantine did and though (no doubt as a concession to Christian sentiment) he made Miltiades of Rome chairman, the Emperor personally selected the

---

[1] Apparently because Gaul had suffered little from persecution, so that the question of the status of *traditores* was not there a burning one.

[2] 'Zum ersten Male in der Kirchengeschichte erscheint die vom Kaiser zu berufende Synode als oberste Instanz: es ist das Vorspiel des nicaenischen Konzils, ja der oekumenischen überhaupt' (Eduard Schwartz, *Kaiser Constantin und die christliche Kirche* (Berlin, 1913), p. 85). Cf. Batiffol, *La Paix constantinienne*, p. 269.

[3] 'Nach den Grundsätzen, die dieser [Constantin] immer befolgt hat, wies er es von sich, in einen innerkirchlichen Streit kraft seiner Hoheitsrechte einzugreifen, und übertrug die Entscheidung dem Bischof Miltiades von Rom, dessen Primat damals schon in der ganzen Christenheit anerkannt war' (Otto Seeck, *Geschichte des Untergangs*, iii. 328-329).

three assessors, Reticius of Autun, Maternus of Cologne and
Marinus of Arles, from the Gallican episcopate.[1] The court was
essentially a commission of royal delegates: Augustine is expressing the matter accurately when he says that the Emperor 'delegated the case to bishops to be discussed and settled',[2] though one
may well doubt his further statement that 'Constantine did not
dare to judge the cause of a bishop'.[3]

It would seem that it was the Pope himself who, by adroitly
exceeding the Emperor's instructions, turned the assembly which
judged the Donatists into something more like the Christian idea
of a synod: for he appears to have added fifteen Italian bishops to
Constantine's nominees.[4] If this interpretation is correct, it is
significant to find as early as 313 a certain uneasiness, at least in
Western Christendom, over the masterful way in which the first
Christian Emperor was already dealing with Church affairs. Be
that as it may, the next stage in the Donatist controversy followed
more closely synodal precedent. Whether because they objected
to the modification of the terms of arbitration they had asked for,
or for some other reason, the Donatists appealed to Constantine
again from the Roman decision and this time the cause was remitted to a council at Arles in 314—an interesting return to
traditional ecclesiastical methods of settling disputes. Its decision
equally went against the Donatists and it dealt with the doctrinal
point involved, in its thirteenth canon, which, besides forbidding
accusations of *traditio* against the clergy to be lightly received,
affirmed that ordinations performed even by convicted *traditores*
were valid.[5]

The reaction of Constantine to this decision is interesting.

[1] See his letter to Miltiades in Eusebius, *H.E.* x. 5.
[2] *Ep.* cv. 8. 'Eam discutiendam atque finiendam episcopis delegavit.'
[3] 'Quia Constantinus non est ausus de causa episcopi iudicare' (*ibid.*).
[4] Optatus, *De schism. Donatist.* i. 23. For this view of the matter cf. Palanque in Fliche et
Martin, *Histoire de l'Église*, vol. iii (Paris, 1948), p. 45: 'Miltiade sut transformer cette commission d'arbitrage romano-gauloise en un véritable concile: ayant convoqué quinze
évêques venus de toutes les provinces italiennes, il renouait la tradition ecclésiastique des
synodes romains, dont l'empereur ne s'était évidemment point soucié'.
[5] 'Si iidem aliquos ordinasse fuerint deprehensi, et hi quos ordinaverint rationales
subsistunt, non illis obsit ordinatio' (Council of Arles, Canon xiii. Hefele-Leclercq,
Histoire des conciles, vol. i (i) (Paris, 1909), p. 289).

Though the authenticity of the letter *Aeterna et religiosa*, which he is said to have addressed to the bishops at Arles on hearing of their proceedings, has been questioned (like that of so many other Constantinian documents),[1] its character, that of *une lettre maussade et découragée*, as it has been described,[2] makes forgery unlikely. In it he praises the judgement arrived at as providential, but goes on to denounce in violent language the 'madness' of the Donatists who have, yet again, appealed from it to the Emperor in person. 'They demand my judgement, judgement from me who myself await the judgement of Christ.'[3] But the decision of bishops should be received as that of Christ Himself.[4] Men who behave thus desert heavenly things for worldly: they are like pagans.[5] But let the bishops have patience: the secular arm will now deal with the schismatics.

Such sentiments, if they are indeed Constantine's, would have come better from him if he had not by a fumbling policy already undermined confidence in episcopal decisions. For in what way was the decision at Arles more definitive than that of the Roman council of the previous year? But the bewilderment of a convert of less than two years' standing, called upon suddenly to deal with matters he barely understood at a time when the synodal system of the Church was still embryonic, may be pardoned. And, since Arles was a larger body than the council which preceded it, we can perhaps see already the origin of the idea, developed by Constantine at Nicaea, that the decision of the world-wide episcopate is final. *Securus iudicat orbis terrarum* may have been the principle towards which the Emperor was feeling his way by trial and error.

[1] By Otto Seeck in *Zeitschrift für Kirchengeschichte*, xxx (1909), pp. 207-208. See also Pierre Batiffol in *Bulletin d'ancienne littérature et d'archéologie chrétienne*, iv (1914), pp. 284-287.

[2] 'Malgré tout, cette lettre maussade et découragée trahit l'irrésolution de l'empereur et l'impuissance du gouvernement' (P. Monceaux, *Histoire littéraire de l'Afrique chrétienne*, vol. iv (Paris, 1912), p. 349).

[3] 'Meum iudicium postulant, qui ipse iudicium Christi expecto' (Appendix to Optatus, C.S.E.L., xxvi. 209).

[4] 'Dico enim, ut se veritas habet, sacerdotum iudicium ita debet haberi, ac si ipse Dominus residens iudicet. Nihil enim licet his aliud sentire vel aliud iudicare, nisi quod Christi magisterio sunt edocti' (*ibid.*).

[5] 'Sicut in causis gentilium fieri solet, appellationem interposuerunt' (*ibid.*).

An even more significant point in this letter is the threat of force against recalcitrants. This was in fact implemented against the Donatists, though without much success. Its importance lies in the fact that as early as 314 there had begun that tradition of persecution in the interests of orthodox conformity which was to mark the Christian Roman Empire and therefore its successor states, the medieval nations.

So long, however, as Constantine lived it was the Church which defined orthodoxy and the State which enforced it. The Nicene Council, by means of which Constantine dealt with the other great ecclesiastical dispute of his reign, that concerning Arius, and with various minor ecclesiastical difficulties, illustrates the fact. As we have seen, although it was summoned by the Emperor, its deliberations seem to have been reasonably free and the civil power accepted its conclusions without question. Towards the end of his reign Constantine showed distinct signs of going back upon this policy, in listening to the enemies of Athanasius. But he could be pardoned for this, in that the Nicene decision was emphatically a snap vote and, as the long-drawn-out history of the Arian controversy shows, a large part, perhaps the greater part, of the Church was not convinced of its truth. It would not have been difficult to persuade the old Emperor that he had been misled and that his Council did not represent the true voice of Christendom. Considerations of State, too, entered into the matter, for Constantine was apparently made to doubt the loyalty of Athanasius. Considering the novelty of the situation in which he found himself—novel alike to him and to the Church— Constantine's efforts to find a *statut* of Church-State relations was not the worst that could be imagined. He inherited from the pagan past the idea that it was the State's duty to regulate religion. Was he not himself *ex officio* the *pontifex maximus*, supreme over the old religion, even though, as a Christian, he did not exercise his duties in person? On the Church's side, there was no clear tradition upon which to rely. Hitherto ecclesiastical affairs had been managed ecclesiastically. But in the age of persecution there was no other way in which to manage them. What if there were a Christian

Emperor? What if what had previously seemed a wild dream came true? Was it a matter of principle that a Christian ruler should be excluded from all say in Church affairs? The Donatists, it is true, were to ask truculently, *Quid est imperatori cum ecclesia?*[1] But they did not do so until they had invalidated their right to raise the slogan by themselves first appealing to the Emperor. There must have been many who felt inclined to answer them like Optatus: *Non enim respublica est in ecclesia sed ecclesia in republica est, id est, in imperio Romano.*[2] The Constantinian revolution was so sudden and complete that neither Church nor State could quickly adjust themselves to it, and precedents were lacking. In the circumstances Constantine did not do so badly in his makeshift devices, unfortunate though some of their implications may have proved later. His system, if it can be so called, at least gave place to the elements which might be thought rightfully to claim some share in the unravelling of ecclesiastical problems, namely the Church on the one hand, as it had existed hitherto, a voluntary society, and the Roman State on the other, the state which was now setting out on a policy of Christianising the society it governed.

His successors were more maladroit. They had suffered, one might say, from a Christian education, which, as then understood, was not always a good thing, as the case of Julian, driven by it back to paganism, reminds us. So they developed a fanaticism from which the soldier-Emperor, who had found his way painfully to Christianity and knew something of the puzzles involved in faith, was more free, despite his blustering denunciations in parade-ground style against pagans, heretics and schismatics. Constantius, the most successful of Constantine's sons, is the supreme example of the amateur theologian-Emperor, who descended himself into the lists of the Arian dispute and set himself to enforce the solution of it which his courtier bishops alleged to be the true one. He seems less to have taken the pulse of the Church (as Constantine commonly did before acting) than to have decided in his own mind what was good for it and then set out to compel the adoption of his ideas. Whether the famous dictum put into his

Optatus, *De schism. Donatist.* iii. 3.   [2] *Ibid.*

mouth by Athanasius (who, it has been pointed out, was far more ready to denounce him behind his back than to his face) be genuine or not, it accurately sums up his policy as it appears on the surface—'What I will, let that be reckoned a canon'.[1] It is noteworthy that he was as tactless with paganism as with the Church, attempting to go beyond his father's policy and suppress it by law, and depriving pagans of the symbols they valued of the old alliance between the gods and the Roman State, such as the Altar of Victory in the Senate House.[2] He, much more than Constantine, tried to make himself the *pontifex maximus* of Christianity.

Let us turn now to the ecclesiastical thought of the age in order to see how the Church reacted to this tendency to Caesaro-papism which, given the ancient pagan background, was bound to emerge the moment the Roman State took the Church under its wing, and which in fact raised its head under Constantine's successors. Here two tendencies can be discerned, the one expressed very fully, the other at first more tacit. We have first uncritical laudation of the idea of a Christian Emperor, of which Eusebius of Caesarea's *Vita Constantini* is the best example. That work cannot be said to express any theory on the subject, for it is merely an extravagant and unqualified panegyric upon every act of Constantine, and its secondary aim is quite clearly to show how intimate its author was with the monarch and what a high opinion Constantine had of him. Eusebius has Boswell's attitude without the diligence which makes Johnson's biographer so photographic. His Constantine is an effigy on a pedestal which comes to life only when the Emperor is allowed to speak for himself in quoted correspondence—in this the exact converse of Boswell's Johnson. But, despite the imperfections of the book as a guide to deeper contemporary thought, it is significant for its very lack of critical insight. Many bishops with far less than Eusebius's limited genius must have thought as he did, or perhaps even more extravagantly, of Constantine in his role of Christian Emperor. Whatever the Emperor did

[1] 'Αλλ' ὅπερ ἐγὼ βούλομαι, τοῦτο κανών, ἔλεγε, νομιζέσθω. οὕτω γάρ μου λέγοντος ἀνέχονται, οἱ τῆς Συρίας λεγόμενοι ἐπίσκοποι. Ἡ τοίνυν πείσθητε, ἢ καὶ ὑμεῖς ὑπερόριοι γενήσεσθε (*Hist. Arianorum*, 33).
[2] Cf. Symmachus, *Relatio*, iii. 4-6 and *Cod. Theod.* XVI. x. 2-6.

in Church affairs was right: theirs not to reason why. The history of the Arian controversy, in which a certain ovine quality marks the doings of the majority of the episcopate, suggests as much. After all, the reactions of the unthinking are often of more importance in history than the considered conduct of the few who reflect.

Our evidence for the general attitude of Christians towards the post-Constantinian Empire is scattered. We are dependent largely upon incidental dicta in books devoted for the most part to other topics, in arriving at an estimate of it. Nevertheless, these are sufficient to enable us to come to some conclusions. One significant phenomenon is the survival of the old pagan vocabulary of divinity applied to the Emperor in Christian documents and the acceptance of it when Christian Emperors use it about themselves. It may be argued with some truth that it was conventional—to some extent it had been so even in pagan times—and meant little more than does the exaggerated phraseology of respect and endearment customary in modern letter-writing. Yet early Christianity had been so much on its guard against even pagan conventions that the fact that no danger was apprehended from this usage tells its own tale. It suggests that Christians were insensibly absorbing something of the supernatural awe felt for rulers, especially in the Near East, from early times. Indeed it is noteworthy that one can observe a difference in the attitude to the Emperor between the two halves of the Empire. In the Latin half we have already seen what appears to have been Miltiades's diplomatic side-stepping of an implied imperial claim to judge the Church. It is no surprise to find there also a greater disposition on the part of bishops to defy imperial attempts to impose forms of Arianism that can be discerned in the East. The difference is partly due to the greater hold of the theology connected with Arianism in the East than in the West. But something must be attributed to a lesser reverence for monarchy and a greater spirit of ecclesiastical independence in the Western provinces, which had never wholly lost the tradition of Brutus.[1] In the East the ideals of Athens had long been overlaid by

[1] It is noteworthy that, whilst in the East $\beta\alpha\sigma\iota\lambda\epsilon\acute{u}s$ was the normal title for the Emperor, in the West the word *rex* was studiously avoided. It returns to common usage only as a term for the barbarian kings of the period of barbarian invasion and settlement.

the longer and more indigenous tradition of divine monarchy. Though, as has been said, they are compromised witnesses to ecclesiastical independence, it is worth noting that the Donatists of the West were the only religious party in the fourth century who kept up a persistent and often very successful resistance to imperial religious policy.

It would, however, be unfair to suggest that zeal for the Church's freedom to manage her own affairs was confined to Western Christendom. Athanasius has already been mentioned. It is worth while recalling that the phrase about him best known to the ordinary man is the hackneyed *Athanasius contra mundum* and that this might at many points of his career be construed as *Athanasius contra imperium*, since much of his lifelong fight for the Nicene faith was a tussle against the Arianising tendencies of the Eastern court, particularly that of Constantius. He may have been reluctant to defy the Emperor to his face—a great thing to demand of anyone in the climate of that age. He may have been a special pleader, ready to use every circumstance he could in his own favour. But he was at least one who regarded truth as the ultimate court of appeal in doctrinal matters and maintained that principle against the princes and rulers of this world. St. Basil, too, as the famous story of his interview with Valens shows, when he rebuked the imperial cook for interfering in theological disputes and had previously informed the Prefect, who resented his boldness, that he had evidently never yet met a bishop.[1] Yet in general the history of the fourth century in the East shows that by the end of it it was becoming more and more difficult to uphold freedom either of doctrine or discipline in the Church as a self-governing society. The tragic fate of St. John Chrysostom and the events connected with the Councils of Ephesus and Chalcedon were to demonstrate this clearly.

Meanwhile, beneath the surface of the sensational disputes which form the dramatic part of the Church history of this period, an integration was taking place between the Church and secular society. This was, in the long run, to have a more decisive

[1] Theodoret, *H.E.* iv. 16. Greg. Naz. *Oratio*, xliii. 50.

effect upon Church-State relations than the more obvious problem of the respective functions of Emperor and hierarchy in the defini-tion of doctrine, since it determined the pattern of Christian civilisation down to comparatively recent times. The outstanding fact is the extent to which the Church was called to take a large share in local administration. The centralisation by which the later Roman Empire sought to combat the military, political and economic crises which threatened the continued existence of the Roman world had virtually annihilated the traditions of municipal self-government. So the bishop, elected by the Christian com-munity of his city (a body more and more corresponding to the entire population), had come to be the sole man of influence still popularly chosen. It is not surprising therefore to find him more and more accepted as leader of the *civitas*, judge by preference of legal disputes, protector of widows and orphans, sometimes even military commander.[1] Here we see the first beginnings of the bishop's position as a local magnate which had so much effect upon later Church history.

This, however, was more especially a Western development, since local government in the West was in a more precarious position than in the East, and it gathered momentum as barbarian rule replaced Roman administration in the fifth century. A fact of more immediate significance is the extent to which the Church was becoming regarded as bound up with the social and economic framework of the Empire. In the West, when imperial govern-ment collapsed with the coming of the barbarians, this was to be a source of strength, for the Church became the supporter of the subject populations and their representative to the new rulers. Before this time, and later in the East, it was sometimes a source of weakness. It is difficult, for example, to explain the strength and persistence of Donatism in North Africa except upon the hypo-thesis that in the minds of many Africans the Catholic Church was associated with a political, social and economic system which they

---

[1] Outstanding examples of bishops fulfilling this last role are Synesius of Cyrene in the Pentapolis and Sidonius Apollinaris at Clermont in Auvergne. See W. S. Crawford, *Synesius the Hellene* (London, 1901), chap. vi, and C. E. Stevens, *Sidonius Apollinaris and His Age* (Oxford, 1933), chap. vii.

regarded as oppressive—an hypothesis which many lines of evidence converge to support.[1] In the East a similar phenomenon becomes apparent with the passage of time. The attractiveness of Nestorianism to Christians outside the boundaries of the Roman Empire is partly to be explained by the fact that its profession differentiated them from the specifically Roman Christianity which their Zoroastrian masters suspected. The adhesion of Egypt and of large parts of Syria to the Monophysite cause is probably not unconnected with that weariness of the imperial system which can be detected in many quarters by this time.[2] It is noteworthy that 'Melchites'—'royalists, emperor's men'—was the derisive epithet applied to the supporters of Chalcedonian orthodoxy by the Monophysites. Monophysitism, indeed, flourished in the two areas where old cultures with a long history had been submerged since the days of Alexander the Great beneath Hellenistic and Roman conquest, and the Monophysites, who adopted Coptic and Syriac increasingly as their liturgical and theological languages, were joining hands with a cultural revolt against the universalism of Graeco-Roman civilisation and perhaps giving it articulate form in religious guise. More than thirty years ago Sir Llewellyn Woodward was the first in England to draw attention to these significant facts,[3] and the progress of historical studies seems more and more to underline their importance.

It is the fate of all religions closely integrated with State systems to share the fortunes of the latter. The Roman Empire in the fourth century was rapidly losing that affection from its subjects which had shown itself in the days of Augustus by genuine,

[1] See on this: W. H. C. Frend, *The Donatist Church: A Movement of Protest in North Africa* (Oxford, 1952), and for some criticisms the review by G. W. H. Lampe in *The Journal of Theological Studies* (New Series, vol. iv, part 2, October 1953, pp. 255-258). A rather different point of view is taken by B. H. Warmington, *The North African Provinces from Diocletian to the Vandal Conquest* (Cambridge, 1954), chap. vii, pp. 76-102.

[2] Cf. the story of the Greek found by the Byzantine envoys to Attila's court, Priscus and Maximin, who preferred life with the barbarians to the burdens of imperial citizenship. (*Historici Graeci Minores* (ed. L. Dindorf, vol. i, Leipzig, 1870), pp. 305 *sqq.*) The same tendency to flee the Roman Empire may perhaps explain some part of the popularity of the monastic life.

[3] E. L. Woodward, *Christianity and Nationalism in the Later Roman Empire* (London, 1916).

spontaneous and, to modern minds, exaggerated demonstrations of loyalty. The fact presented a real, if perhaps unconscious, problem to the Church which had so recently been offered and had accepted the patronage of the imperial government. There was a price to pay for the conversion of Constantine, a price for which the bill was not presented all at once.

CHAPTER IV

BYZANTINE THEOCRACY

A basic principle of modern scientific research technique is that of the 'control' experiment. It has been increasingly recognised that it is possible to go very far astray in studying the behaviour of some substance or organism in specialised conditions unless one possesses also exact data about its behaviour in more ordinary or different circumstances. Thus, for example, to judge whether a species of microbe is stimulated or inhibited in its development by unusual heat, it is necessary not only to observe the growth of a colony subjected to warmth, but also that of a colony of the same strain in similar conditions but living in a more normal temperature. If one is to examine the efficacy of a new remedy for disease, one must have, side by side with the group of patients receiving it, another group to whom it is denied. Only so can the effects of that common logical fallacy, *post hoc, ergo propter hoc*, be eliminated.

The historian, by the nature of his study, is debarred from exactly imitating this technique, for unfortunately he cannot experiment upon human societies. Occasionally, however, historical circumstances produce for him something analogous to the natural scientist's isolated groups of *corpora vilia*. Societies, akin at least in composition and historical background, become by the accidents of time isolated from each other and subjected to different historical environments. It is then a reasonable supposition that the divergences which they develop are to be attributed primarily to the varying circumstances in which they have been compelled to live. A reasonable supposition—but one attended in practice by many dangers. For human life is a very complex thing; and human environment consists of a multitude of factors not easily separable, not always indeed recognisable, especially when evidence about the past is scanty. Simplification is the historian's besetting sin. Upon how many history collection papers in this University have been pencilled the words: 'Generalisation from insufficient evidence'? The same phrase might well be written in the margins of many historical works commonly accepted as standard.

Despite this *caveat*, it seems not wholly rash to suggest that the cultural and political schism which became increasingly apparent in the world of the Roman Empire from at least the fifth century A.D.—and indeed earlier—is an isolating factor which justifies our applying the technique, or rather the reasoning, of experiment and control to what we may begin to call the Eastern and the Western Christian worlds. I will not enter into the dangerous and complicated question of when we can speak of that schism as definitive. Nevertheless, whether with Pirenne[1] we see the crucial moment in the age of Muhammadan conquest, or, with his critics, regard the establishment of the barbarian kingdoms in the West nearly two centuries earlier as effecting the break,[2] in neither case can we regard the increasing isolation of the Roman and Hellenic halves of the Roman Empire as without significance. I do not ignore the fact that the seeds of division can be observed long before either of the suggested crucial centuries:[3] no historical events fail to throw their shadows backwards, because historical causes are commonly slow and cumulative in operation. But such considerations have comparatively little to do with my purpose, which is to argue that, from at least certain points of view, the Byzantine world can be regarded historically as a control experiment for determining the factors governing the evolution of the West, and vice versa. Since, however, these lectures are chiefly concerned with Western Euro-

[1] 'De quelque côté qu'on l'envisage, la période inaugurée par l'établissement des Barbares dans l'Empire n'a donc rien introduit dans l'histoire d'absolument nouveau. . . . Bref, le caractère de la *Romania* reste méditerranéen' (H. Pirenne, *Mahomet et Charlemagne* (5e édit., Paris and Brussels, 1937), p. 123).

[2] 'My own belief is that the unity of the Mediterranean world was broken by the pirate fleets of Vandal Carthage and that the shattered unity was never restored' (N. H. Baynes in *Journal of Roman Studies*, vol. xix (1929), p. 233). See also on this question R. S. López, 'Mohammed and Charlemagne: A Revision', in *Speculum*, vol. xviii (1943), pp. 14-38; H. Laurent, 'Les Travaux de M. Henri Pirenne', in *Byzantion*, vol. vii (1932), pp. 495 *sqq.*; G. I. Bratianu, 'Une Nouvelle Histoire de l'Europe au moyen-âge: la fin du monde antique et le triomphe de l'Orient', in *Revue belge de philosophie et d'histoire*, vol. xviii (1939), pp. 252-266.

[3] Some would trace this division back even as far as the first century A.D. See Ettore Lepore, 'Un sintomo di coscienza occidentale all' "apogeo dell' impero"', in *Rivista storica italiana*, anno lx (Naples, 1948), pp. 193-203.

pean history, it will be convenient to take Byzantium as the 'control' and the West as the *corpus vile* subjected to new influences rather than the other way round.

Such a method can be justified, in the writer's opinion, by indisputable facts, especially in the matter of Church and State. For, whatever the developments—and they were not wanting—the way in which Church and State were related in the Byzantine Empire shows a more obvious continuity with the past than anything which can be observed in the West. Byzantium at least was conscious of no change, nor can any event or chain of events be pointed out which resulted in a revolution in ideas or facts concerning this link between the sacred and the secular in the East during the whole period up to 1453. It seems at first sight a paradox that, despite the innumerable political revolutions in Byzantine life, the constitutional and administrative history of the Empire presents a spectacle of unbroken evolution, much as England, reputed in the Middle Ages and later to be one of the most revolutionary of states, is yet to the historian almost the supreme example of historical continuity. *Plus ça change, plus c'est la même chose,* might be the final judgement upon both societies. At no point in Byzantine history can one lay a finger and say: 'Here is an absolute dividing line'.

In the West, as we shall see, it is far otherwise. Between the old system of the Roman Empire and the polities of the barbarian successor states, between these and the Carolingian experiment in Empire, between that and the feudal world, between feudalism and the beginnings of modern nationalism, there are great gulfs fixed, however numerous the bridges that span them. The fact can be illustrated by the consideration that to the Byzantine the classical world, however remote, remained also comprehensible. To the Westerner it had become, even by the eighth century, a fairyland transfigured by the mists of time. Nor can its rediscovery by the humanists of the later Middle Ages be regarded as much more than an artificial *tour de force*. From Petrarch to Erasmus, those who tried to live classically got about as near to the objects of their *mimesis* as Marie-Antoinette to the life of a dairymaid.

67

Between Byzantium and the West there is all the difference between an ancient family which has retained the essentials of its heritage through all the turns of fortune and a proletarianised *noblesse* which, with the return of wealth, endeavours to recapture the life of its ancestors.

Not that Byzantium received no new influences. The extent to which those who still laid claim to the titles of Hellenes and Romans—both of which names in Gibbon's jaundiced view they disgraced[1]—became in fact Orientalised, is still a matter of dispute among Byzantinists, and whilst scientific Byzantine studies are still relatively in their infancy it behoves the non-specialist to maintain a respectful silence. Nevertheless, it would seem that the effect of influences upon Constantinople coming from the further East, from Persia and beyond, cannot be denied. But, for our purposes at least, such influences can be regarded as slight in their incidence in the ecclesiastical field. For Christianity had been so thoroughly coloured by Helleno-Roman culture by the fifth century, and in the process so standardised, that even in the Eastern Empire it was impervious to most Oriental influences other than those it had received at its birth. The best proof of this is the way in which religious schism and cultural change went together in the East—a matter referred to in the last lecture. It was not until, in the Nestorian and Monophysite schisms, the churches of Persia, Syria and Egypt had broken ecclesiastically and politically with Constantinople that they reverted wholly to a Christianity expressed in Syriac or Coptic. Even now the embalmed Greek words which still stud the liturgy and theology of these bodies bear witness to the indissoluble connection between developed Christianity and Hellenism, whilst even later it was partly through nominally de-Hellenised Christians that Greek philosophy in Syriac translation reached the Arabic world and was thence transmitted to the West.[2] On the Church's side there was no conscious break away from the

---

[1] 'But the subjects of the Byzantine empire, who assume and dishonour the names both of Greeks and Romans, present a dead uniformity of abject vices, which are neither softened by the weakness of humanity nor animated by the vigour of memorable crimes' (*Decline and Fall*, chap. xlviii, vol. v, p. 170).

[2] See De Lacy O'Leary, *How Greek Science passed to the Arabs* (London, 1949).

past and it is therefore unlikely that we shall find any essential change in the Christian outlook upon the State.

In a similar way the Byzantine state maintained many of the traditions of the Roman Empire. During the whole period of the Dark and Middle Ages the Eastern Empire, for this very reason, stands out as a unique form of government in Christendom. 'The contrast of political structure between East and West', says Ludo Moritz Hartmann, 'is the most characteristic feature of the Early Middle Ages. The riddle of Byzantium, which remained a great power despite all territorial losses, finds its solution in its economic and social organization.'[1] The same author points out the differences which distinguished the Eastern Empire from the increasingly decentralised barbarian succession states of the West, namely an hierarchic lay civil service under the Emperor, a system of taxation which permitted standing military forces, and a control and utilisation of trade and industry. 'The more highly developed economy of Byzantium could feed a denser population, while its organisation was capable of combining and utilising the resources at its disposal in a much more effective manner than the Western states, based on natural economy, were able to do.'[2] And Hartmann explains by this fact the position of the Byzantine Church, as compared with that attained by the Church in the West. Calling it (with some exaggeration) 'always a department of state organization', he says: 'There was no possibility of an independent evolution, because the organs of the state interfered everywhere and there was no room for ecclesiastical autonomy. Those secular functions, which elsewhere were taken over by the church, had in Byzantium retained the character of public services.'[3]

There is clearly much truth in this view. The Church in the East, down to the time of the overwhelming of Eastern Christendom by Islam, was not in partnership with relatively rudimentary forms of political organisation such as it confronted in the West once the framework of Roman administration withered before the

[1] Ludo Moritz Hartmann, *The Early Mediaeval State: Byzantium, Italy and the West* (Historical Association Pamphlet, General Series, G.14, London, 1949), p. 9.
[2] *Ibid.*   [3] *Ibid.*

growing barbarisation of the new kingdoms. It stood within the old tradition of the *polis*, now grown to be a world state. And, as every student of Platonic and Aristotelian political thought is aware, from the early days of Greek civilisation the city had been regarded as the be-all and end-all of the citizen's life. Nothing seemed so alien to the classical mind as any claim of an individual to live a life apart from the community. The specious individualism of classical paganism is a deceptive and accidental growth upon an older and deeper tradition of collectivism: indeed much of it has been read into classical thought by modern individualists of the Swinburne type. And, once the pressure of economic necessity and foreign invasion began to be felt in the later days of the Roman Empire, the imperial system reverted to a totalitarianism as relentless as that of ancient Sparta, if less crude and primitive. There could therefore be no room for a doctrine of *imperium in imperio* in Byzantium. The conception of a free church in a free state could never arise either in the Constantinian polity or in the Byzantine system which succeeded it, still less the notion of a state subjected to the Church in some or all of its functions. How that latter could arise in the West we shall later see. By the shores of the Bosphorus it did not enter men's minds.

But political and social circumstances do not explain all. It is not merely the absence of certain ideas, but the strong influence of their opposites which normally governs the evolution of societies. In Byzantium two streams of thought about the nature of imperial authority flowed together to enhance the Emperor's place in the Church. On the one hand was the old pagan conception of the divinity of rulers, strongly held at Rome, yet more indigenous still in the Eastern lands ruled from Constantinople, reinforced by the universal view of the ancient world that the king was responsible for the due worship of the gods by his people. On the other hand, once the Empire became Christian this idea could be, and was, baptized into that of a divinely authorised Christian kingship, akin to the Davidic monarchy of the Old Testament. Byzantine iconography illustrates this last conception. Thus, in the illuminations of a Paris manuscript David appears in the robes of the Basileus. In the mosaics of San Vitale at Ravenna, Melchizedek, the mysterious priest-king of Jerusalem, wears the same vestments, familiar to every subject of the Empire. So, too, in Byzantine pictures the majesty and authority of the Emperor is associated with that of the kingly attributes of Christ, from whom the Emperor is seen receiving his power and before whom, as in one of the mosaics of St. Sophia, he prostrates himself in worship. For the Augustus is the vicegerent of God, just as formerly he had been regarded as, though divine himself, the servant of the higher gods.[1]

Here again continuity tells. The conception of divine kingship was not lacking in the Western barbarian states, the kings of which laid claim to descent from Teutonic deities. But, whatever their boasts of divine lineage, and later of divine appointment, the barbarian kings were not the heirs of Augustus. The *parvenu* can never have the self-assurance of the born aristocrat.[2] Though the idea that it was the people who raised the Emperor to his throne never disappeared at Byzantium (derived, as it was, from the tradition of the *lex regia* by which the Roman people delegated its power to the *princeps*)[3] yet for centuries no non-Roman Western ruler dared to claim the unique position of the Emperor by popular election or otherwise. Indeed it was long before the West dared even to reject the shadowy but venerable overlordship of the distant Augustus at Constantinople. Not by ordinary hereditary right, but by continuity of political succession, did the Basileus of Byzantium claim authority over the whole world, the οἰκουμένη, and in particular of that part of it subject to his direct power. Against such a claim no secondary authority, not even that of the Church, could establish a valid counter-claim.

Are we then to accept as the explanatory formula for Church-State relations in the Roman Empire of the East the much can-

---

[1] See André Grabar, *L'Empereur dans l'art byzantin* (Publications de la Faculté des Lettres de l'Université de Strasbourg, fasc. 75, Paris, 1936), pp. 95-97 and 98-122.

[2] Their realisation of this fact is perhaps to be discerned in the hesitation of any barbarian leader before the time of Charlemagne to take the imperial title. Even powerful chiefs like Alaric and Ricimer set up puppet emperors of Roman origin rather than claim the purple themselves. [3] Justinian, *Institutes*, I. ii. 6.

vassed phrase 'Caesaropapism'? Only, I think, if we shut our eyes
to the complexity of a situation which does not admit of statement
in simple terms. We have seen already that we are dealing with a
different situation from that of Western Europe. Byzantium was
emphatically not a state which had abdicated to local or inferior
centres of authority any of its prerogatives: it was not an interim
type of state interposed between classical and modern conceptions
of sovereignty. Consequently we should not expect to find evidence of the existence of, or even desire for, ecclesiastical independence of the kind the West was to know in days when often the
Church stood as the sole barrier to localised anarchy. If we are to
regard the Eastern Emperors as Caesarean Popes, we must
eliminate from our definitions of Papacy all those functions of
temporal power added to spiritual which are suggested by the
names of Hildebrand, Innocent III and Boniface VIII. If the
Basileus was a Pope he was not, and could not be, a spiritual ruler
attracting to himself temporal power. The reverse was the case.
Whatever divinity hedged the person of the Augustus was derived
from his temporal position and not vice versa. This may seem a
truism unnecessary to state. Yet one wonders whether the currency
of Caesaropapist terminology has not unconsciously been influenced by the connotations of the word 'Pope' to Western ears.
What has really to be determined is rather whether the Emperors
arrogated to themselves spiritual prerogatives to which Christian
tradition gave them no right.

The most obvious basis for the charge that they did so lies in
imperial activity in the doctrinal sphere. Some of the most sensational episodes in Byzantine history turn upon the efforts of successive Emperors to enforce interpretations of the Faith contained
in imperial decrees. We have already noticed the tendency in the
days before one can talk of an Eastern Empire at all, those of
Constantius or Valens, and have noted the fact that the policy was
normally more sustained and successful in the Eastern provinces
than in the Western. As imperial authority wanes in the West such
incidents become more frequent and more blatant. There are
three classical examples. In 484 Zeno, by his *Henoticon* or Edict of

Union, attempted a compromise with the Monophysites by a doctrinal formula which ignored, though it did not contradict, the decrees of the Council of Chalcedon. In the sixth century, Justinian, in the course of a tortuous and changeable religious policy, forced upon Pope Vigilius, with the aid of a General Council, the condemnation of the famous 'Three Chapters', writings of theologians of the past who had been left in good odour at Chalcedon. In 565, at the end of his reign, he declared by edict in favour of that form of Monophysitism which proclaimed the incorruptibility of Christ's human body. In the next century Heraclius, by the *Ecthesis* of 638 , attempted to make Monothelism, the doctrine of a single will in the Incarnate Christ, the orthodoxy of the Empire—a policy modified by the same method in 648 by his successor, Constans II, whose *Type* demanded neutrality upon the issue by forbidding any discussion of the existence of one or two wills in the Lord.

Such attempts at officially determined and officially enforced theology look at first sight singularly like Caesaropapism of the most radical type. Yet what is commonly ignored is the fact that all of them, with the exception of the condemnation of the Three Chapters, failed dismally. None of the others became part of the tradition of the Church or even of the Byzantine Empire. All in the long run were treated as heretical vagaries. And the one exception proves the rule. For the Three Chapters, however cavalierly treated at the Second Council of Constantinople, according to Justinian's demand, were at least suspect of Nestorianism, a heresy already rejected by the Church. Indeed, Theodore of Mopsuestia, author of one part of the anathematised writings, would by common consent today be regarded as more clearly Nestorian than Nestorius himself.

It cannot be too strongly emphasised that the Emperors of the East succeeded in making their doctrinal policies prevail only when these were in accord with what history on the long view shows to have been the mind of the Church. It may be argued that this was so merely because the West (which, before the medieval schism between Rome and Constantinople, could still make its

opinion felt) resisted. The long arm of the Emperor did not reach
so easily to the West as to the East. But this explanation, though it
fits to some extent the history of imperial intervention in the long-
drawn-out Monophysite disputes, breaks down when one examines
the Iconoclastic controversy of the eighth and ninth centuries.
Then, with even more brutal force, a series of Emperors tried to
suppress the veneration of images—a matter which touched
popular religion even more directly than more abstract questions
about the being of Christ. The West, it is true, took the opposite
side, at least so far as the Papacy was concerned. But the West
was by no means unanimous: its chief temporal ruler, Charlemagne, criticised both Iconodules and Iconoclasts. If one studies
the long and complicated history of the matter, it seems clear that
what ultimately defeated Iconoclasm was the firm attachment of
the majority of the Byzantine people, led by the monks (who
occupied in popular regard a position not unlike that of the Old
Testament prophets), to the use of images and to the conviction
that the prohibition of it derived from unorthodox views, akin to
Monophysitism, of the nature of the Incarnation. There is, indeed,
much more to be said of the controversy than that: but there is the
basic fact which explains the ultimate failure of Iconoclasm.

In short, one cannot point to any instance in Byzantine history
in which emperors, however autocratic, succeeded finally in turning the current of belief in a direction opposed to Church tradition
and to the convictions of the majority of churchmen, clerical or
lay. In the last resort they always found themselves opposed by a
force of passive resistance which, if more amorphous than Western
insistence upon the rights of the ecclesiastical power, was just as
deadening to the blows of Erastianism.[1] Nor could rulers defy
with impunity the moral rules of the Church, at any rate to the
extent of expecting the Church to canonise breaches of the moral
code. When Leo VI persisted in entering upon a fourth marriage in
906, by marrying his mistress Zoë, he was excommunicated by the

[1] 'C'est un fait que, malgré leur puissance, ni Justinien, ni les Héracléides, ni les empereurs
iconoclastes n'ont jamais pu faire triompher dans l'Église d'Orient des dogmes qui lui
semblaient contraires à l'orthodoxie' (Louis Bréhier, *Les Institutions de l'empire byzantin*
(Paris, 1949), p. 441).

Patriarch, Nicholas Mysticus. Though Nicholas's objections were ultimately overruled by Rome and the other patriarchates, to which the rule prohibiting fourth marriages was not sacrosanct, a virtual schism resulted from the excommunication, which convulsed the Empire and had severe political repercussions. Indeed, the conception of the bishop as guardian of the sacraments, with power to repel from them the unworthy and the unorthodox, always remained alive in Byzantium, however often threatened in its working by brute force—as indeed it often was in the West.

The undoubted influence of Byzantine Emperors in Church affairs is therefore a phenomenon more impressive at first sight than under close analysis. To see the Basileus as king and priest is a superficial way of viewing the matter and cannot be maintained when one examines history more closely. Thus, for example, it is erroneous to imagine that the efforts of emperors to establish dogmatic standards by imperial decree were made completely on their own initiative or authority. Rarely or never was this the case. Zeno's *Henoticon* was issued in close accord with Acacius, the Patriarch of Constantinople, whom the Emperor had consulted. Justinian, as already related, obtained, however forcibly, the assent of both Pope and Oecumenical Council to his condemnation of the Three Chapters. Procopius has left us the vivid picture of the Augustus burning midnight oil in long and anxious conference with theologians, endeavouring to plumb to the depths the mysteries of Christology.[1] Even the launching of Iconoclasm by Leo the Isaurian in 725 was, in answer to the objections of the Patriarch Germanus, given some measure of ecclesiastical authority by a *silentium* held in 729 or 730—a mixto-clerical and lay imperial council, not unlike the Anglo-Saxon *Witenagemot*. In the following reign of Constantine V an oecumenical council of the Church was summoned to put the whole matter upon what was regarded as a firm dogmatic basis. At no time could the imperial will decide religious matters in complete isolation from the Church.

[1] ὃς δὴ κάθηται ἀφύλακτος ἐς ἀεὶ ἐπὶ λέσχης τινὸς ἀωρὶ νύκτωρ, ὁμοῦ τοῖς τῶν ἱερέων ἐσχατογέρουσιν ἀνακυκλεῖν τὰ Χριστιανῶν λόγια σπουδὴν ἔχων (Procopius, *History of the Wars*, VII. xxxii. 9 (Loeb Edit. by H. B. Dewing, vol. iv, London and New York, 1924), p. 422).

What then was the Byzantine idea of the Emperor's role in the Church, if he was not its unquestioned master? The question is not easy to answer, chiefly because the problem depended, not upon precise constitutional formulation, but upon a living and changing tradition. It was suggested in the last chapter that, because of the relatively sudden change in Constantine's day, by which the Church passed from outlawry to imperial patronage, no theory of the Emperor's position in Christendom could then be formulated, so that this vital question was left to be solved *ambulando*. I would suggest now that, at least in the East, that state of uncertainty lasted longer than we are apt to imagine—perhaps throughout Byzantine history. In legal codes the Emperors sometimes threw out *obiter dicta* giving expression to their own idea of their ecclesiastical responsibilities in this or that matter. But no comprehensive statement was ever made, either by them or by the Byzantine Church.[1] It remained a subject for discussion, and often for controversy, as concrete problems arose. Students of English constitutional history will recognise here something not unfamiliar to them—the flexibility of a constitution never reduced to full written definition and changing with changing times, though its main outlines remain the same. That in itself suggests the impracticability of trying to reduce Byzantine theories of Church and State to formulae. Caesaropapism, the Church viewed as a department of State, theocracy—these suggested phrases all fail to catch the Protean character of the historic reality.

It would be unwise to rush in with an attempted definition where so many great men have failed to give satisfaction. 'Prudence is cautious how she defines.' Let this brief consideration of the 'control experiment' conclude rather by drawing attention to a series of points necessary to be borne in mind if we are even to approach, not a definition (which is perhaps in the nature of things impossible), but any understanding of the phenomenon at all.

(1) Let us remember the observations with which we began. We must always remember that the Byzantine Church was in

[1] The ideas involved are well discussed by Bréhier, *op. cit.* pp. 431 *sqq.*

partnership, not with young, semi-barbarian, primitivistic states like the kingdoms of the West, but with a centralised, economically developed and administratively evolved State with long traditions. New Rome was in many ways Old Rome writ large. We cannot therefore expect to find the kind of ecclesiastical independence which we find developing in the West and which even there came only slowly and with many struggles.

(2) Byzantium, too, was for centuries a widespread empire ruling many different peoples—one which without absurdity could be thought of as the οἰκουμένη, the inhabited world, or all of it that mattered. Consequently the Emperors had to view religious policy from a wide angle. Too often it is not appreciated that, for example, the Monophysite question involved more than pure theology. Monophysitism by historic chance became closely associated with the growing tendency of the less Hellenised provinces to shake free from the Empire, to recover their old independence of centuries before and their ancestral culture. So to attempt to conciliate and reunite to the Church the opponents of Chalcedon was an apparent political responsibility facing every Emperor from the mid-fifth century to the time of the Muhammadan invasions, which ended the problem by swallowing up the dissident provinces. In the same way, though opinion varies about the genesis of Iconoclasm, it is difficult to believe that it was not, at least in part, a movement determined by Moslem criticism of popular Christianity—and Islam was the major anxiety of the Byzantine Empire in the eighth century. So, in taking an active part in doctrinal disputes, the Emperors of the East were by no means invading a sphere remote from their most immediate duties.

(3) It is coming more and more to be realised that, however irresponsible and absolute the Emperors may appear in their ecclesiastical doings, they were in fact often party leaders and subject to party pressure, rather than arbiters. Byzantium was throughout most of its history a home of faction. It is perhaps not fanciful to see in its politics the continuance of that tradition of party strife, στάσις, which dogged the footsteps of Greek city

states and at certain periods vexed Rome also. Recent research has thrown light upon what seems to us the fantastic relationship between the circus factions of Blues and Greens and religious quarrels.[1] 'Eastern Christianity', says Dvornik, 'was erected on a rational basis, which gave the average faithful active participation in the divine service and Church life and facilities to give their opinion on even the subtlest points of theology. Popular organizations such as the Blues and the Greens thus offered themselves as rallying centres for champions of doctrines true or false to help them in their respective activities.'[2] Even after Heraclius attempted to stifle the revolutionary power of the factions by incorporating them into the machinery of State, party strife, on somewhat different lines, continued and, as the same author has shown, played a great part in later religious disputes. It follows that we must be prepared to see, not so much an imperial dictatorship over the Church in Byzantium, as an inextricable mingling of politics and religion at all times, complicated by a participation of laity, as well as clergy, in doctrinal disputes to a degree rarely, if ever, to be found in the West.[3]

(4) This consideration leads in turn to something of even more fundamental importance. In realising the nature of religious disputes in Byzantium as party conflicts in which, to a greater or lesser extent, all members of the State take part, we are really observing one minor consequence of a supreme fact. That is that to speak of Church-State relations in the East is really a glaring anachronism which only the need to use technical language in history excuses. We have to find words in which to discuss our analysis of the past, but often we shall find ourselves using them in senses which would have conveyed no meaning in the past described. I believe that the conception of Church and State as rival societies in partnership or conflict would have been mean-

---

[1] Those familiar with Scottish and Irish football matches may find the association less extraordinary than it seems to the Englishman.

[2] F. Dvornik, *The Photian Schism* (Cambridge, 1948), p. 7.

[3] See also, on this, Bréhier, *op. cit.* pp. 195 *sqq.*; F. Dvornik, 'The Circus Parties in Byzantium, their Evolution and Suppression', in *Byzantina-Metabyzantina*, vol. i (New York, 1946), pp. 119-133, and G. Manojlović (trs. and ed. H. Grégoire, in *Byzantion*, vol. xi (1936)), pp. 655-665.

ingless to a Byzantine. He was not conscious of belonging to more than one society—the people of God, a flock which had indeed shepherds of different kinds, priests and emperors, but was nevertheless one flock, one people, in every aspect of its life the *respublica Christiana*. We do not necessarily speak nonsense in arguing whether at Constantinople the State ruled the Church or the Church the State. But we must remember that the question thus asked has meaning only in the light of subsequent Western European history. To a man of the age of Justinian or Heraclius it would have been barely intelligible, and scarcely more so to one who lived by the Golden Horn in 1453. We shall see that even in the West it took centuries before that question could be clearly posed: and the West was, as I have tried to show, an infinitely less stable society than that of East Rome, with the almost Chinese quality of conservatism it displayed even in its very real evolution. Had one put the enquiry to a Byzantine he might, if philosophical enough to understand one's meaning, have replied with Rousseau in another context: *Cette question ne paraît difficile à résoudre que parce qu'elle est mal posée.*[1]

It was suggested above that in the Byzantine Empire we meet with a relatively unchanging society which can to some extent be used as a 'control' for our analysis of the varying relations of Church and State in the West. What was then adumbrated can now be made clearer. Does not our brief review of the facts suggest this conclusion? That there is always a problem posed by the fact that Christianity claims to be a supernatural society living in the same world and under the same conditions as the natural society of mankind. The Byzantine reaction to this problem was in fact an attempt to continue the *modus vivendi* between religion and everyday life traditional up to Constantine's day. In other words, though genuinely Christian in desire and fact, Byzantium had assumed that the Christian Church could be incorporated into the State very much to the same degree and in the same manner as the ethnic religions of the past. Society *vis-à-vis* the gods and *vis-à-vis* itself had hitherto never been thought to be essentially

---

[1] *Du contrat social*, ii. 5.

different or distinct: such was the all but universal opinion of antiquity. It was natural to continue the assumption when Christianity made good its claim to be a fit religion for universal empire. As we maintained in the last chapter, that assumption was very generally accepted in the Christian Roman Empire before Byzantium can be thought of as a separate entity. Byzantium, its most authentic heir and continuation, never saw reason to re-examine the matter, however often convulsed by the practical problems resulting from a conception it regarded as axiomatic. In doing so it may or may not have been right: that is barely a question for pure history. But only such a view of Byzantine history can give any real clue, I hold, to a puzzle which has seemed as perplexing to many, especially from the time when scientific history, with Gibbon, became aware that after the fifth century the Roman Empire was not represented solely by Hobbes's crowned ghost on its Roman tombstone, the Papacy.[1]

[1] *Leviathan*, iv. 47.

CHAPTER V

THE WESTERN CHURCH AND THE
POST-ROMAN WORLD

The break-up of civilisations is a phenomenon which directly invites the deadliest disease of historiography, undue dramatisation. Apocalyptic is a literary *genre* which has its due and proper place in theology: it is woefully out of place in history, where it produces dangerous misunderstandings of evidence and distortions of sober fact. It is natural that the age of the overrunning of the Western Roman world by barbarians should have suffered more than most from mythologising. Its events, looked at through the foreshortening glass of time, appear intensely dramatic. As a result a whole series of different and highly coloured treatments of the fifth and following centuries have appeared and produced pictures which still colour the thought of those not professionally concerned with exact history.

Gibbon to some extent corrected the old idea of the barbarian invasions as incursions of locust-like beings wiping out civilisation. He wrote: 'Our fancy may create, or adopt, a pleasing romance that the Goths and Vandals sallied from Scandinavia, ardent to avenge the flight of Odin, to break the chains, and to chastise the oppressors, of mankind; that they wished to burn the records of classic literature and to found their national architecture on the broken members of the Tuscan and Corinthian orders. But, in simple truth, the northern conquerors were neither sufficiently savage nor sufficiently refined to entertain such aspiring ideas of destruction and revenge. The shepherds of Scythia and Germany had been educated in the armies of the empire, whose discipline they acquired, and whose weakness they invaded; with the familiar use of the Latin tongue, they had learned to reverence the name and titles of Rome; and, though incapable of emulating, they were more inclined to admire than to abolish, the arts and studies of a brighter period.'[1]

[1] *Decline and Fall*, chap. lxxi, vol. vii, pp. 308-309.

It would have been well if such a sober estimate of the real state of the case, however in need of correction in detail, could have held the field. But there followed in the nineteenth century (ironically enough partly as a result of the propaganda of the ingenious French aristocrat, the Comte de Gobineau)[1] an opposite myth to that decried by Gibbon, which prospered because it fitted in well with newly discovered German nationalism at a time when the Germans were developing modern historiography. By this the coming of the barbarians was represented as a great cleansing process, replacing the vices of decadent Greco-Roman civilisation by the manly virtues of the Teutonic races. Propagated in England by the doctrinaire ardour which made the learning of E. A. Freeman such a dangerous thing, and popularised by the less documented sentimentalism of Charles Kingsley, this fairy-tale still survives among those whose historical reading is dated. It has indeed behind it the authority of a contemporary witness of the period, Salvian of Marseilles, who, however, even in his own day had difficulty in making such a superb homiletic theme fit the known facts. A reading of Gregory of Tours should be enough to dissipate in any mind the notion of a new and edifying society of simple barbarian saints displacing a corrupt world of refined debauchery. The Merovingians had little to learn from Nero, Commodus or Heliogabalus, not to mention later examples of Roman vice.

It is the social and economic historians who have been foremost in delivering us from romanticism. They have shown us the increasingly precarious economic condition of the later Roman Empire, a society which, from at least the third century onwards, was living beyond its resources. They have insisted, too, upon the increasing pressure of taxation and compulsory service imposed by the fourth-century emperors upon the ordinary citizen, as a factor both sapping active loyalty to Rome and causing men to try to build for themselves a simpler and more direct economy. Already in Constantine's day we are made aware, from legislative attempts to check it, of the growing independence of the great

[1] J. A. de Gobineau, *Essai sur l'inégalité des races humaines*, 4 vols. (Paris, 1853–55).

rural landlords, who were making their domains into strongholds to some degree impervious to the central power. By the fifth century Sidonius Apollinaris complains of men rejecting family traditions of service to the Empire in favour of the life of country squires—an exchange he himself later made.[1] The peasants, too, were revolting against both State and landlords. In general, especially in the West, municipal life, upon which Roman civilisation had chiefly depended, was giving place to a decentralised society based upon the land before ever the barbarian conquests began.

The breakdown of Roman administration in large areas naturally accelerated and confirmed the process, and the new barbarian kingdoms were rural rather than urban in character. The barbarians themselves did not love cities and preferred to settle upon country estates. This suited the situation, for, since land was increasingly recognised as the only sure source of wealth, the warriors of Gothic, Vandal or Frankish armies were rewarded by their leaders with landed estates, because, even had they preferred them, money payments would have been difficult to find. So in the old provinces of the West there sprang up a new, mixed society composed partly of townsfolk and peasants of the old provincial stock, partly of landowners largely of the new conquering races. The new society was organised into independent kingdoms under barbarian kings, who engaged in internecine wars and conquests, the kaleidoscopic results of which were enhanced by the Teutonic tradition of dividing kingdoms among a deceased monarch's sons. Of such a character were the Visigothic kingdom in Southern Gaul and later in Spain; the Ostrogothic régime in Italy; and, destined to become the greatest and most enduring, the Frankish kingdom which at the turn of the fifth and sixth centuries conquered all Gaul and made it France. Such was everywhere the new social and political background against which the Western Church had to live after the Christian Roman Empire had ceased to exist in that half of Europe.

Before judging the effect of this situation upon the relations of

[1] *Epp.* i. 6.

Church and civil power in the West, the structure of the new society must be examined further, for on it many things were to depend. First of all we must realise that the idea of Rome was not lost. The passage from Gibbon quoted earlier[1] expresses rhetorically a profound truth easily substantiated in detail. Many among the new peoples were no strangers to the Empire. Before they attained independent political power they had served Rome, either as individual enlisted men or as *foederati*, mercenary troops fighting under their own native leaders with their own weapons and discipline and settled in time of peace upon lands allotted to them by the Roman authorities. The Goths were admitted within the confines of the Empire on these terms in the fourth century and, despite their many revolts and plunderings, had the service of Rome as a national tradition. Indeed, the great march of the Visigoths under Alaric and later Athaulf from Illyricum to Italy and thence, after the sack of Rome in 410, to Gaul, resembles more a military mutiny for pay and supplies than a barbarian invasion proper. The same cannot be said of the breaking of the Rhine frontier by the Alans, Sueves and Vandals. Yet soldiers of these nations also had for long served in Roman armies. Scarcely one barbarian people which colonised the West was completely new to Roman life and tradition.

So it is not surprising to find among them a real respect for Rome, even a strange reluctance to usurp or to cut free from the Empire. The well-known story, related upon good authority by Orosius, or Athaulf, Alaric's brother and successor, gives articulate expression to thoughts which may well have passed in the minds of other barbarian leaders. Athaulf, so he told a Roman friend, had once wished to destroy the Empire, substituting for the old Romania a new Gothia. But experience had taught him that the Goths were too lawless and barbaric to found a civilisation and he had changed his aim. He wished now to re-establish the Empire by the force of Gothic arms and to be its protector rather than its destroyer.[2] From these, or less well-defined motives, the new

---

[1] Above, p. 81.
[2] Crosius, *Historia contra paganos*, vii. 43.

kings scrupulously respected the tradition that no barbarian could assume the imperial purple. They regarded themselves, though of regal rank in relation to their own nation-armies, as no more than vicegerents of the Roman Emperor in the provinces in which they settled. They gladly accepted and cherished Roman titles such as *magister militum*, *patricius*, and the like, and paid at least formal homage to the Augustus. Admittedly their obedience was nominal, and, as time passed, their subjection became more and more unreal. Yet the Empire possessed the force characteristic of all ideas and was sufficiently real to maintain a tradition which did not finally end until the last *soi-disant* Roman Emperor of the West abdicated that title in 1806.

Moreover, the idea was to some extent translated into action. No attempt was made formally to abolish or replace the institutions of the Empire in the barbarian-ruled lands. For the subject provincial populations the authority of Roman law was recognised, even though their barbarian conquerors lived under their own traditional and primitive legal systems. So far as possible the Roman bureaucracy was used by the barbarian kings, until changing times, the decline of education and increasing decentralisation whittled it away. In Gaul even the old system of taxation lingered on.[1] Some more enlightened barbarian kings, such as Theodoric in Italy, tried to patronise learning and urged their own tribesmen to acquire Roman *civilitas*. There was a real, if limited, effort for continuity. The theory held in most of the new kingdoms was that the barbarian armies were occupying Roman land on a system of *hospitalitas*, as allied troops permanently billeted upon the provincials.[2]

How then did the Western Church accommodate itself to these new circumstances, political and social?

It was faced at the outset by one circumstance rarely understood fully at the present day, though in fact it underlies many modern

[1] Ferdinand Lot, *L'Impôt foncier et la capitation personnelle sous le Bas-Empire et à l'époque francque* (Bibliothèque de l'École des Hautes Études, fasc. 253, Paris, 1928), pp. 83 *sqq.*

[2] See Ferdinand Lot, 'Du régime de l'hospitalité', in *Revue belge de philologie et d'histoire*, vol. vii (1928), pp. 975-1011. Cf. Marc Bloch, 'Une Mise à point: les invasions', in *Annales d'histoire économique et sociale*, vii. 33-46 and viii. 13-28 (Paris, 1945).

political problems—religious disunion. The barbarians, with the exception of the Franks, were not pagans, for they had been evangelised before entering the Empire. But the missions to them began at a time when the Arian controversy was at its height and the policy of the imperial government inclined towards Arianism. So it was not the Nicene faith, after 381 the assured orthodoxy of the Empire, which they held. They were Arians, and more than nominal Arians: already that faith had become their national tradition. It may well be that a theology making the Second Person of the Trinity a demigod appealed to those newly converted from a polytheistic belief in Odin and his family. In any case it was not until the eighth century that Germanic Arianism finally disappeared with the conversion of the Lombards to Catholicism. Up to that time some at least of the ruling class in the West were Arians and in the fifth century most of them were so.

We have, no doubt, moved away from the incomprehension of the eighteenth and nineteenth centuries, which, partly because it found the idea irritating, failed to recognise the profound effect of religious dissensions upon history. We have, indeed, come to see the converse of that fact—the equally profound influence of political, social and economic factors upon religious history. But, unlike our grandparents, we realise that theology is not a negligible factor in human development. We can therefore appreciate better than they the very considerable consequences of the historic accident (if it can so be called) of the Western barbarians' Arianism, which were manifested in two ways. First of all there was added to the racial, social and cultural barriers already separating Roman and Teuton a sharp cleavage in religion. So any real assimilation between the subject populations and their overlords was prevented. It may well be that this was the decisive factor preventing the re-establishment of a new Empire in the West of the type hoped for by Athaulf.[1] Already, by the fifth century, Rome had lost much of the assimilative power which had made her what she was. There is apparent, after the death of Theodosius I in 395, a

[1] See above, p. 84.

racialist feeling absent in earlier times.[1] Thus, Stilicho was disliked because of his Vandal origin: as Orosius puts it, he was of the 'cowardly, avaricious, treacherous and crafty race of the Vandals'.[2] A similar feeling may have had much to do with the Roman government's failure, at a very critical time, to come to terms with Alaric and his Goths. In any case, therefore, the building of united barbaro-Roman states would have been hindered by the prevailing temper of mind upon the Roman side. When to racial and cultural prejudice was added religious abhorrence the thing became virtually impossible.

Except in Vandal North Africa, where they bitterly persecuted Catholics, the barbarian rulers were not greatly to blame for this. Most of them showed real tolerance towards the Catholic Church, and persecution, or even oppression on religious grounds, was the exception rather than the rule. But hatred of Arianism, springing from memories of the fourth century, nursed in their Roman subjects a sullen spirit of non-co-operation which defeated even such promising ventures as Theodoric's attempt to build up a Romano-Gothic state in Italy.

The fact that the first real co-operation between the two elements of the new society took place in Merovingian Gaul illustrates this point. For the Franks were the great exception to the rule that barbarism and Arianism went together. Clovis was converted in 496 direct from paganism to Catholic Christianity. Henceforth he found the Catholic Church throughout Gaul on his side: indeed it proved an active Fifth Column in the Visigothic kingdom when he turned his armies towards the South. Had the other Teutons held the faith of Nicaea the amalgamation of the newcomers and the old populations might have been achieved far more rapidly and successfully than it was. In particular, Teutonic Catholicism would have deprived Justinian's efforts in the sixth century to reconquer the West of much of their justification in the

---

[1] See Santo Mazzarino, *Stilicone: la crisi imperiale dopo Teodosio* (Rome, 1942) and E. Demougeot, *De l'unité à la division de l'empire romain, 395-410* (Paris, 1951) for discussions of this matter.

[2] 'Vandalorum inbellis avarae perfidae et dolosae gentis genere editus' (*Historia contra paganos*, vii. 38).

eyes of contemporaries and might even have averted them. And it was his devastating war in Italy which did as much to destroy the weakened remains of Roman civilisation in what had been the nucleus of the Roman West.

Here then is one great factor militating against an adequate *statut* of Church-State relations in the post-Roman West. The Church there was confronted, not by orthodox, but by heretical governments. Another increased the difficulty. Arianism, unlike Catholicism, had no universal organisation. The Arian churches were national and became, as the nations settled, what German historians designate *Landeskirchen*. They had no recognised form of intercommunication, still less the Catholic pattern of patriarchates centering in the Papacy. Less other-worldly than the Catholic Church, the Arian bodies had also a married priesthood and discouraged asceticism. Both characteristics tended to inhibit in the barbarian kingdoms the notion of the Church as a universal supernatural society in competition with the State or of its clergy as raised above worldly concerns. In fact the Arian churches appear, from what is known of them, to have been closely under royal control. This is not surprising, even apart from the facts already mentioned, for, as in the case of all other ancient peoples, German religion in pagan times was linked closely with kingship. And, therefore, as Karl Voigt says: 'One can assume that the part which a German ruler played in pagan times in matters of religion and worship exercised a strong influence in the development of the Germanic State-Church idea.'[1]

If we remember also the fact that before the fifth century the Germanic peoples were migratory nations we can still better understand the situation. To quote Voigt again: 'The development of a Gothic tribal church must evidently have been much helped by the fact that the Goths after the turn of the fourth and fifth centuries entered once again on their wanderings. Whilst they journeyed from country to country without any fixed abodes,

[1] 'Und man wird annehmen dürfen, dass die Rolle, die der germanische Herrscher in der heidnischen Zeit in Sachen der Religion und des Kultes gespielt hatte, einen starken Einfluss auf die Ausbildung des germanischen Staatskirchentumes ausgeübt hat' (Karl Voigt, *Staat und Kirche von Konstantin dem Grossen bis zum Ende der Karolingerzeit* (Stuttgart, 1936), p. 118).

close ecclesiastical relations with their bishops, who were ever more closely identified with them alone (especially since those bishops had no definite territorial districts) must have developed.'[1]

We have seen already that the tradition of the Roman Empire implied a close union of Church and State. It is easy to understand how this would be strengthened by inoculation from a parallel tradition of the same kind, a tradition strengthened by the peculiar circumstances of the conversion of the Germanic tribes and given a twist away from the universalist outlook of the Roman Empire and its Church. In short, Arianism gave birth to the idea of national Christianity in something like its modern, particularistic form.

Not surprisingly, then, we find the Western Church tending to develop under barbarian rule into a series of national bodies, each closely linked with the state it served and relatively independent of neighbouring churches. A tendency only, nevertheless. For there were factors working the other way. The Catholic Church in barbarian lands was for long the church of those who did not confess what their kings would no doubt have liked to make the state religion. It was a church of the subject people, not of the *Herrenvolk*. Hence, for support and encouragement it looked outside the frontiers and was not anxious to ally itself too closely with the immediate ruling power. Moreover it had a territorial organisation going back to the days of the undivided Empire. It possessed a provincial system in which the city bishops were subject to the bishop of the provincial capital, the metropolis. This configuration was not at once overthrown by the new territorial groupings. Thus, in Visigothic Southern Gaul, some suffragan sees of the Province of Arles were in Burgundian territory, whilst we find bishops from outside the Visigothic kingdom taking part in the appointment of bishops within it.[2] Later on in the Lombard kingdom of North Italy we find some Lombard bishoprics

---

[1] 'Die Ausbildung einer gotischen Stammeskirche wurde dann weiter offenbar dadurch sehr gefördert, dass die Goten seit der Wende des 4. und 5. Jahrhunderts wieder Wanderungen antraten. Während sie ohne feste Wohnstätten von Land zu Land zogen, mussten sie mit ihren Bischöfen immer mehr zu einem nur sie umfassenden, zunächst noch mit keinem bestimmten räumlichen Gebiete verknüpften kirchlichen Verbande verwachsen' (Voigt, p. 117).   [2] See Voigt, p. 117.

dependent upon the metropolitan authority of Rome and others under the Archbishop of Ravenna, who was himself a subject of the Roman Emperor in the East.[1]

But these recalcitrant factors in the situation tended to disappear with time: they did not long survive the appearance of the Catholic Franks and the conversion to Catholicism of the Goths in Spain, both events which gave barbarian kings more hold over the Catholic Church in their realms. In France and Spain *Landeskirchen* were formed. The principle of the identity of political and ecclesiastical circumscriptions was from the first adopted in the Frankish realm. In 511, fifteen years only after Clovis's baptism,[2] the first national council of the Frankish Church met at Orléans.[3] It soon became the recognised rule, to quote Voigt, that 'the boundaries of the ecclesiastical system must coincide with those of the realm' and that 'no part of the realm should be under a bishop who had his see outside the realm'.[4] In consequence, for example, when Theudebert I made conquests, three bishoprics were removed from the ecclesiastical province of Aquileia. When the

[1] Voigt, pp. 217-218. As the author remarks, 'Die katholische Kirche des Langobardenreiches hatte keinen scharf ausgeprägten landeskirchlichen Charakter' (p. 217).

[2] The traditional date of 496 for the baptism of Clovis is adopted here without prejudice to the considerable criticism to which it has been subjected by historians who argue in favour of the date of 506 or later, and, in some cases, for Tours rather than Rheims as the scene of the baptism. For the most recent arguments against the tradition see A. van de Vyver in *Revue belge de philologie et d'histoire*, vol. 15 (1936), pp. 859-914, vol. 16 (1937), pp. 35-94 and vol. 17 (1938), pp. 793-813; the same author in *Le Moyen-Age*, vol. 53 (1947), pp. 177-196; Sir Francis Oppenheimer, *Frankish Themes and Problems* (London, 1952); J. M. Wallace-Hadrill in *Transactions of the Royal Historical Society*, 5th series, vol. i (1951), especially pp. 25-45; Ernest Stein, *Histoire du bas-empire*, vol. ii (Paris-Brussels-Amsterdam, 1949), pp. 147-148. On the other side see F. Lot in *Revue belge*, vol. 17 (1938), pp. 63-69; J. Calmette in *Académie des inscriptions et belles-lettres: comptes-rendus*, 1946, pp. 193-202, and reviews of Sir Francis Oppenheimer's book by J. M. Wallace-Hadrill in *The English Historical Review*, vol. lxviii (1953), pp. 454-455, and by Margaret Deanesly in *The Journal of Ecclesiastical History*, vol. iv (1953), pp. 98-99. Mr. Wallace-Hadrill of Merton College (to whom I am indebted for these references) allows me to say that, whilst not having come to a final conclusion, he is at present inclined to favour the traditional date and place of the baptism.

[3] Voigt, p. 239. Already, in 506, we find the Visigothic monarchy permitting, and perhaps encouraging, the assembling of a council of Catholic bishops of the kingdom at Agde (Voigt, p. 134; Mansi, *Concilia*, viii. 359 sqq.).

[4] 'Die katholische Kirche im Frankenreiche war grundsätzlich Landeskirche, die Grenzen der kirchlichen Organisation mussten sich mit denen des Reiches decken, kein Teil des Reiches durfte einem Bischof unterstehen, der seinen Sitz ausserhalb des Reiches hatte' (Voigt, p. 238).

Lombards ceded Alpine areas to King Guntram, he founded a new bishopric of Maurienne in order to withdraw them from their ancient dependence upon the Bishop of Turin, and Pope Gregory the Great's attempt to get the new arrangement reversed was unsuccessful.[1] The conversion of the Spanish Visigoths to Catholicism in 589 was followed in 610 by the establishment of Toledo, the royal capital, as a metropolitan see in place of Cartagena, then under Byzantine rule. As late as 633 St. Isidore of Seville, and not the Archbishop of the city, presided at Toledo itself over a national council, a fact which shows that the political eminence of Toledo was still not recognised as giving it ecclesiastical primacy in Spain. But later councils met under the presidency of Toledan archbishops, whilst in 681 the holders of this see were given the right to install all bishops in Spain, outside their ecclesiastical province as well as within, once they had been nominated by the King and approved by the Archbishop, who thus virtually became Primate of Spain.[2]

National churches of this type naturally fell closely under the authority of kings. With variations in detail, it was to the monarchs increasingly that the nomination of archbishops and bishops fell, the old principle of election by the clergy and people of the diocese becoming more and more a dead letter.[3] We find,

---

[1] Voigt, *ibid.*

[2] 'Illud quoque collationi mutuae decernendum nobis occurrit, quod in quibusdam civitatibus, decedentibus episcopis propriis, dum differtur diu ordinatio successoris, non minima creatur et officiorum divinorum offensio, et ecclesiasticarum rerum noscitur perditio. Nam dum longe lateque diffuso tractu terrarum, commeantium impeditur celeritas nunciorum, quo aut non queat regis auditibus decedentis praesulis transitus innotesci, aut de successore morientis episcopi libera principis electio praestolari, nascitur semper, et nostro ordini de relatione talium difficultas, et regiae potestati, dum consultum nostrum pro subrogandis pontificibus sustinet, incuriosa necessitas. Unde placuit omnibus pontificibus Hispaniae, ut salvo privilegio uniuscuiusque provinciae, licitum maneat deinceps Toletano pontifici, quoscumque regalis potestas elegerit, et iam dicti Toletani episcopi iudicio dignos esse probaverit, in quibuslicet provinciis, in praecedentium sedibus praeficere praesules, et decedentibus episcopis eligere successores. . . . Hanc quoque definitionis formulam, sicut de episcopis, ita et de ceteris ecclesiarum rectoribus placuit observandam' (Can. 6, Mansi, xi. 1033-1034). The whole passage throws an interesting light upon Spanish ideas of the respective parts of king and ecclesiastics in Church appointments at this time. Cf. also A. K. Ziegler, *Church and State in Visigothic Spain* (Catholic University of America, Washington D.C., 1930), p. 49.

[3] ¿Era la confirmación una mera fórmula, o un derecho real y efectivo de los monarcas, que podían suspender y dejar sin efecto lo acordado en los concilios? No ocurrió en la

too, a close relationship between councils of Church and State. National ecclesiastical assemblies meet at the royal summons. Here indeed there was no change from imperial practice: it was the Emperor who summoned oecumenical councils of the Christian Roman Empire. We find also that to have effect conciliar legislation needs royal sanction—another legacy in part of Roman imperial practice.[1] The *agenda* of councils is determined, at least in part, by the king. For example, a feature of the Visigothic national councils at Toledo, from the middle of the seventh century onwards, was the king's *tomus*, laid before the council at its opening, which determined the matters to be discussed and expressed the king's will about the decisions to be reached, sometimes even prescribing the punishments to be attached to breaches of canons as yet unpromulgated. Sometimes laws already issued by royal authority were adopted by ecclesiastical councils as canons.

Indeed in Western Europe of the Dark Ages it is often difficult to distinguish between civil and ecclesiastical assemblies. To use Visigothic Spain once more as our example, one finds there state officials and the royal court taking part in the councils of the national church, which, as has been said, 'had . . . in a certain degree the character of assemblies of the realm, the functions of which they had taken over'.[2] They handle both properly ecclesiastical matters and what would today be regarded as secular ones, and one finds spiritual penalties, such as excommunication, attached to the violation of political laws and, on the other hand, secular punishments threatened for spiritual offences.[3]

It is a well-known fact that this intermingling of matters civil

España visigótica ningun conflicto de esta especie: jamas rey alguno negó su aprobación a los canones de los sínodos nacionales; mas no era tampoco posible que estallaran estas disidencias, porque las asambleas no habían de decretar nada contrario a la volundad del rey, dada la estrecha subordinación del episcopado y del oficio palatino al trono' (E. Pérez Pujol, *Historia de las instituciones sociales de la España goda*, vol. iii (Madrid, 1896), p. 325). Cf. Ziegler, pp. 43-44 and Voigt, pp. 135 *sqq*.

[1] Voigt, p. 138; Ziegler, pp. 42-43.

[2] 'Die Konzilien erhielten dadurch in gewissem Masse den Charakter von Reichsversammlungen, deren Funktionen sie auch übernommen haben' (Voigt, pp. 138-139). But it is not clear that the lay members (who were always fewer than the clerics) had decisive votes in other than secular matters. See Pérez Pujol, iii. 297-313.

[3] See Voigt, pp. 140-142.

and ecclesiastical reached its height in the Frankish Kingdom of Carolingian days. The considerable mass of legislation contained in the Capitularies of Charlemagne and his son, Louis the Pious, embodied in a large but still incomplete code by Ansegisus, Abbot of St. Wandrille in 827,[1] deals as much with Church affairs as with those of the State. Most of it emanates ultimately from the will of the monarch, even though promulgated in assemblies of clergy and laity, who, however, seem to have deliberated separately in the first instance.[2] For Charlemagne regarded it as his function to rule the Church, no less than the State. 'Nobis, quibus, in huius saeculi procellosis fluctibus ad regendam commissa est':[3] such is the relationship in which, to quote his own words, he conceives the Frankish Church, indeed the Church of the whole West, to stand to him. Primarily, no doubt, his function appeared to be the defence and extension of Christendom by military force. But equally he believed the reform of the Church to be his duty: he was empowered to watch over and control its day-to-day activities and to force all his subjects to accept its faith and observe its discipline, as he understood them.

For Charlemagne's interest in and control of ecclesiastical affairs did not stop short at administrative matters or moral discipline— the natural first concern of a ruler. He took a most active part in doctrinal controversy, following in this the example of the Roman Emperors whose successor he was proclaimed to be before the end of his life. In 794 the Council of Frankfort was summoned by his orders, and, with the Pope's legates on either side of him, he presided over it. The parallel with Constantine at Nicaea is complete. Two main matters were dealt with, the Adoptianist heresy in Spain and the Iconoclast controversy, now raging in the East. In the first, Charlemagne did little more than lend his support to a condemnation already effected by the Pope. The Spanish bishops

---

[1] Text in M.G.H. *Leges*, i. 256-325. See on the code E. Amann, *L'Époque carolingienne* (Histoire de l'Église, edd. A. Fliche and V. Martin, vol. 6 (Paris, 1947), pp. 75-76.

[2] L. Halphen, *Charlemagne et l'empire carolingien* ('L'Évolution de l'humanité', vol. xxxiii, Paris, 1947), pp. 161 *sqq.*

[3] M.G.H. *Concilia*, vol. ii, Suppl. (ed. H. Bastgen, Hanover and Leipzig, 1924), p. 2. Cf. n. 1 *ibid.* for parallel expressions.

who supported Felix of Urgel, the protagonist of the heresy, had appealed to Charlemagne from this, but, since they were not his subjects (being under Moslem rule), their appeal was not respectfully couched. The monarch, as his opening speech made clear, had no desire to listen to defences of Adoptianism. He left the decision to the bishops present and, when they had condemned the teaching, contented himself with exhorting the Spanish episcopate to fall into line if they wished for his help against the Moors.[1]

The other controversy shows him in a very different light. The question at issue was the endorsement of the work of the Second Council of Nicaea in 787, which, with the Pope's approval, had condemned Iconoclasm and defended the veneration of images. One must admit that the information about it was very faulty. Its acts had been translated into Latin by one of those ill-equipped translators who in all ages rush in to do work at which angels might tremble. (Anastasius the Librarian later described him as one who knew neither Greek nor Latin adequately.)[2] Though we do not possess his translation in full, sufficient fragments remain to make clear that at important points he seriously misrepresented the teaching of the Council. Certainly, to the Frankish mind his work suggested that it had approved idolatry. That must have shocked Charlemagne, under whose name appeared the famous *Capitulare de Imaginibus* (better known as the *Libri Carolini*). Like many royal treatises on theology it cannot be regarded as all his own work. Charlemagne's always limited scholarship—he was indeed technically illiterate[3]—could never have produced it, and Alcuin, his English friend and theological adviser, has been sug-

---

[1] Text in M.G.H. *Concilia*, vol. ii (Hanover and Leipzig, 1906), pp. 157-164. 'Ecce ego [*sc.* Carolus Magnus] vestris petitionibus satisfaciens congregationi sacerdotum auditor et arbiter adsedi. Discernimus et Deo donante decrevimus quid esset de hac inquisitione firmiter tenendum' (p. 161). See also Amann, p. 145.

[2] 'Non quod ante nos minime fuerit interpretata, sed quod interpres pene per singula relicto utriusque linguae idiomate, adeo fuerit verbum e verbo secutus, ut quid in eadem editione intelligatur, aut vix aut nunquam possit adverti, in fastidium versa legentium, pene ab omnibus hac pro causa contemnatur' (*Praef. Anastasii in Septimam Synodum ad Joannem VIII*, P.L. cxxix. 195).

[3] 'Temptabat et scribere tabulasque et codicillos ad hoc in lecto sub cervicalibus circumferre solebat, ut, cum vacuum tempus esset, manum litteris effigiendis adsuesceret, sed parum successit labor praeposterus ac sero inchoatus' (Einhard, *Vita Caroli*, 25).

gested as the most likely author.[1] What is of interset, however, is the attitude taken up by Charles, who fathered it. He rejects both the Iconoclastic council of 753 and the assembly of 787 and subjects the acts of the latter to a detailed scrutiny, denying the relevance and force of the Biblical and patristic passages they cite and at the same time attacking the council's claim to oecumenicity. Instead he sets forth a doctrine of his own. Images are lawful and right, but are merely the books of the illiterate and therefore not to be worshipped. This definition he caused to be endorsed by the Council of Frankfort.[2]

The outcome was embarrassing to the unfortunate Pope, Hadrian I, who had already approved the Second Council of Nicaea unofficially in his negotiations with the East, though he had not yet pronounced formally for it. He was now faced by a declaration in the opposite sense made by a council which represented virtually the whole West, a council at which his own legates had been present. He temporised with Charlemagne. He explained that the Eastern theologians had not really intended to set the worship of images upon a level with the adoration of God, as the Franks imagined, and refused to reject their work in so many words. But at the same time he suggested the unworthy expedient, if the Frankish king should insist upon some reprobation of the East, of being ready to declare the Eastern Emperor a heretic on another ground, namely that of refusing to return to Roman jurisdiction territories filched from the authority of the Holy See in South Italy during the Iconoclastic quarrel.[3] Eventually the matter became merged in another quarrel between Frankish theologians and Constantinople over the Double Procession of the Holy Spirit and in the complicated diplomatic difficulties with Byzantium resulting from Charlemagne's coronation as Roman Emperor in 800. But in effect it caused a doctrinal tension between the Franks and the Papacy which lasted during the remainder of Charlemagne's reign.

[1] Amann, p. 125 and n. 2.
[2] M.G.H. *Concilia*, vol. ii, *Capitulare Francofurtense*, 2, p. 165. For the varying orders of events suggested by different historians, see Amann, p. 157, n. 2.
[3] M.G.H. *Epist.* vol. v (Berlin, 1899), pp. 6-57.

The interest of this curious affair, as already indicated, lies for us in the light it throws upon Charlemagne's idea of his function in the Church. On the one hand the King of the Franks complained bitterly that the very important section of the Church over which he presided as temporal ruler had never been consulted about what claimed to be an oecumenical decision.[1] He was protesting against the Byzantine policy which virtually identified the universal Church with that of the East—for Rome, which had been consulted, was viewed at Constantinople, as part of the Eastern Empire.[2] On the other hand, however, Charlemagne was claiming, at least in Western Christendom, the historic rights of the Emperor in doctrinal disputes, namely to cause their settlement by means of imperially summoned councils whose decisions would be imperially enforced. 'It is not certain,' says M. Amann of the Frankish Church, 'that its temporal head was already thinking of taking the imperial title which would make him the equal of the Greek *Basileus*. But quite certainly—and the prologue to the *Caroline Books* can leave no doubt upon the subject—he thought of himself as possessed in ecclesiastical matters of the same rights as the sovereign of New Rome.'[3]

The remark raises an important question with the discussion of which this lecture may well close. It seems to me that underlying

[1] M.G.H. *Conc.* ii, Suppl. '. . . dumque suorum gestorum ordinem volunt mandare memoriae posteritatis, discindant vinculum ecclesiasticae unitatis' (p. 3).

'Nam si novas constitutiones ecclesiae ingerere iactantia est, scisma est, quod tamen in ecclesia fieri non debet. Quod si scisma est, macula est, quae in sponsa esse negatur. Si igitur novas constitutiones ecclesiae ingerere iactantia est, macula procul dubio est, quae in sponsa esse negatur' (p. 4).

'Contra cuius errores ideo scribere compulsi sumus, ut sicubi forte aut manus tenentium aut aures audientium inquinare temptaverit, nostri stili divinarum Scripturarum auctoritate armati invectione pellatur et inertem vel potius inermem orientali de parte venientem hostem occidua in parte per nos favente Deo adlata sanctorum patrum sententia feriat. Quod opus adgressi sumus cum conhibentia sacerdotum in regno a Deo nobis concesso catholicis gregibus praelatorum, non arrogantiae supercilio, sed zelo Dei et veritatis studio' (p. 5).

[2] Amann, p. 124.

[3] 'Que son chef temporel songeât des lors à prendre le titre impérial, qui ferait de lui l'égal du basileus grec, ce n'est pas certain. Mais, à coup sûr,—et le prologue des *Livres carolins* ne peut laisser à ce sujet aucun doute—il se considérait comme investi, en matière ecclésiastique, des mêmes droits que le souverain de la Nouvelle Rome. Comment dès lors aurait-il pu admettre que des questions doctrinales fussent décidées par la seule initiative de l'Église d'Orient?' (Amann, p. 125).

all the complications of this confused period of transition from classical to medieval society there is one fundamental point which we have already encountered in casting our eyes upon Byzantium. We saw there that the peculiar and almost indefinable relationship between Church and State is best understood by realising that in distinguishing the two we are making use of a category of thought alien to contemporary minds. To the Byzantines both were but aspects of one Christian society, inseparable as two facets of a jewel. In the light of what we have just considered, we have to ask ourselves whether such a distinction would not have been in the Dark Ages as meaningless in the West as in the East. It is easy to exaggerate the effects of the political division caused by the barbarian conquests and to assume that because of them the West must necessarily have viewed Church-State relations in a wholly different way from Byzantium. Is that assumption correct? On the one hand, as we have seen, the idea of the Empire was never lost in the West and could easily be revived by Charlemagne. (Indeed it received an important revival in the sixth century, when Justinian reconquered much of the barbarian-held territory.) On the other hand, every Western State, be it as barbarised as one pleases to think—and none was wholly barbarian—thought of itself as in a sense a microcosm of the old Empire. We have seen that the powers claimed by barbarian kings over the Church were largely revivals of imperial custom, and with Charlemagne we witness a startling resurrection of what may be called the Constantinian view of Christian imperialism. We must, then, not be too hypnotised by what might seem to be the novel phenomenon of the *Landeskirche*. Teutonic it may have been in its actual historical emergence. Coloured it probably was by a background of Teutonic paganism and early Teutonic Arian Christianity. But, given the ineluctable fact of the breakdown of unified administration in the Western world, it was only in the form of the *Landeskirche* that the old constitution of the Christian Roman Empire could now be continued and express itself. The Roman subjects of the barbarian kings may well have seen no revolutionary difference between the relation of Church and State in the new kingdoms from that which folk memory recalled of the old system as it had existed from Constantine to Honorius. The idea of an almost absolute identity between Church and Christian State did not need to be created by the Teutons: it was there already in the soil they conquered. However much we take for granted today a distinction between the spiritual and the secular community, we must not antedate its emergence. As I have tried to show, that distinction is the very antithesis of the habitual thinking of almost all early societies and in particular of the Greco-Roman world. Like Charles II, the notion of an identity of Church and State took an unconscionable time dying.[1]

[1] 'We would say that in the early Middle Ages, that is to say, up to the Investiture struggle—and perhaps inclusive of it—the conflict is habitually considered as between the Sacerdotium and Regnum or Imperium, and, in nine cases out of ten at least, as taking place in the Ecclesia, rather than in the Respublica. Only in the later Middle Ages are Respublica and Ecclesia used as convertible terms for Regnum and Imperium and Sacerdotium respectively: and the conclusion we would draw is that, when this happens, the conception of the single society is breaking up' (C. N. S. Woolf, *Bartolus of Sassoferrato: His Position in the History of Medieval Political Thought* (Cambridge, 1913), p. 104).

CHAPTER VI

THE MEDIEVAL ATTEMPT AT PAPAL THEOCRACY

'When a strong man armed keepeth his palace, his goods are in peace.'[1] This dictum of the Gospel is not without its bearing upon the history of Church and State. We have seen already that it was pre-eminently the character of the Byzantine State which preserved the Roman tradition of centralised professional government, and thereby effectively prevented in the East the rise of ideas of ecclesiastical independence. We saw, too, in the last lecture, that the tradition of a close unity of civil and ecclesiastical power survived the breakdown of Roman rule, partly because of the establishment of *Landeskirchen* (which adapted the old idea to the smaller territorial units of the new Western polity), partly because of the survival, in theory if not in practice, of the ideal of centralised government. Kingship was very much a reality in the barbarian kingdoms set up upon Roman soil and its prestige lasted long enough to allow the resuscitation of the imperial ideal under Charlemagne. So far, the State, as a strong man armed, had maintained, with whatever practical limitations, the conception of sovereignty.

We pass now to a period in which this is no longer true. When one remembers the disorders of Merovingian France or Lombard Italy, it may seem paradoxical to suggest that it was not the first series of barbarian incursions, in the fifth and sixth centuries, which gravely weakened the conception of state sovereignty in Western Europe, but the second, those of the Scandinavians and Magyars in the ninth and tenth centuries. Yet for such a judgement a good case could be made. For, if the over-mighty subject was already a problem in Constantine's day and throughout the period following it, as the laws against the *potentiores* bear witness,[2] and, even if the authority of Merovingian kings was limited by

---

[1] Luke xi. 21.
[2] There is an excellent short account of the power acquired by great proprietors in the time of the Later Empire in Ferdinand Lot, *La Fin du monde antique et le début du moyen-âge* ('L'Évolution de l'humanité', vol. xxxi, Paris, 1927), Part I, chap. vii, pp. 147 *sqq.*

the power of their nobles, we do not yet find a doctrine of contractual sovereignty based upon an inchoate idea of the State as
composed of a series of authorities and communities with rights of
their own. Between the practical breakdown of a political concept
and its replacement by another much time may elapse. Thus, in
England the fact that effective power had passed from the king
personally to the majority in the House of Commons was recognised only a long time after it had become a reality. So, it was
not until a social evolution caused by the exigencies of the times
had run its full course that the Western world realised, even dimly,
that the notion of the State had changed.

To speak more precisely, we have now to consider the appearance of the state of society called, for want of a better name,
feudal, and to estimate its effect upon the problem we are studying.
We have first to see how far this arrangement of society modified
the idea of political power with which hitherto the Christian
Church had been in contact. For it is not too much to say that
without such a change of outlook the medieval attempt at papal
theocracy, which is my theme in this lecture, would have been
impossible. In the East, as we have seen, there was no essential
transformation of the idea of the State throughout the Byzantine
period, and therefore no essential alterations of the relations
between it and the Church. It is therefore reasonable to connect
the vastly different history of Church-State relations in the West
at least partly with changes, conscious or unconscious, in political
thinking.

The evolution of feudalism is still a subject upon which research
has not said its last word, though upon much of the story there is
agreement.[1] Let it suffice me to draw attention to some facts
which may be regarded as established. In essentials one may trace
back the origins of feudalism to the later days of the Roman

[1] See Marc Bloch, *La Société féodale* ('L'Évolution de l'humanité', vols. xxxiv and xxxiv
bis, Paris, 1939 and 1940); F. L. Ganshof, *Qu'est-ce que la féodalité?* (2e édit., Neuchâtel
and Brussels, 1947), E.T. by Philip Grierson, *Feudalism* (London, 1952), with corrections
and additions; Carl Stephenson, *Mediaeval Feudalism* (Cornell Univ. Press, Ithaca, N.Y.,
1942); Carl Stephenson, 'The Origin and Significance of Feudalism', in *American Historical
Review*, vol. xlvi (1940-41), pp. 788-812; J. Calmette, *La Société féodale* (4e édit., Collection
Armand Colin, Paris, 1938).

Empire in the West. Already then there was a shifting of the balance of power and influence from town to countryside, so that great landowners were establishing themselves as almost independent potentates upon their estates.[1] But this is not what is technically meant by feudalism. As we saw, the idea of central government and of sovereignty remained long after this process had begun. The influence of the *potentiores* was usurped, rather than recognised by law, even though *patronatus* (a right not unlike later feudal lordship) became a feature of society.[2] It was later on, in Merovingian and early Carolingian times in France, that we see the rise of vassalage, the maintenance by kings and great men of private armies of men bound to them by contracts implying on the one side faithful service, on the other protection. With the growth of a habit of rewarding vassals with gifts of land to ensure their livelihood—the only possible method of so doing in an age of natural economy—the conditions are present which will give rise, almost inevitably, to classic feudalism, the system by which land is held from a lord on condition of military service. When this appears, a complex chain of relationships comes into being, since the lesser man needs the lordship of the greater and the greater the service and support of the lesser, at every level of a graded society.

In itself this system could have led to a centralised state even more closely knit together than that of the classical world. For at every point the ordinary bond between sovereign, intermediate authority and simple subject was reinforced by the additional tie of feudal fealty and homage confirmed by oath. In practice it had quite the reverse effect. The reason is not far to seek. On the one hand, the feudal relation, implying as it did a two-way responsibility, was looked upon as contractual and therefore as liable to repudiation, at least in the free classes of society. On the other hand, the feudal tenant, as immediate landlord, came, in an age of disorder, to be thought of and to think of himself as the one political authority upon his estate, as ruler of it, no less than owner.

[1] See Lot, *La Fin du monde antique*, pp. 147-148.
[2] The subject of *patronatus* has been studied in detail by Francis de Zulueta ('Patronage in the Later Empire', *Oxford Studies in Social and Legal History*, vol. i (Oxford, 1909)).

'Chaque baron,' says an expounder of feudal law, 'est souverain dans sa baronie.'[1] Here, indeed, feudalism hardly needed to innovate. The power of landlords to judge and tax their tenants began early in the Dark Ages: feudalism proper merely increased and made general what had originally been exceptional. It added momentum to a process of political decentralisation which had been growing for centuries.

One thing only was needed to make definitive this parcelling out of political authority. That was the recognition of the principle of heredity in the feudal fief. What was later to be known as the *feudum* or fief, went earlier under the name of *precarium* or *beneficium*—both words which of their nature emphasise the will of the overlord who grants the land.[2] But in a society in which ties of blood were highly valued, the right of son to succeed to father in the possession of land could and did easily prevail over the element of arbitrariness in the original conception of the bargain by which land was granted. How easily hereditary right could be assumed can be shown by a neat example cited by Marc Bloch. In 876 Charles the Bald granted to a certain Aldebert the land of *Cavaliacus* for his lifetime and that of his son as a *beneficium*. In 914 Alger, Aldebert's son, is found giving the same estate to the canons of Limoges upon the pretext that it was his hereditary *allodium*, or estate free of all service.[3] If even the fact of dependent tenure could thus be forgotten or disregarded in the interests of heredity, how much more easily could feudal tenants establish their right to

[1] 'Pour de que nous parlons en cest livre en pluseurs lieus du souverain et de ce qu'il puet et doit fere, li aucun pourroient entendre pour ce que nous ne nommons conte ne duc, que ce fust du roi; mes en tous les lieus la ou li rois n'est par nommés, nous entendons de ceus qui tienent en baronie, car chascuns barons est souverains en sa baronie. Voirs est que li rois est souverains par dessus tous et a de son droit le general garde de tout son roiaume, par quoi il puet fere teus establissemens comme il li plest pour le commun pourfit, et ce qu'il establist doit estre tenu. . . . Et pour ce qu'il est souverains par desseus tous, nous le nommons quant nous parlons d'aucune souveraineté, qui a li apartient' (Philippe de Beaumanoir, *Coutumes de Beauvaisis*, ed. Am. Salmon, vol. ii (Paris, 1900), chap. xxiv, no. 1043, pp. 23-24). See also on this subject Marcel David, *La Souveraineté de les limites juridiques du pouvoir monarchique du IXᵉ au XVᵉ siècle* ('Annales de la faculté de droit et des sciences politiques de Strasbourg', Paris, 1954).

[2] *Precarium*—that which is obtained by request, *preces*; *beneficium*—a 'benefit' conferred by a superior upon an inferior.

[3] Marc Bloch, *La Société féodale: la formation des liens de dépendance* ('L'Évolution de l'humanité', vol. xxxiv, Paris, 1939), p. 265.

transmit their fiefs to their sons under the continued lordship of those from whom they had received them? So it is not surprising to find that, by about the eleventh century, the principle of hereditary succession to feudal estates was becoming established as a custom not to be broken except as a legal punishment for crime —and custom in the Middle Ages had the force of law, indeed in Northern Europe *was* law. Nor was it land only which went by right of descent. In many cases public office followed the same rule, so that, for example, the Carolingian *comes*, the appointed representative of the king in local government, became the *comte* of the hierarchy of feudal hereditary nobility.

It seems no exaggeration to see in this development of land-holding from something governed by royal will to something controlled by hereditary right, the feature which most of all marks the change from the classical unitary conception of the State to that of the State as a complex of individual or communal sharers of power characteristic of the Middle Ages proper. It is dangerous and easy to be too precise. The idea of kingship and even the idea of sovereignty never perished wholly: the balance between centripetal and centrifugal forces varied greatly at different times and, more especially, in different parts of Western Europe. Sir Maurice Powicke, in his valuable essay entitled 'Reflections on the Medieval State,[1] has warned us, with all the authority of his unrivalled knowledge, of the danger of generalisation. We can neither generalise beyond a certain point nor dogmatise. Nevertheless no one can fail to see that in the centuries separating the Carolingian Age from that of the Renaissance men have largely ceased to think of society as a homogeneous single corporation ruled by one absolute law and a single central power. They have come rather to view it as a complex balance of different and quasi-independent centres of power, each with its own rights and duties.

At times this went to almost anarchical lengths. The notorious formula of election supposed to have been employed by the *ricos hombres*, the highest order of nobility in Aragon, in choosing their king runs thus: 'We who are as good as you choose you for our

[1] In *Ways of Medieval Life and Thought* (London, 1949), pp. 130-148.

ruler and lord, provided that you observe our laws and privileges, and if not, not'.¹ The text is of doubtful authenticity but, as Hallam said, it is 'sufficiently agreeable to the old government' of Aragon in practice.² Aragon indeed was an extreme instance of devolution, a state in which even the right of *desnaturalización*, formal renunciation of allegiance to the Crown after due notice given, was enjoyed by all the nobility,³ so that political obligation was virtually reduced to a contractual basis. But, as Fritz Kern has pointed out, the same idea is in fact involved in all oaths of fealty, which were the cement of the early medieval state. 'Fealty, as distinct from obedience, is reciprocal in character, and contains the implicit condition that the one party owes it to the other only so long as the other keeps faith.'⁴ Always in the medieval West there is implicit the idea of rights as derived not solely from the state, but from the status of the individuals which make up the political community.⁵

¹ 'Entre otros fueros ordenaron el fuero que se llamava de la unión, que contiene dos partes dignas de ser sabidas, y muy al proposito de la información que voy dando. La una, *Que siempre que le rey les que brantasso sus fueros, pudiessen eligir otro rey, Encará que sea Pagano*. Palabras formales del fuero que trata desto. Y assy es de saber el modo antiguo de jurar a su rey les Aragoneses, que es, *Nos, que valemos tanto como vos, os hazemos nuestro rey, y Señor, con tal que guardeys nuestros fueros, y libertades, y fino No'* (*Las obras y relaciones de Anton. Pérez. Imprimido por Pietro Chouët [Geneva] MDCLIV*).

² *State of Europe during the Middle Ages*, chap. iv (reprint of 4th ed., London, 1869, p. 274). On the question of the genuineness of the oath, for which Antonio Pérez, Philip II's minister, is the authority, see W. H. Prescott, *The Reign of Ferdinand and Isabella*, Sect. II (new edit. revised in one vol., pub. Routledge, London, n.d., p. 23). Vinogradoff treated the formula as authentic. (*Cambridge Medieval History*, vol. iii (1922), pp. 460-461.)

³ H. J. Chaytor, *A History of Aragon and Catalonia* (London, 1933), p. 110. Cf. the remarkable powers of the *Justicia* of Aragon (Chaytor, pp. 119-120), who has been described as combining in his own person 'the powers of the Lord Chancellor of England with those of the Supreme Court of the United States'. 'He was regarded as a power between the king and the people—the controller of the one and protector of the other' (H. E. Watts, *Spain* ('Story of the Nations' series, London and New York, 1893), pp. 155-156). As R. W. and A. J. Carlyle point out, the idea of an independent judge between king and nobles, such as was the Aragonese *Justicia*, is but one example of the 'general principle that the feudal court was normally supreme in all questions between the king and his vassals' (*A History of Mediaeval Political Theory in the West*, vol. v (Edinburgh and London, 1928), p. 110). Aragon was but an extreme example of medieval particularism; there, as Alfonso III said, 'había tantos reyes como ricos hombres'.

⁴ Fritz Kern, *Kingship and Law in the Middle Ages* (E.T. by S. B. Chrimes, Oxford, 1939), p. 87.

⁵ 'Der Staat des Mittelalters ist ebensogut Adelsstaat wie Herrscherstaat. Aber die Abgrenzung der Teilgewalten von der Zentralgewalt musste immer wieder zu Auseinandersetzungen führen, und diese sind verschieden verlaufen' (Heinrich Mitteis, *Der*

It is not difficult to see how in such an atmosphere the idea of the Church as an institution separate from the State and possessed of its own authority—an idea ultimately derived from the Biblical notion of the Kingdom of God—could develop into that of the Church as an *imperium in imperio*. So long as the classical idea of sovereignty persisted such an evolution was inconceivable or barely possible. But, given feudal conditions, the way was open. For the Church had a history infinitely longer and more impressive than that of the feudal fief. It could claim independence with far better title than any feudal landlord.

Yet this was far from being the immediate outcome of the Church's finding itself living in the new type of society which developed, as the result of a long evolution, towards the end of the first millennium A.D. On the contrary, in the breakdown of centralised power, the Church suffered a loss of independence and not without reason is the volume of the great Fliche et Martin, *Histoire de l'Église,* covering the period 888 to 1057, given the title *L'Église au pouvoir des laïques*.[1] To understand the reasons we need to turn to a phenomenon in Church history for the elucidation of which we are indebted to comparatively recent historical scholarship—a phenomenon of which the existence was barely recognised before the nineteenth century. I refer to the notion of the 'private church', the *Eigenkirche* as it is technically known. It was in October 1894 that Ulrich Stutz delivered his now classical inaugural lecture in the University of Basel entitled *Die Eigenkirche als Element des mittelalterlich-germanischen Kirchenrechtes* (Berlin, 1895),[2] and thereby set in motion a series of studies and controversies which have to a great extent transformed our notions of ecclesiastical development in the early Middle Ages. It is not my purpose to discuss the disputes which have arisen about the origin of the institution then described by Stutz—disputes which have

Staat des hohen Mittelalters (3rd edit., Weimar, 1948), p. 502). For a discussion of the evolution of the feudal contractual idea into that of the *régime des estats,* see G. de Lagarde, *La Naissance de l'esprit laïque au déclin du moyen-âge,* vol. iv (Paris, 1942), chap. ii, pp. 67-131. A fuller treatment is given by É. Lousse, *La Société d'ancien régime : organisation et représentation corporatives* (Louvain, 1943).

[1] By Émile Amann and Auguste Dumas (Paris, 1948).
[2] E.T. by Geoffrey Barraclough in *Mediaeval Germany,* vol. ii (Oxford, 1938), pp. 35-70.

been so strangely complicated and embittered by nationalistic feeling, as German and French historians have contended on behalf of Teutonic and Latin claims to the doubtful honour of inventing the private church. (These contests remind one of the rivalry between Ipswich and Sudbury to be regarded as the original of Dickens's Eatanswill, for only an idealist could regard the private church as a blessing to mankind or to the Church.) It would probably now be agreed that Stutz's attempt to identify the institution he discovered with a peculiarity of Germanic paganism carried on into early German Arian Christianity and thence into medieval Catholic polity has failed, and that the proprietary church is but one example of the phenomena produced by the general decay of centralism in the decline and fall of the Roman Empire in the West.[1] Let us content ourselves with considering its importance in the history of Church-State relations.

What was an *Eigenkirche*? It was a church built by a landlord on his estate for the spiritual benefit of himself and his dependants. In accordance with the spirit of the times the Dark Ages landlord regarded his foundation as his own property and both Church and State perforce admitted his claim to possess it. Not only was the church and its income his, but he retained also the right to nominate its priest—a right which has survived in this country and in some other parts of Europe in the form of lay parochial patronage, even though other vestiges of the private church system have vanished. In its heyday the landlord claimed not only to appoint but to control his priest. Furthermore, he conceived himself to possess the right to dispose of his church by gift, sale or testamentary disposition, to third parties, if he did not leave it to devolve upon his heir. Short of secularising the building (which

---

[1] See the documented and judicious discussion of the issues by Professor David Knowles in his *Monastic Order in England* (Cambridge, 1940), pp. 562-568. P. Imbart de la Tour, at the suggestion of his master, Fustel de Coulanges, had already studied some aspects of the private church in his Sorbonne thesis, *De ecclesiis rusticanis aetate carolingica* (Bordeaux, 1890), more than four years before the appearance of Stutz's lecture.

There is a valuable summary of the whole matter in G. W. O. Addleshaw's two pamphlets, *The Beginnings of the Parochial System* and *The Development of the Parochial System from Charlemagne (768–814) to Urban II (1088–1099)* (St. Anthony's Press Publications, nos. 3 and 6, London, 1953 and 1954).

would have been sacrilege) he could do almost anything with it, whilst over its incumbent his powers were often greater than those of the diocesan bishop.

The obvious friction between lay and ecclesiastical authority occasioned by this claim of the laity to the ownership of what were to become the parish churches of medieval Europe needs no stressing. What is of even greater significance is the extension, by a natural transition of thought, of a parallel claim to lay control of the larger units of ecclesiastical jurisdiction and property, bishoprics and monasteries. Kings and lesser magnates, accustomed to the idea of owning and controlling churches upon their domains, thought it natural to claim similar rights over the sees and religious houses they had in many cases founded or endowed and of which in any case they were the protectors. In regard to bishoprics there was the earlier precedent of imperial and royal control of episcopal elections to aid their claim: monarchs had long been accustomed to think of the bishops of their realms as *their* bishops. With the decline of royal power in favour of that of local lords, it was equally natural for these latter to regard the greater churches within their sphere of influence as subject to them. So one finds a curious rivalry between kings and nobles for the control of episcopal elections. For example, of 77 sees in eleventh-century France, the king had the control of about 25: the rest were in the hands of dukes, counts or viscounts. That control was exercised chiefly in determining the occupant of the see. The temporal lord might either concede the election to the clergy and people, subject to his own confirmation, or himself appoint a candidate direct.[1] But it did not limit itself to this. The idea of the private church, as we have seen, involved more than the mere right of appointment to it: the church was the lord's property. This notion, too, is applied to bishoprics. The see, with its lands and property, comes to be regarded as an 'honour'; the same word is used as that increasingly current to describe a lay fief. As such it is in the overlord's gift. He expects from its tenant homage, fealty

[1] The classic book on this topic is P. Imbart de la Tour, *Les Élections épiscopales dans l'Église de France du IXe au XIIe siècle* (Paris, 1890).

and military service: he claims the right to invest him with the honour and when it is vacant take it 'into his own hand' until the time comes to grant it again to its newly chosen incumbent.

Here we come face to face with another aspect of the influence of feudal ideas upon ecclesiastical affairs. When political power is localised to the extent required by a feudal organisation of society, and is bound up with the holding of land, it is inevitable that the Church should become, to a greater degree than ever before, a sharer in that power. For, before the development of money investments and finance, endowment of the Church can only be in land. And when land is the measure of power, the greater ecclesiastical landlords, bishops, abbots, cathedral churches and other prelates or corporations, must of necessity be important units in the State, responsible for military service, local jurisdiction, and supervision of agricultural economy. And if they are such, the State cannot be indifferent to their identity. Even in their spiritual capacity, as men wielding great powers of spiritual persuasion and coercion, bishops and other prelates are formidable and we have already seen that the State, from the moment it became Christian, interested itself profoundly in ecclesiastical appointments. But when to spiritual power was added, under feudal conditions, temporal authority over wide areas of territory, bishops and abbots became personages about whose loyalty the State could not take chances. In England the prince-bishop in the full sense, as found in, for example, Germany, was a rare, indeed a unique phenomenon. Yet who can look at Durham Castle and reflect upon the key position of the Palatinate of Durham in the defence of the Scottish border without realising that no King of England could remain indifferent to the outcome of an election to that see?

The temporal importance of prelates was the ultimate and legitimate reason upon the State's side for its retention of at least some degree of control over ecclesiastical personages and property, a control which came to be regarded by zealous churchmen as out of harmony with any adequate notion of the Church's freedom. For the Church, too, had a strong case for demanding self-government. The State, in making ecclesiastical appointments, was not likely to pay great heed to spiritual qualities, as compared with docility to state policy, skill in administration or even warlike ability. (It is one of the ironies of history that Bruno of Toul, who was to become the first of the great eleventh-century reforming Popes as Leo IX, owed his elevation to episcopal rank chiefly to his powers of generalship.)[1] Nor was this the worst possibility. An unscrupulous ruler might sell ecclesiastical office as readily as temporal to the highest bidder, so countenancing and encouraging the peculiarly deadly sin of simony. Equally the general neglect in the later Dark Ages of the canons prohibiting clerical marriage, combined with the general drift towards hereditary office, opened the possibility of feudal warrior-priest dynasties of Hasmonean type. A feudalised Church meant a Church dominated by lay power and lay mentality, and also set up serious obstacles to a spiritual revival such as the low clerical morals of the age, so horrifically depicted in the lurid pages of St. Peter Damian's *Liber Gomorrhianus*,[2] quite obviously demanded.

These inner contradictions of a feudalised Church did not at first become apparent when in the tenth and eleventh centuries, as the disorders brought about by the second great wave of barbarian invasion died away, men of the better sort set their hands to Church reform. There were so many obvious Augean stables to cleanse that the ultimate question of the source of the troubles of the Church did not need to be faced. Attention has often been drawn recently to the great contrast between these first reform movements and what we are accustomed to call the Hildebrandine spirit. The distinction lies chiefly in the fact that before the middle of the eleventh century the reformers concentrated upon extirpating the more glaring abuses, with a certain indifference to the means by which this could be effected. If emperors and kings were willing to use their power directly to put down simony and to recall the clergy to a higher standard of life, well and good. Even though such a method of reform meant some perpetuation, or even extension, of lay control of the Church, they did not object

---

[1] Marc Bloch, *La Société féodale: les classes et le gouvernement des hommes* (Paris, 1940), p. 107.   [2] P.L. cxlv. 159-190.

to it, provided that it was effective, and they were the more easily able to maintain this attitude in that they retained an idea of kingship as divinely ordained for the Church's benefit.

But when Hildebrand became Pope in 1073, under the title of Gregory VII, a change was almost at once perceptible, a change to be attributed almost solely to the powerful personality of one of the most original figures of the Middle Ages. Of the two greatest reforming zealots of the period immediately preceding, St. Peter Damian (who died in 1072) and Cardinal Humbert (who had disappeared from the scene some ten years earlier), only the latter can be considered in any real sense a precursor of the great Pope in his views. Damian held to the old tradition. He wished for collaboration between Pope and Emperor in the work of reform, a union so close that 'the King shall be found in the Roman Pontiff, the Roman Pontiff in the King', for, as he said, 'in one Mediator of God and man, these two, the *regnum* and the *sacerdotium*, are bound together by a divine mystery'.[1] A similar ideal had been held in the previous century by Pope Silvester II (the famous Gerbert of Aurillac) in his close alliance with the Emperor Otto III.[2] Damian held on to a hope which in the eyes of Hildebrand came to be forlorn and, indeed, based upon illusion. Damian could even exhort the young Emperor, Henry IV, destined to become Hildebrand's bitter enemy, to show himself a new Constantine,[3] a

[1] 'Sicut in uno mediatore Dei et hominum, haec duo, regnum scilicet et sacerdotium, divino sunt conflata mysterio; ita sublimes istae duae personae tanta sibimet invicem unanimitate iungantur, ut quodam mutuo glutino et rex in Romano pontifice, et Romanus pontifex inveniatur in rege; salvo scilicet suo privilegio papae, quod nemo [nemini] praeter eum usurpare permittitur' (*P.L.* cxlv. 86-87). Cf. A. Fliche, *La Réforme grégorienne*, vol. i (Louvain and Paris, 1924), p. 229.

[2] 'In diesem Satz liegt das Zugeständnis an das Papsttum, dass, wenn auch seine verbrieften Rechte aufgehoben seien, die bisher gültige theoretische Basis nicht angefochten würde: es blieb die Zwei-Gewaltenlehre zur Regelung der Beziehungen zwischen Papsttum und Kaisertum, es blieb das Nebeneinander von regalis potestas und sacrata auctoritas pontificum, von regnum und sacerdotium, das Leo von Vercelli im Jahre 998 in seinem Gregor-Rhythmus fixiert hatte' (Percy Ernst Schramm, *Kaiser, Rom und Renovatio: Studien und Texte zur Geschichte des römischen Erneuerungsgedankes*, Teil I, Studien der Bibliothek Warburg hersg. von Fritz Saxl, XVII (Leipzig and Berlin, 1929), p. 169). Cf. F. Dvornik, *The Making of Central and Eastern Europe* (London, 1949), pp. 138 *sqq.* and *passim*.

[3] 'Porro si Cadaloum cito velut alter Constantinum Arium destruis, et Ecclesiae, pro quo Christus mortuus est pacem reformare contendis; faciat te Deus in proximo de regno imperiale fastigium scandere, et a cunctis hostibus tuis insignis gloriae titulos reportare' (*Ep.* vii. 3, *P.L.* cxliv. 442).

title he had earlier, and with better reason, accorded to Henry's father, Henry III.[1] Yet even Damian had believed the Roman Church to be superior, not only to every other ecclesiastical authority, but to every lay power also, and enunciated the maxim, *Terrenus imperator non habet in Romana Ecclesia potestatem.*[2] This thought was developed much more powerfully by Cardinal Humbert, who used the comparison, which became a common-place later in the Middle Ages, of soul and body as expressing the true relations of the spiritual and temporal powers. It was for the spiritual power, as the directing force of the body of Christendom, to decide what should be done, for the temporal to put the decisions into effect.[3]

Here we see already adumbrated the germ of the Gregorian ideas. Nevertheless, Gregory VII carried the seminal notions of his predecessors in reform much further than they. It would seem that he felt driven to do so by a realisation that the temporal heads of Christendom were bruised reeds. In a letter written within four months of his accession one indeed finds him comparing the spiritual and temporal powers to the twin eyes of Christendom[4] and his earliest negotiations with Henry IV (already under papal ban before Hildebrand became Pope) are marked by a desire for good relations. In the view of Fliche, it was not until two years later, in 1075, that Gregory, almost in despair, turned to a more

[1] 'Videtur itaque imperator iste Constantino Caesari adversus catholicae hostes Ecclesiae non supparem obtinuisse victoriam' (*P.L.* cxlv. 152-153).

[2] *P.L.* cxlv. 71. Cf. *ibid.* 'Quoniam ubi principatus sacerdotum, et Christianae religionis caput ab imperatore coelesti constitutum est, iustum non est, ut illic imperator terrenus habeat potestatem.'

[3] 'Unde qui sacerdotalem et regalem dignitatem vult irreprehensibiliter et utiliter conferre, dicat sacerdotium in praesenti ecclesia assimilari animae, regnum autem corpori, quia invicem se diligunt et vicissim sese indigent suamque sibi operam vicissim exigunt et impendunt. Ex quibus sicut praeeminet anima et praecipit, sic sacerdotalis dignitas regali, utputa caelestis terrestri. Sic ne praepostera, sed ordinata sint omnia, sacerdotium tanquam anima praemoneat quae sunt agenda; regnum deinde tanquam caput sui corporis omnibus membris praemineat et ea quo expedit praecedat. Sicut enim regum est ecclesiasticos sequi, sic laicorum quoque reges suos ad utilitatem ecclesiae et patriae; sic ab una earum potestate populus doceri, ab altera debet regi, quarum neutra populum inconsiderate sequi' (*Adversus simoniacos*, iii. 21, in M.G.H. *Libelli de lite*, vol. i (Hanover, 1891), pp. 225-226).

[4] 'Nam sicut duobus oculis humanum corpus temporali lumine regitur, ita his duabus dignitatibus in pura religione concordantibus corpus Ecclesiae spirituali lumine regi et illuminari probatur' (*Ep. xii ad Rodolfum Sueviae Ducem.* Reg. i. 19, *P.L.* cxlviii. 302).

intransigent policy, which was marked by the decree of February 1075, forbidding lay investiture of bishops with their sees, and by the document known as the *Dictatus Papae*.

Let us consider the scope of these two pronouncements. Lay investiture, the juridical act symbolised by the giving of the episcopal ring and staff to the elected bishop, was the means by which the 'honour' of a bishopric was conferred, and this demonstrated in the most vivid way possible the control claimed by the temporal power over local church, accompanied as it was by the spoken formula, *Accipe ecclesiam tuam*. It had already been forbidden, though in rather vague terms, by Nicholas II in 1059. Gregory had hitherto not enforced this decree and had recognised bishops appointed by lay investiture. Though we do not possess the exact terms of his prohibition of 1075, it seems clear that it must have been more precise and formal than that of his predecessor, and therefore to be regarded as a declaration of war against a custom regarded hitherto as a normal expression of royal authority in the Church.

Far more significant, however, is the teaching contained in the *Dictatus Papae*, a list of papal prerogatives drawn up in succinct and aphoristic form. An Italian scholar, G. B. Borino, has recently made the interesting suggestion that this series of short sentences was originally the list of *capitula* attached to a catena of canonical *auctoritates* collected at Gregory's orders to give precedents for the programme he proposed to follow.[1] The supposition is very probable when one considers the degree to which the whole reforming movement saw itself as an attempt to restore the Church's forgotten canon law. The articles of the *Dictatus* are largely concerned with papal supremacy over the Church and may indeed have been determined largely by the attempts Gregory had been making to persuade the Eastern Church to recognise papal authority. But the document also lays down in its twelfth article that the Pope has the right to depose emperors.[2] It is noteworthy

---

[1] G. B. Borino, 'Un' ipotesi sul "Dictatus Papae" di Gregorio VII', *Archivio della R. Deputazione romana di Storia patria*, nuova serie, vol. x, annata xvii (Rome, 1944), pp. 237-252.   [2] 'Quod illi liceat imperatores deponere.'

that Caspar, who has traced canonical precedents for most of the other propositions in it, found none for this. It would be interesting to know, if Borino's idea is correct, what texts were originally cited under this heading in the canonical collection to which, as he conjectures, the *Dictatus* supplied headings.[1]

Here, indeed, is something novel. Arquillière, describing it as *une conclusion théologique nouvelle*, remarks with reason: 'This is real theocracy, and all the attempts which have been made to deprive Gregorian thought of this characteristic will always come up against this short and formidable formula.'[2]

With the enunciation of a theory of spiritual supremacy over temporal affairs began the great contests between *regnum* and *sacerdotium* which are the central interest of medieval history between the eleventh and the fourteenth centuries. To describe them in detail would be wearisome and unprofitable, and would add nothing to a task many times performed by others. One fact must be noted. The quarrels began with what is loosely termed the Investiture Contest, extending from the days of Gregory VII to the settlement achieved between his successor, Calixtus II, and the Emperor Henry V, Henry IV's son, in 1122, the Concordat of Worms. The expression is unhappy because, as the late Professor Z. N. Brooke argued, the original dispute between Hildebrand and Henry IV turned far more upon freedom of episcopal elections than upon investiture itself. It was Gregory's successors who turned it into a contest about investiture and the right of monarchs to grant to ecclesiastics the temporal possessions annexed to great churches. In so doing, Brooke argued, they lost sight of what Gregory had been chiefly anxious to secure, namely, the Church's right to select its own higher personnel.[3] The principle behind lay

[1] H.-X. Arquillière, *Saint Grégoire VII: essai sur sa conception du pouvoir pontifical* (Paris, 1934), p. 134.

[2] 'C'est bien de la théocratie, et tous les efforts qui ont été faits pour en dépouiller la pensée grégorienne se heurteront toujours à cette brève et formidable formule' (Arquillière, *ibid.*).

[3] 'But by concentrating upon it [the abolition of lay investiture] they lost their ultimate aim. The king had something with which to barter; by renouncing investiture he gave up the shadow and retained the substance—all that part of the customary procedure which ensured his control over the appointment of bishops and over the bishops when appointed. So Gregory's purpose was defeated when what he intended as a means became an end. It

CHRISTIANITY AND THE STATE

investiture was far greater than that of the ceremony itself and it was lost sight of in the struggle. Moreover, as suggested earlier, it was a matter upon which both Church and State could put forward a plausible case: indeed in the matter of appointments to sees and abbeys the internal contradiction implicit in the fact of a feudalised Church was at its most acute, for the men whose choice was in question had by force of circumstance to be great figures in Church and State alike. Only once, it would seem, was the question roundly faced, in 1110 and 1111, when, on the occasion of Henry V's coronation, the unworldly Paschal II proposed a solution of the problem by which the Church would renounce temporal possessions in return for the abandonment by the State of all claims upon the selection and control of prelates. The proposal outraged alike ecclesiastics reluctant to abandon worldly position and lay magnates wishing to retain full rights of patronage and control of local churches, and the idea collapsed in scenes of riot. Nevertheless the root of the difficulty was then uncovered, even if all men shrank from recognising it.[1]

With the settlement, or patching up, of the investiture dispute by an agreement which left to the Emperor the substance of his claim to nominate prelates at the price of his more shadowy right to invest them with the symbols of power,[2] the essential dispute changed character. More and more the point at issue is the theoretical relationship of the spiritual and temporal powers. This was the heart of the matter in the struggle between Frederick Barbarossa and the Holy See, and in the later epic conflict between Frederick II and the Papacy, even though many concrete political issues, such as the status of the Italian city states, entered in. At the time the question was commonly posed in directly theological terms. Does the Emperor hold his power directly from God, or only mediately through the Pope? Nowadays it would probably

was a Pyrrhic triumph for the Papacy when the king was left in possession of the field' (Z. N. Brooke, 'Lay Investiture and its Relation to the Conflict of Empire and Papacy', Raleigh Lecture, in *Proceedings of the British Academy*, 1939, p. 244).

[1] For some reflections upon this bizarre incident, see my essay, 'Feudal Episcopacy', in *The Apostolic Ministry*, ed. K. E. Kirk (London, 1946), pp. 372-374.

[2] M.G.H. *Leges*, Sect. iv, *Constitutiones imperatorum*, vol. i, ed. L. Weiland (Hanover, 1893), nos. 107 and 108, pp. 159-161.

be differently phrased. Are Church and State aspects of one society or are they two independent powers? In either case, are there two sources of authority on earth or one only? In some such way as this the problem—which has been with us ever since— would present itself to a modern mind.

It is, however, important to notice, in order to understand a vital difference between medieval assumptions and our own, that the former question was never asked in that precise form in the Middle Ages. It is always common ground to both sides in Church-State disputes that there is one Christian society only, one Christendom, one *respublica Christiana*. (For example, Gregory VII, in his simile of the two eyes of Christendom, mentioned above,[1] speaks of the *sacerdotium* and the *imperium* as two *dignitates* in the one body of the Church.) On the other hand, one of his opponents, the author of the treatise, *De unitate ecclesiae conservanda*, wrote a treatise accusing him of causing schism in the Church by excommunicating the Emperor.)[2] The idea of unity is the starting point of all discussion of the subject: what is in dispute is the relationship between the two principles distinguished within that unity, the spiritual and temporal powers, *sacerdotium* and *regnum*. From at least the time of Pope Gelasius I in the fifth century the existence of these two principles, corresponding to the dual nature of man, body and soul, spirit and matter, had been recognised: indeed Gelasius's affirmation of the independence of the two powers, each in their own sphere, became a *locus classicus* in later discussion.[3] But, as all experience of condominium shows, it is easier to assert the existence of parallel authorities than to determine their relations and the limits of their power. In this specific case it was all the more difficult to do this, in that the distinction could

---

[1] See p. 111, n. 4.

[2] In M.G.H. *Libelli de lite*, vol. ii (Hanover, 1892), pp. 173 *sqq.*

[3] 'Duo quippe sunt, imperator Auguste, quibus principaliter mundus hic regitur: auctoritas sacra [*al.* sacrata] pontificum, et regalis potestas. In quibus tanto gravius est pondus sacerdotum, quanto etiam pro ipsis regibus Domino in divino reddituri sunt examine rationem. Nosti etenim, fili clementissime, quod licet praesideas humano generi dignitate, rerum tamen praesulibus divinarum devotus colla submittis, atque ab eis causas tuae salutis expetis [*al.* expectas], inque sumendis caelestibus sacramentis, eisque (ut competit) disponendis, subdi te debere cognoscis religionis ordine potius quam praesse' (*P.L.* lix. 42).

easily become too absolute. To say, as was commonly done, that it was the State's function to direct man to his earthly goal, the Church's to prepare him for heaven, was to overlook the fact that on Christian principles no act of man, however mundane, is without relevance to his eternal destiny, and that no supernatural human activity, be it never so spiritual, is without repercussions upon his everyday life. (This last consideration is perhaps best illustrated by the fact, familiar to every medieval man, that even withdrawal from the world in order to pursue a life of heavenly contemplation is an act which may have far-reaching effects upon society. Monasticism was one of the most important social phenomena which had to be taken into account by every medieval state.)

If we have been right in supposing that, when first an alliance of Church and State upon Christian terms became possible, the problem posed by the Christian conception of the Church as a supernatural society existing nevertheless partly in visible form on earth was never roundly faced, then we shall understand more easily why the great contests of Church and State in the eleventh and following centuries were, in a sense, predestined to occur. For the first attempt to solve the half-recognised problem was, as we have seen, to continue half-consciously the relationship between civil society and religion of pagan days, making the necessary adaptations by makeshift means. In the gradual transformation of Western Europe, begun by the barbarian invasions and deepened by later insecurity, the difficulties evaded earlier became acute. Hence the sharp conflict we have been considering.

It is easy to say that by greater good-will on either side the crisis could have been averted. But that is really an historical subterfuge. No doubt there is some truth—not to say truism—in the assertion. But the fact that the same phrase forms today the cheapest and most unilluminating homiletic comment upon contemporary troubles, varying from labour unrest to the schism between Eastern and Western ideologies, suggests that it is always superficial. Men are most usually quarrelsome when they are in perplexity, and no mere exhortations to charity, which do nothing to lighten the obscurity which is straining it, effect anything of value. In the case we are considering this banal comment about the need for good-will ignores the series of unresolved contradictions in medieval Church-State relations. To one of these attention has already been drawn. It lies in the fact that whilst an unendowed Church would have had very little chance of independence in an insecure age, that very endowment, necessarily in territory, involved the Church ineluctably in mundane concerns and so drew upon it the jealousy of the civil power. But two others remain to be noticed.

There is first the consideration that it was not only the position of the Church as feudal landowner on a large scale which hampered the efforts of the eleventh-century reformers to free the clergy from worldly cares and lay control. There was also the fact that in the West, in contrast to Byzantium, there was no educated laity capable of staffing a civil service, which had therefore to be clerical in composition. We speak loosely of conflicts of Church and State at this time, meaning conflicts of clergy and laity, forgetting all too easily that those who upheld the rights of the State were themselves predominantly clerics. The most anti-clerical medieval king or emperor would have been helpless in any conflict with the Pope without his own clerks to argue his case. This, no less than the civic importance of prelates as landholders, made the claim of the medieval clergy to the status of an international privileged caste, exempt from lay jurisdiction and control, an anomaly.

Finally, at a deeper level, there lay the fact that the clergy claimed—and was bound to claim if it was to fulfil its apostolic commission—a power of censorship over lay morals. Now politics, as everyone up to Renaissance times would have agreed, is a part of morals. If so, ecclesiastical censure must necessarily sometimes involve indirect interference in the sphere normally appropriated to the temporal power. And such interference would be the more arbitrary in that centuries of dealing with a semi-barbarous society had imbued the Church with the spirit of the stern parent or schoolmaster, rather than that of the urbane spiritual adviser, in dealing with its children. It proceeded by means of excommunication and penitential discipline rather than by exhortation when breaches of the moral law were in evidence, and expected the State to enforce its censures by the weight of the secular arm if need be. How can the independence of the State from the spiritual power be a reality when the State is thought of as standing to the Church in the relation of child or pupil?

This last was the issue which really lay behind the contest over the relations of *regnum* and *sacerdotium*. In the last resort, the power of the Pope over kings or emperors, by whatever metaphysical or technical theological arguments it may be defended, rests upon the papal pastoral mission. 'These different arguments', says M. Arquillière of Gregory VII's polemic, 'tend towards a single end, which is seen by him with a clear inevitability': to show the pre-eminence of the priesthood over the royal office as that of the 'father' over the 'son' or of the 'master' over the 'disciple'. 'The royal office is in the Church. It exists for the Church; even dynastic heredity does not give it a right which may not be touched. . . . In the last resort it exists by the Church. . . . This [Gregory's attitude] is the exercise of the power of the keys, in a society where the accepted faith recognises no other limit to it than the sanctity of its usage.' As the same author rightly says, 'we come here upon the bases of medieval civilisation'. So he can claim, if perhaps with some exaggeration, that 'if we wish to keep profoundly within the atmosphere of the age, as the historian must always try to do, we cannot say that Gregory VII thought that he was committing the least usurpation. He never goes outside his strictly spiritual attitude. Only, kingship, in assuming, chiefly with Charlemagne, a weighty religious mission—in absorbing into itself the old idea of the Empire, in making of itself a magistrature spiritual as much as political—kingship thus conceived was condemning its representatives one day or another to be dominated by the supreme head of the Church.'[1]

[1] 'Ces divers arguments tendent à un unique but, qui lui apparaît avec une évidence éclatante; montrer la prééminence du sacerdoce sur la royauté comme celle du "Père" sur le "fils" ou du "maître" sur le "disciple" . . . La royauté est dans l'Église. Elle existe pour l'Église; même l'hérédité dynastique ne lui confère pas un droit intangible . . . Enfin

The wheel has come full circle. The king who sought, or felt it his duty, to control the Church, by that very fact finds himself subject to the Church's judgement. The fateful sequel to lay control of ecclesiastical matters noted by Arquillière was necessarily involved by the social evolution of a religion which by its charter deeds committed, not to kings, but to apostles, the spiritual guidance of its adherents. The medieval crisis of Church and State is in the last resort but the acute perception of the dilemma almost necessarily involved, that the State must either dominate the Church or be dominated by it.

elle existe par l'Église . . . c'est l'exercice du pouvoir les clés, dans une société où la croyance commune ne lui reconnaît d'autre limite que la sainteté de son usage . . . Nous touchons ici aux bases de la civilisation médiévale. Et si l'on veut rester profondément dans l'esprit du temps, comme l'historien doit y tendre, on ne peut pas dire que Grégoire VII ait pensé commettre la moindre usurpation. Il ne sort jamais de son point de vue strictement spirituel. Seulement, la royauté, en assumant, principalement avec Charlemagne, une lourde mission religieuse—en y absorbant la vieille notion de l'Empire, en faisant une magistrature spirituelle autant que politique,—la royauté ainsi conçue condamnait un jour ou l'autre ses représentants à être dominés par le chef suprême de l'Église' (Arquillière, *Saint Grégoire VII*, pp. 286-287).

CHAPTER VII

THE BREAK-UP OF THE MEDIEVAL WORLD

I do not believe that anyone can study the history of the Middle Ages without being gripped by the feeling that at some point in it something failed seriously in civilisation.

> *Nequaquam, quoniam medio de fonte leporum*
> *Surgit amari aliquid quod in ipsis floribus angat.*[1]

Lucretius's words, though in a very different context, express exactly the impression gained. The whole period which in French usage is described as *le haut moyen-âge*, that which extends roughly from the eleventh to the thirteenth century, is unmistakably an age of promise. There is much in it that is crude and childish, much that is morally deplorable, much that is obviously experimental. Yet always there remains the note of promise. Whether one looks at it from the political angle and considers the many interesting experiments in government, development of the technique of centralised justice, taxation and consultation, whether one considers the growth of town life, commerce and agriculture, or whether, in the deeper matters of mind and spirit, one observes the growing maturity of philosophy and theology, or the broadening of popular religion as a result of the work of men like St. Bernard and the early friars—in all these aspects of human life the atmosphere is that of spring, of spring with its sudden frosts and gales, its floods and its unaccountable outbursts of animal madness, but equally of spring with its returning warmth and sunshine, its freshness and tenderness, and, above all, its note of expectancy. History seems to stand on the brink of fresh revelation.

And yet this spring seems to pass into autumn without any intervening high summer. By the early fourteenth century there is quite obviously a chill in the air. A note of cynicism pervades all the rest of the Middle Ages. Huizinga has examined the loss of nerve characteristic of the fifteenth century:[2] but the tendency

---

[1] Lucretius, *De natura rerum*, iv. 1133.
[2] J. Huizinga, *The Waning of the Middle Ages* (E.T., London, 1924).

analysed could be traced much further back. Indeed it seems more and more apparent that the real dividing line between confidence and its loss lies further back even than the turn of the thirteenth and fourteenth centuries. For the later thirteenth century was an age of disillusionment. In political affairs it was the period of the breakdown of the Holy Roman Empire in its idealistic and effective form, the age also of the ruin of the crusading ideal, of discontent and civil war in England, of the beginnings of tyranny replacing republicanism in Italian cities. In the world of thought, the confident alliance of faith and reason characteristic of the earlier part of the century was already being undermined by the beginnings of the scepticism which proved such a solvent of constructive thought in the centuries to follow. Economic friction and, in some respects, repression can be seen. Impossible as it is to lay a finger upon any precise year, or even decade, difficult as it is to isolate any one cause or symptom, yet it seems clear that the *malaise* began in what many (notably Bishop Lightfoot in a great essay)[1] have regarded as the period of the greatest flowering of medieval culture, the age which did indeed leave the greatest legacy to the future.[2]

Why should this be so? It would require more space and greater powers than those at my command fully to discuss the question. One wonders whether the problem is capable of a definitive answer at all. Disease in its earliest stages is as difficult to detect in human society as in the human body. Yet I feel sure that one clue is to be found in the topic I am trying to trace—the relations between Church and State, between religious and secular society.

In the last lecture we saw that the notion of papal theocracy was in some ways an inevitable outcome of the problem posed by the fact that Christianity never was or could be an ethnic religion like its predecessors. Christ's institution of an apostolate as the formative and regulative organ of His new society made that for ever impossible. Side by side with the hierarchy of the State there

---

[1] 'England during the Latter Half of the Thirteenth Century', in J. B. Lightfoot, *Historical Essays* (London, 1895). '. . . a magnificent and precocious age' (p. 181).

[2] It is not necessarily implied that all the symptoms of decay began at the same moment. Stability, or even development, in one field of human life can co-exist with decadence in another.

would always be in a Christian community the hierarchy of the Church, a clergy, which, as its very name implied, was in origin and function distinct from the corps of wielders of temporal power.[1] The unavoidable intermingling of the two hierarchies, produced by the conversion of Europe and the peculiar evolution of Western society, in the long run—a period of nearly a thousand years—brought out the underlying tension produced by parallel authorities in one community. We saw in the last lecture the confusion caused by the share in political affairs necessarily taken by a clergy which nevertheless claimed at the same time, negatively, immunity from State control, and positively, the right to a coercive censorship over lay morals and politics. From that last claim, as we saw, there sprang by logical stages, almost unconsciously, the notion of a theocracy exercised through the Vicar of Christ over all aspects of human life.

But in what way in fact was that theocracy exercised? Sometimes, often indeed, with wisdom and righteousness. But not always. A. L. Smith's Ford Lectures of 1905 on *Church and State in the Middle Ages* end with a striking passage, familiar perhaps to many readers. 'Dante', says the lecturer, 'puts in the black starless air of the outer circle of the Inferno the shade of him *che fece lo gran rifiuto*. Of all Dante's tremendous verdicts, none has such a bitter ring of scorn as this. It is generally interpreted of one individual Pope; but it might well stand as judgement on the whole Papacy of the thirteenth century, when it bartered spiritual leadership for temporal rule, the legacy of St. Peter for the fatal dower of Constantine.'[2] Is this a fair statement of the case? One cannot help thinking that the author laid his finger upon the real worm in the bud of thirteenth-century civilisation in those few words. The policy of Innocent IV and his successors, of which he is there speaking, the vendetta they pursued against the whole House of Hohenstaufen, their mobilisation of all resources, spiritual,

[1] κλῆρος—the body of men which is the Lord's 'lot' or portion, which depends upon God and not upon man, and therefore stands apart from the rest of the community. The idea comes from the Old Testament. See Num. xviii. 20 and 24, Deut. x. 9 and xviii. 1-2 Josh. xiii. 14 and 33.
[2] A. L. Smith, *Church and State in the Middle Ages* (Oxford, 1913), p. 245.

diplomatic, military and economic, against it in the spirit of modern total war—all this appals the more in that it is not easy to say for what great moral end all this force was applied. However it had begun, upon whatever memories of the Church's subjection to Emperors in times past it was nourished, the Papacy's campaign against Frederick II and his heirs resembles far too closely the action of a kingdom of this world menaced by encirclement, a desperate struggle carried on to a bitter end. There was in fact a real strategical encirclement produced by the union of Germany and Southern Italy in the hands of a man of Frederick's political zeal and determination: the Papacy, on its territorial side, was as a nut in the jaws of powerful nutcrackers. Indeed this dread of *Einkrei- sung* can be traced in its effects upon papal policy right to the end of the Middle Ages: the sensitiveness felt by all Popes about the possibility of the Kingdom of Naples's once again falling into the hands of a powerful external power illustrates the fact. To this partly can be traced the later decline of the Papacy to the moral status of a purely Italian power playing the huckster's policy which is the perennial temptation of Italian diplomacy.

> 'O! it is excellent
> To have a giant's strength, but it is tyrannous
> To use it like a giant.'[1]

And not uncommonly the misuse of great resources leads to the impoverishment of those resources themselves.

One may very well enquire what such a policy as just described had to do with the vocation of moral arbiter of Europe, in the name of which the Papacy originally laid claim to power in the temporal sphere. In the last resort very little. Yet, how logical, how inevitable almost, was the descent to Avernus! Gregory VII claimed a deposing power, to be exercised in the last resort by military force unleashed at the Pope's command, in the name of justice or righteousness, *iustitia*—that favourite word of his. To love of justice he attributed his death in exile. The word *iustitia* has been reckoned to occur more than two hundred times in the great

---

[1] *Measure for Measure*, Act i, sc. 2.

Pope's extant writings.[1] It is claimed by Arquillière that it bears, in Gregorian language, a wider sense than that of mere negative equity.

'It is theological justice, that which results from incorporation into Christ by the sacraments, by sanctifying grace, by observance of the divine commandments, by the banishment of sin in all its forms.'[2] How far the claim is true, or how far Gregory was conscious of the full implications of his favourite term, we need not now enquire. But that he was not primarily under the influence of merely political motives in his actions, nor that of coarse love of power, the *cupiditas dominandi* pilloried by St. Augustine, seems clear. The way in which he threw away his political advantage by refusing, after the specious penance of Henry IV at Canossa in 1077, to take sides for or against the royal penitent, so losing the support of Henry's rebellious German subjects, seems sufficient evidence of this. He was then the pastor rather than the politician.[3]

But such a detached attitude becomes less and less characteristic of his successors. The contest of Papacy and Empire can be regarded as a long war, extending from the eleventh to the thirteenth century and beyond. It is a common experience that the continuance of a war obscures more and more the distinctness of the issues which began it and blurs moral outlines. So it proved in this case. The scrupulosity which made Gregory VII a bad ally to his political confederates was not shared by Alexander III when he encouraged the Italian cities to war against Barbarossa. By the time of Innocent IV, in whose policy (to quote once again A. L. Smith) 'everything spiritual, everything religious, became a means to one

---

[1] Arquillière, *Saint Grégoire VII*, p. 261, citing Bernheim.

[2] 'C'est la justice *théologique*, c'est celle qui résulte de l'incorporation au Christ par les sacrements, par la grâce sanctifiante, par l'observation des préceptes divins, par l'éloignement du péché, sous toutes ses formes' (Arquillière, p. 270).

[3] 'D'un geste Grégoire VII a dissipé tous les avantages péniblement accumulés au cours de l'année 1076, mais le geste est sublime et inspiré par le plus pur sentiment chrétien. Si le pape avait maintenu son exigence première et refusé d'ouvrir les portes du château au pécheur suppliant, il aurait laissé la réputation d'un politique énergique, d'un diplomate aussi tenace que clairvoyant; en pardonnant, il a prouvé qu'il était un vrai chrétien, capable de renoncer à des succès d'ordre temporel pour se conformer aux exigences de la charité' (A. Fliche, *L'Europe occidentale de 888 à 1125* (Histoire générale fondé par Gustave Glotz: Histoire du moyen-âge, vol. ii, Paris, 1941), pp. 403-404).

political end',[1] it had disappeared almost entirely. The only Pope after Hildebrand who had something of Hildebrand's detachment from mere expediency, was the great Innocent III (1198–1216), who, out of zeal for what he conceived to be the interests of strict justice, protected the infant Frederick II in his Sicilian kingdom and procured his election to the Empire, thereby creating the dangerous situation against which Gregory IX and Innocent IV struggled so hard. Yet he, too, in other matters could show opportunism, as when, having denounced the iniquity of the sack of Constantinople by the Fourth Crusade in 1204, he nevertheless legalised its results and used them to advance the interests of the Latin Church in Eastern Christendom.

What are the reasons for this cumulative moral suicide? The slowness with which opinion turned against the Papacy, the long delay of the revolt against it, which began in the fourteenth century and ended in the Reformation, is evidence that its claim to the position of judge of mankind, had struck chords in many minds. It was not by minor mistakes that goodwill was lost and impetus given to the movement towards secularism in politics, which is so obvious in the fourteenth and fifteenth centuries.

Some suggestions can be made, which, though not complete explanations, perhaps throw light upon the problem.

(1) One has been mentioned before and need but be epitomised here. Arbitration necessitates detachment in the arbitrator. Yet the Church, of which the Papacy was the head, was never ready to disentangle itself fully from the secular community it professed to judge. In one sense it could not do so: as has been said before, no Western State could dispense with the services of the clergy in civil administration. Yet there is little evidence of a desire even for detachment. In the last lecture the storm aroused by Paschal II's sudden proposal in 1111 to abandon ecclesiastical property in return for the abandonment of lay investiture of bishops was mentioned.[2] The clergy were horrified at the prospect of abandoning the *regalia* of the Empire, the 'towns, duchies, marches,

---

[1] A. L. Smith, *Church and State*, p. 228.   [2] See above, p. 114.

counties, mints, market dues, markets'[1] and so forth held by ecclesiastical persons and corporations. Another piece of evidence shows that those who asked to be recognised as a caste segregated from common life were not willing to accept the logical outcome of their separation from the world. In the struggle for clerical privilege and immunity no distinction was commonly made between ecclesiastics engaged in directly spiritual duties and those who might be described in medieval phrase as *clerici clericaliter non viventes*—the large number of ordained men occupied in primarily secular business and the cares of state. 'The common [canonical] opinion set aside absolutely any lay jurisdiction over clerks which resulted from the offices they fulfilled', says Génestal, the historian of clerical immunity in medieval France.[2] The Church wished to have matters both ways, to retain its influence and share in civil society and yet to contract out of it. No man will accept an umpire who insists upon taking a hand in the game and moreover has a stake upon its issue.

(2) To this involvement in temporal affairs may perhaps be traced in part an even deeper secularisation of the Church in spirit, namely the extent to which priestly, and in particular papal, authority was assimilated in theory to political power. 'My kingdom is not of this world' was a text understood too often by the medieval Church in a restricted sense, as if it meant merely that the sources of ecclesiastical authority were from above, not from below, instead of at least implying some condemnation of

---

[1] ' Interdicimus etiam et sub districtione anathematis prohibemus, ne quis episcoporum seu abbatum, presentium vel futurorum, eadem regalia invadent, id est civitates, ducatus, marchias, comitatus, monetas, teloneum, mercatum, advocatias regni, iura centurionum et curtes que manifeste regni erant, cum pertinentiis suis, militiam et castra regni, nec se deinceps nisi per gratiam regis de ipsis regalibus intromittant . . . Oportet enim episcopos curis secularibus expeditos curam suorum agere populorum nec ecclesiis suis abesse diutius' (M.G.H. *Leges Sect. IV: Const. imperatorum*, vol. i (Hanover, 1893), n. 90, p. 141).

[2] 'Eugène III, dans le c. *sacerdotibus*, avait décidé que les clercs officiers de laïques, qui seraient arrêtés pour quelque fraude dans leur administration, ne devraient pas être protégés par l'Église . . . Ce texte que vise une perte partielle du privilège pour la répression des fautes commises dans l'exercice des fonctions défendues, avait été interprété par certains grands canonistes du XIIIe siècle dans le sens d'une déchéance complète. Mais l'opinion absolument opposée avait triomphé. L'opinion commune écartait absolument toute compétence laïque sur les clercs à raison des offices exercés' (R. Génestal, *Le privilegium fori en France du décret de Gratien à la fin du XIVe siècle*, vol. i (Paris, 1921), p. 195).

the exercise by priests of the type of power enjoyed by the kings of the Gentiles. In short, there was a marked tendency to think of *regnum* and *sacerdotium* as different in origin rather than in character. For this, much of the blame must be laid at the door of the canonists. It has already been pointed out that the eleventh-century reformers made the canon law, often forgotten or disregarded before, in a sense their Bible. From it were drawn their arguments for a reform of clerical life and habits and for the right of the Church under the Pope to control its own affairs. Given the medieval passion for precedents and *auctoritates* the policy was an obvious one and possessed cogency in its age. But it was to prove mischievous, especially when the scientific study of the canons developed in the twelfth century, the age of Gratian and of the systematised canon law which became the code of the late medieval Church. For the twelfth century was also the age of the virtual rediscovery and close study of Roman civil law, pursued in those same centres, such as Bologna, which were hives of canonist activity.

'Every fresh step in the development of the canon law after Gratian brought with it a still further infiltration of legal ideas, so that ere long a study of the civil law became an indispensable preliminary to the education of the canonist, who became in consequence less and less of a theologian, and more and more of a lawyer.'[1]

There may be some exaggeration in this statement—the great canonists were by no means ignorant of theology and some contributed to it—but it is true in essence.

Now it should be remembered that the Civil Law, as the Middle Ages received it, was that canonised by Justinian and so was moulded by the authoritarianism of the later and less sunny Roman Empire. The Code, Digest and Institutes themselves proceeded from the will of an omnipotent Emperor, and, although the law contained in them retained traces of earlier ideas of government by consent and popular sovereignty, which were not without influence, yet it was shot through and through with

[1] Hastings Rashdall, *The Universities of Medieval Europe* (new edit., by F. M. Powicke and A. B. Emden, Oxford, 1936), i. 133-134.

absolutist conceptions of the authority of rulers and of their legislative omnicompetence. It is well known that the influence of Roman law upon medieval Europe was increasingly in the direction of reviving the concept of royal power, and that by the 'reception' of it as the law of the State in several countries of the West at the end of the Middle Ages absolutism received a considerable stimulus. It is not surprising to find in such an atmosphere an increasing and less and less judicious assimilation of the Pope's authority to that of an absolute secular legislator, having the laws in his breast. This was noticed by Gierke in the nineteenth century,[1] who even attributed the growth of the notion of absolute sovereignty in later medieval Europe to the influence of canonical *dicta* about the papal *plenitudo potestatis*.[2] Recently Dr. Ullmann of Cambridge has made the extravagance of some canonical ideas of papal power even more clear with the help of unpublished canonical texts.[3] It does not need the citation of Acton's now hackneyed remark about the absolutely corrupting effect of absolute power[4] to indicate the outcome of such a way of conceiving the highest office in the Church. Let it suffice to mention the illuminating fact that the famous *Consilium de emendanda ecclesia*, drawn up in 1537 by a committee which included Cardinal Pole, singled out as the first cause of the disorders which had provoked the Reformation and the religious crisis of the sixteenth century, the flattery of the canonists who had told Popes that their will was law.[5] 'This', says the committee, 'is the

---

[1] Otto Gierke, *Political Theories of the Middle Age*, trs. F. W. Maitland (Cambridge, 1900).

[2] 'It was within the Church that the idea of Monarchical Omnipotence first began to appear. It appeared in the shape of a *plenitudo potestatis* attributed to the Pope.' (Gierke, p. 36.)

[3] Walter Ullmann, *Medieval Papalism: The Political Theories of the Medieval Canonists* (London, 1949).

[4] 'Power tends to corrupt, and absolute power corrupts absolutely. Great men are almost always bad men, even when they exercise influence and not authority: still more when you superadd the tendency or the certainty of corruption by authority' (Letter of 1887 to Mandell Creighton. Extracts printed in Louise Creighton, *Life and Letters of Mandell Creighton*, vol. i (London, 1904), p. 372).

[5] 'Ita quod voluntas pontificis, qualiscunque ea fuerit, sit regula qua eius operationes et actiones dirigantur; ex quo proculdubio effici ut quicquid libeat, id etiam liceat. Ex hoc fonte, sancte pater, tanquam ex equo Troiano, irrupere in ecclesiam Dei tot abusus et tam graves morbi, quibus nunc conspicimus eam ad desperationem salutis laborasse' (B. J. Kidd, *Documents illustrative of the Continental Reformation* (Oxford, 1911), n. 126, p. 308).

Trojan horse out of which all abuses and dire diseases have invaded the Church.' Such an idea of irresponsible papal power was not only the source of the excesses which lost the Popes their moral right to be censors of kings. It also, by a natural reaction, encouraged kings to compete with popes in extravagant claims to absolute authority, and so led to the secularist conception of unitary sovereignty which was to break up the whole basis of medieval Church-State relations.

(3) One other matter may be mentioned more briefly, as being more obvious, though scarcely less important. There is a real anomaly in the spectacle of a ruler who claims universal power paying undue attention to territory controlled by him directly and so entering at this lower level into direct competition with supposedly lesser potentates. It was such a competition for local power which, after the Great Interregnum of the thirteenth century weakened the prestige of the Holy Roman Emperors, compelled, after the loss of the imperial demesne lands, to depend upon their family possessions as sources of power. By a process in some ways parallel, the Papacy, with its increasing zeal for the retention and enlargement of the Papal States, forfeited something of its international position and gave occasion to men to regard it as an Italian principate, one among the many territorial powers of Europe. So, in the sixteenth century, even Sir Thomas More, who was to die a martyr for the spiritual and universal authority of the Papacy, could warn Henry VIII against emphasising papal power too strongly when writing against Luther, on the ground that the Pope was a prince like other princes, with whom the king might later be politically on bad terms, so that he might live to repent his generous attitude to the Pope.[1] It is a maxim of federal systems of government that the federal power should itself be too unimportant territorially to compete with the component states—a

---

[1] 'The Pope, as your grace knowethe, is a prince as you are, and in league with all other Christian princes. It may hereafter so fall owte that your grace and he may varye vppon some pointes of the league, whereuppon may growe breach of amitye and warre betweene you bothe. I thincke it best therefore that that place be amended, and his aucthority more sclenderly touched' (*The Lyfe of Sir Thomas Moore, knighte, written by William Roper, Esquire*, ed. E. V. Hitchcock (Early English Text Society. Original Series, n. 197, London, 1935), p. 68).

principle of which the District of Columbia stands as a permanent witness. If the Popes aimed at governing a federated Europe they were transgressing this as yet unformulated but vital principle in making so much of the Papal States. One can see this obscuring of the wider by the narrower sovereignty already in the earlier medieval conflict of Papacy and Empire, when papal policy was at least partly determined by considerations of political power in Italy. As the Middle Ages grow old, it becomes much more obvious and blatant and ends in the unedifying spectacle of an Alexander VI acquiescing in the building up in the papal territory of a centralised base for the benefit of his son, Cesare Borgia.

The first sign of decadence in the notion of papal theocracy is commonly taken to be the conflict, at the turn of the thirteenth and fourteenth centuries, between Boniface VIII and Philip the Fair, of France, and rightly so. That colourful and sensational series of incidents, extending from 1296 to 1303, did serve to bring out in sudden and stark relief the extent to which new forces of national monarchy had arisen to challenge, and challenge successfully, the papal claim to control the secular world. Significantly, they began with a dispute about the right of the State to tax the clergy upon their professional, spiritual revenues. The clerical claim to contract out of control by the civil power, whilst at the same time retaining the advantages the clergy derived from association with it, was attacked at the point at which it could be made to seem most vulnerable. The controversial literature produced by Philip IV's supporters, some of the earliest masters of the modern art of political propaganda, did not fail to make the argument cogent.[1] After a truce caused by Boniface's skilful but humiliating withdrawal from a tactically weak position, the quarrel was renewed upon an issue arising out of another aspect of clerical privilege. The affair of Bernard Saisset, the unedifying Bishop of Pamiers, who was arrested by the French royal authorities on charges of treason, provided the *casus belli*. But this second dispute, though started on a particular issue, soon assumed a general scope,

---

[1] This is well studied in Jean Rivière, *Le Problème de l'Église et de l'état au temps de Philippe le Bel* (Spicilegium Sacrum Lovaniense, fasc. 8, Louvain and Paris, 1926).

for it brought out in the most specific way the underlying principle of papal power in the temporal field. Boniface, trying to found his contentions upon the unassailable rock of dogma, affirmed his rights, as he conceived them, in the bull *Unam Sanctam*, which affirmed, with all the solemnity of a doctrinal decree, that obedience to the Holy See was absolutely necessary to eternal salvation. And the context makes clear that what was in his mind was obedience not only in spiritual, but in temporal matters as well. The whole history of the rest of the fourteenth and of all the fifteenth century is a commentary upon the practical futility of such a claim, in fact of the new temper of European thought. The termination of the dispute by the temporary imprisonment of the Pope at Anagni by a band of bravoes under the direction of Philip's agent Guillaume de Nogaret, and Boniface's speedy death (due, it is said, to mortification at the insult), is but a symbol of what was to happen. By the time that the pretension to direct temporal authority was tacitly laid aside, partly under the influence of Bellarmine, in the seventeenth century, the papal claim was already a practical anachronism.[1]

It has been argued by no less a thinker than Jacques Maritain, in his *Primauté du spirituel*,[2] that, even in the Middle Ages, the Papacy never formally claimed direct temporal supremacy.[2] With all due respect, I cannot regard the argument as more than special pleading. Partly it depends upon the view taken of the technical theological scope of the operative words of Boniface's bull just mentioned. That is a matter outside my subject. But Maritain is constrained to admit that, even if the Popes themselves made no such claim, some of their supporters did so for them.[3] Historically,

[1] See on this 'Pouvoir Directif I and II' in Robert Hull, S.J., *Medieval Theories of the Papacy and other Essays* (London, 1934), pp. 104-130.

[2] 'Dans leur enseignement et dans leur action comme chefs de l'Église, ce n'est pas à la théorie du pouvoir direct, c'est à la doctrine du pouvoir indirect et de la suprématie du spirituel sur le temporel, libre lui-même et souverain dans son domaine . . . que les Papes, du onzième au quatorzième siècle, ont rendu témoignage. . . .' (Jacques Maritain, *Primauté du spirituel* (Paris, 1927), p. 187. E.T. by J. F. Scanlan, *The Things that are not Caesar's* (Unicorn Books, London, 1939), p. 126.)

[3] '. . . les exagérations violentes où certains canonistes du quatorzième et du quinzième siècles étaient tombés: se portant à l'extrême opposé des prétentions régaliennes des légistes, ceux-ci voulaient que tout droit, tout juste domaine et toute légitime possession soient

that is what matters. For it is the teaching current about prerogative, and the actions based upon such teaching, which determine historical events and attitudes much more than the actual formal utterances of the power claiming prerogative. It was not so much James I's *True Law of Free Monarchies* and his homilies to his subjects which brought about the revolt against Stuart government, as the use made of prerogative by him and his son and the decisions of the justiciary about it. So, in this matter of papal power, it was the combined influence of papal activities and of the canonical justifications offered for them which led to questioning and finally to rebellion. And the actions were precise and definite enough, and arbitrary too, as when Boniface VIII himself claimed the right to nullify an election to the Empire or objected to Albert of Austria as Emperor on the ground that he was a one-eyed man with an ugly face, whose wife came of the serpent brood of Frederick II.[1]

The wider revolt was not long in making its appearance. The controversial literature of the quarrel between Boniface and Philip, interesting as it is, does not stray widely outside the traditional medieval area of debate. On the papal side, protagonists like Giles of Rome and James of Viterbo endeavour to show, with greater or less radicalism, that the unquestioned spiritual prerogatives of the Pope necessarily involve a right of supremacy in temporal matters. On the other side, writers like John of Paris, the Dominican, argue the reverse from *auctoritates* of the same kind as those adduced by their opponents, Scripture, the Fathers, canon law and historical precedent. As John of Paris himself puts it: 'Many like [*sc.* auctoritates] can be produced to show that the Lord Pope does not possess both swords, nor jurisdiction in

---

enfermés comme en un écrin dans la poitrine du Souverain Pontife, de telle sorte que celui-ci pût régulièrement intervenir de façon directe dans les questions de propriété ressortissant au droit civil, et que l'on pût régulièrement en appeler à lui de toute sentence portée par les juges séculiers; ils regardaient comme illégitime le pouvoir des princes païens sur les peuples infidèles, et, en définitive, niaient la légitimité des pouvoirs terrestres fondés sur le droit naturel. Pourtant l'Église ne fait pas plus cette légitimité que la grâce ne fait la nature' (Maritain, p. 184, E.T. p. 123).

[1] 'Est homo monoculus et vultu sordido, non potest esse Imperator' (cited, James, Viscount Bryce, *The Holy Roman Empire* (new edit., London, 1906), p. 217, note *q*).

temporal matters, unless they should be granted to him out of devotion by a prince'.[1] Here can be seen the older Gelasian tradition of the separate origin and equal authority in their own spheres of the spiritual and temporal powers—a tradition never entirely submerged by the theocratic theory and now still at loggerheads with the newer view. So far, there is little innovation.

That was to come later in the century. Shortly after the Bonifacian controversy, Dante, in his De monarchia,[2] still tries on orthodox lines to avoid the conclusion which the papalists claimed as inevitable, that supremacy in things spiritual carries with it as a consequence supremacy in things temporal. But the next great Church-State controversy of the century, that between the Emperor Lewis the Bavarian and the Avignon Papacy, sounded a new note.

He who struck it was Marsilius of Padua, a thinker whose influence, though greater after his death than in his lifetime, was that of a portent. For it was he who returned upon the papalist writers their own favourite dilemma. They had argued that either a man must accept the political authority of the Pope or prove himself a heretic by denying the prerogatives of Peter. Marsilius's solution of the difficulty is precisely to attack those prerogatives, without apparently feeling conscious of unorthodoxy or caring for the fact that he was attacking a cherished belief. Peter, he asserts, had no more authority than the other Apostles: therefore the Pope is not, by divine right, supreme even in the Church.[3] It is not actually the fact that Marsilius was the first medieval

---

[1] 'Et multa consimilia adduci possunt ad ostendendum dominum papam non habere utrumque gladium nec iurisdictionem in temporalibus nisi sibi concedatur a principe ex devotione' (John of Paris, De potestate regia et papali, cap. x). (Text ed. Jean Leclercq, O.S.B. in Jean de Paris et l'ecclésiologie du XIIIᵉ siècle (Paris, 1942), p. 198.

[2] 'Quapropter cum solis concertatio restat, qui, aliquali zelo erga matrem Ecclesiam ducti, ipsam, quae quaeritur, veritatem ignorant. Cum quibus illa reverentia fretus, quam pius filius matri, pius in Christum, pius in Pastorem, pius in omnes Christianam religionem profitentes, pro salute veritatis in hoc libro certamen incipio' (Dante, De Monarchia, iii. 3 (ed. E. Moore with intro. by W. H. V. Reade, Oxford, 1916, p. 365)).

[3] 'Similiter autem nec iurisdictionem coactivam habuit Petrus in reliquos apostolos plusquam econverso, nec per consequens ipsorum successores invicem' (Defensor Pacis, II. xvi. 11 (ed. C. W. Prévité-Orton, Cambridge, 1928, p. 281)).

to attack the Petrine claims. That mysterious individual, the 'Anonymous of York', had done so over two centuries before, by his conclusion that 'by divine institution no one among the Apostles was the greater: none had magisterial authority or pre-eminence over the others'.[1] But the views of this radical became as obscure as his personality. (Z. N. Brooke has doubted whether he was connected with York, as Böhmer, who disinterred him, sup-posed, or whether the collection of tractates to which his name is given are all by his hand.)[2] It is therefore virtually true to say that Marsilius was the first man of note thus to lay his axe to the root of the tree of papal theocracy. Moreover, he was both original and unique in his own day. It is worth noticing that William of Ockham, Lewis the Bavarian's other great supporter, keeps to the old, well-trodden path of conceding to the Pope his power in ecclesiastical matters (with some reservations, due to Ockham's belief that the Papacy had grievously erred in defining Franciscan poverty) whilst denying that it may lawfully be extended to temporal matters. He regards the Pope as less than absolute, even

[1] 'Divina institutione nullus inter apostolos maior fuit, nullus magisterium vel princi-patum in alios habuit' (text edited in Heinrich Böhmer, *Kirche und Staat in England und in der Normandie* (Leipzig, 1899), p. 475). Cf. also other parts of the text ed. Heinrich Böhmer in M.G.H., *Libelli de lite*, vol. iii (Hanover, 1897), pp. 642-690.

[2] See Z. N. Brooke, *The English Church and the Papacy* (Cambridge, 1931), pp. 158-160. The problem of the 'York Tractates' has more recently been fully treated in a scholarly work by George Huntston Williams, *The Norman Anonymous of 1100 A.D.* (Harvard Theological Studies, no. xviii, Harvard Univ. Press, Cambridge, Mass., and London, 1951). He is inclined to attribute all of them, with one exception, to a single author, who is possibly to be identified with Archbishop Bona Anima of Rouen or with his archdeacon, Fulbert. Williams discounts the supposed connection of the writings with York and would term the writer 'The Anonymous of Rouen'. This new study (which prints some parts of the MS. hitherto unpublished) is also extremely critical of the outlook revealed in the Tractates. 'By corrupting the Gelasian principle in the interests of an Anglo-Norman Territorial Church, the Anonymous threatened the very heart of Christianity in the measure that he may have been influential in reducing the Faith to the proportions of a merely ethnic religion, a religion of the *polis*, whose chief usefulness is to serve as the cement of society and to provide the latter with the appropriate solemnities for its own glorification. To be sure, Christianity as a Religion, shares, within self-imposed limits, these same functions with the ethnic and in our day the politically inspired pseudo-religions of blood, soil and class; but the Church as the bearer of Revelation ceases to be the universal Church of Christ whenever it supposes her principal office to be discharged therein' (pp. 202-203). This attitude to a writer some have regarded as an apostle of evangelical freedom from the Papacy interestingly reflects the effects of a growing know-ledge of the real meaning of the *Eigenkirche* tradition, the appreciation of modern totali-tarianism and an American environment.

in the Church: but he does not question papal authority in general.[1] Nevertheless, it was with Marsilius rather than with Ockham that the future lay. It is not merely that Marsilius anticipated Luther's rejection *in toto* of the Papacy as a necessary part of the Christian Church. It is rather that he was the founder of the secularist view of the State, a view which was to gain ground more and more, in practice if not in theory, until the Lutheran tradition of Protestantism, so to say, canonised it. To Marsilius, as later to Luther, the 'spiritual estate' was not a body with independent rights peculiar to it, except in the sense that he admitted that the sacraments were committed solely to the priesthood for administration.[2] Otherwise, even in matters of doctrine, the priesthood has no exclusive or final voice, which belongs to the whole body of Christian peoples.[3] In affairs of State the clergy has no voice at all: on the contrary, in such matters it is subject to the State.[4] It matters little that Marsilius, an Italian inheriting republican traditions, was by no means an advocate of absolute monarchy—a fact which necessitated a bowdlerising of his *Defensor Pacis* when Henry VIII and Thomas Cromwell had it reissued in 1535, as a wholesome doctrine for Englishmen.[5] Marsilius's State, whatever its

[1] On Ockham see: E. F. Jacob, 'Ockham as a Political Thinker' (chap. v of *Essays in the Conciliar Epoch*, 2nd edit., Manchester, 1952, pp. 85-105 and notes, pp. 245-247; Richard Scholz, *Wilhelm von Ockham als politischer Denker und sein Breviloquium de principatu tyrannico* (Stuttgart, 1944); Léon Baudry, *Guillaume d'Occam: sa vie, ses œuvres, ses idées sociales et politiques*, vol. i (Paris, 1949); G. de Lagarde, *La Naissance de l'esprit laïque au déclin du moyen-âge*, vols. iv, v and vi (Paris, 1942-46); Robert Hull, S.J., 'Ockham and the Papacy', in *Medieval Theories of the Papacy* (London, 1934), pp. 48-59. The edition of Ockham's political works planned by the Manchester University Press has been delayed by the untimely death of the original editor and is now in process of revision and completion. *Guillelmi de Ockham Opera Politica*, vol. i, ed. J. G. Sikes (Manchester, 1940), is available.

[2] 'His siquidem *character sacerdotalis*, sit unus aut plures, potestas est per quam sacerdos consecrare potest ex pane et vino corpus et sanguinem Christi benedictum cum certa verborum pronuniatione ac reliqua ecclesiastica sacramenta ministrare; per quem etiam solvere potest et ligare homines a peccatis' (*Def. pacis*, II. xv. 2, Prévité-Orton, pp. 264-265).   [3] *Def. pacis*, II. xix-xxi, Prévité-Orton, pp. 312-342.

[4] *Def. pacis*, II. iv, Prévité-Orton, pp. 128-143.

[5] On the importance of Marsilius's book during the Henrician Reformation see Philip Hughes, *The Reformation in England*, vol. i (London, 1950), pp. 331 *sqq.* and reff. there given. On April 1, 1534, William Marshall announces to Thomas Cromwell that he has now begun to print the translation of it, held up for a year by lack of money, in reliance upon Cromwell's promise of a loan of £20. *Letters and Papers of the Reign of Henry VIII*, vol. vii, ed. James Gairdner, n. 423, p. 178.

constitution, is a Leviathan which can brook no rival power: like Rousseau, he thought that a republic, in respect of other communities within its boundaries, should be as absolute as any emperor. What he was really attempting to destroy was the whole medieval idea of the State as a balance of power. As he says, 'To no single person, or whatever rank or status, and to no corporation belongs any right of government or of coercive jurisdiction over anyone in this world, unless this authority be given him directly by a divine or human legislator.[1]' That is a trenchant statement of the idea of unitary sovereignty.

In thus rejecting the earlier medieval view of the State, Marsilius, whether consciously or not, spoke in harmony with a whole series of tendencies, as yet indistinct, yet, taken collectively, characteristic of the age, tendencies destined to work together in the production of one complex pattern—that of the post-medieval world. We cannot better end our survey of the later Middle Ages, nor introduce ourselves more conveniently to the subject of the next lecture, than by considering some of these and in trying to see their hearing upon the relations of the spiritual and temporal powers, which is our main theme.

Anyone attempting to deal with them is at present hampered by the incompleteness of scholarly work upon late medieval thought, which, not unnaturally, has received less attention than that of the medieval heyday. Not all the sources have been published: I feel sure that there are manuscripts in our libraries which will tell us much when they have been read and edited. Valuable investigations have been undertaken by authors such as Vignaux and de Lagarde. But there is still much more to be done, in the fields alike of philosophy, theology and political thought. Yet, already, some conclusions may be drawn from the facts so far known.

(1) It seems clear that the sceptical type of thought which,

---

[1] 'Nulli personae singulari cuiuscumque dignitatis aut status existat, neque collegio cuipiam convenire principatum seu iurisdictionem aliquam cuiusquam in hoc saeculo coactivam, nisi per legislatorem divinum aut humanum immediate sibi tradita fuerit auctoritas ista' (*Def. pacis*, I. xvii. 13, Prévité-Orton, p. 96).
See also on Marsilius, C. W. Prévité-Orton, 'Marsilius of Padua' (Annual Italian Lecture, read May 29, 1935, in *Proceedings of the British Academy*), 1935, pp. 137-183, and A. P. D'Entrèves, *The Medieval Contribution to Political Thought* (Oxford, 1939), pp. 44-87.

as the fourteenth century progressed, replaced the confident rationalism of much thirteenth-century scholasticism, was leading to a *mystique* of will, human and divine, destined to influence deeply later theological and political thought. Despair of producing irrefragable natural proofs of the foundations of Christianity—an attitude especially associated with Occamism—led to increased stress upon Divine revelation as the one ultimate authority. That in turn directed men's thoughts to the Divine Will, rather than to the Divine Intelligence, as the attribute most characteristic of God. By analogy, the human will, the faculty most operative in the act of faith, was highly estimated in comparison with the human intellect. It is not difficult to see how consonant this was with the growing parallel *mystique* of despotism already apparent in fifteenth-century Italy, which was destined to enthrall large parts of Europe in the sixteenth and following centuries. Not reason, as in the Middle Ages, but will is increasingly regarded as the effective source of law and right. *Hoc volo, sic iubeo: stet pro ratione voluntas.*[1]

(2) Applied to pure theology the renewed interest in Divine Will led on the one hand to revived predestinarianism,[2] and on the other to a type of moral theology which saw in right and wrong, not so much a reflection of the Divine Nature and of what is logically opposed to it, as arbitrary enactments of God, the supreme legislator.[3] Both tendencies have consequences in the

[1] Juvenal, *Satire* III, 223.

[2] The most noteworthy exponent of predestinarianism in the fourteenth century was the Englishman, Thomas Bradwardine, who died in 1349 shortly after his consecration as Archbishop of Canterbury. His *De causa Dei contra Pelagium* taught that 'every act of human will is determined from eternity by the omnipotent and omniscient will of God' (Meyrick H. Carré, *Phases of Thought in England* (Oxford, 1949), p. 170). His attitude seems to derive partly from a revived Augustinianism, partly from the Ockhamist conviction of the absolute and sovereign freedom of God. (See Frederick Copleston, S.J., *A History of Philosophy*, vol. iii (London, 1953), p. 124 and cf. Étienne Gilson, *La Philosophie au moyen-âge* (new edit., Paris, 1944), pp. 618–619.) 'The Calvinist theology is the heir to Thomas Bradwardine' (Carré, p. 193). On the continuing importance of controversy about predestination in the fifteenth century see Léon Baudry, *La Quérelle des futurs contingents* (Louvain, 1465–75) (Paris, 1950).

[3] 'Hatred of God, stealing, committing adultery, are forbidden by God. But they could be ordered by God; and, if they were, they would be meritorious acts. No one can say that Ockham lacked the courage to draw the logical conclusions from his personal theory of ethics' (Copleston, iii. 105). Cf. de Lagarde, *Naissance de l'esprit laïque*, vi. 55 sqq.

theology of politics. To Wycliffe, for example, the Church was pre-eminently the *corpus praedestinatorum*, and since the body of the elect must of necessity be invisible on earth, more impetus was given to the growing idea, shared to some extent by Wycliffe himself, that ecclesiastics cannot rightly exercise coercive jurisdiction, since their proper sphere of authority is not a visible kingdom.[1] On the other hand, if right and wrong are freely determined by the arbitrary will of God, the hitherto accepted notion of a Law of Nature, implanted in man's reason and the ultimate source and censor of all human positive law, is weakened. With it goes much of the Church's right to criticise the policies of the State, which has an unchallengeable autonomy and can issue and change legislation at its pleasure.[2]

[1] 'Quamvis autem ecclesia dicatur mulipliciter in scriptura, suppono quod sumatur ad propositum pro famosiori, scilicet congregacione omnium predestinatorum. . . . Ista autem ecclesia secundum partem pregrinantem non habet aliquem prescitum partem sui, sicut non habet secundum partem triumphantem. . . . Patet ergo ex fide et signacione *quid nominis ecclesie catholice* quod ipsa est omnes predestinati presentes, preteriti et futuri' (*Johannis Wyclif: Tractatus de ecclesia*, ed. Johann Loserth (Wyclif Soc., London, 1886), pp. 2, 3-4 and 5). Note Wycliffe's refusal to draw any distinction between membership of the visible and invisible church.

[2] Wycliffe is more concerned to denounce the accumulation and misuse of temporal *possessions* by the Church, and to condemn the involvement of ecclesiastics in secular administration and office, than to discuss ecclesiastical independence and the Church's right to enforce the moral law upon the temporal power. Nevertheless it is noteworthy that he teaches the absolute unlawfulness of active resistance to temporal authority in a way contrary to ordinary medieval teaching.

'Sed quia contingit prepositum abuti sua potestate ideo secundum glossam, est taliter distinguendum "Vel illata est iniuria quo ad causam propriam vel pure quo ad causam dei. In primo casu post exhortacionem evangelicam paciencia est optima medicina. Si pure in causa dei cristianus debet, post correpcionem evangelicam, preposito suo usque ad mortem, si oportet, confidenter et obedienter resistere. Et sic utrobique innitendum est paciencie, comittendo humiliter deo iudicium iniuriam vindicandi." Et qui excedit hanc regulam resistit dampnabiliter potestati et dei ordinacioni, ut faciunt hi qui rebellant precipue, id est affecione comodi temporalis personalis. Contempnunt enim magis bonum ordinatum a deo, et eligunt temere minus bonum. Deus enim ordinavit persecucionem tyranorum, ad exercitationem et coronam suorum martirum' (*De officio Regis*, ed. A. W. Pollard and Charles Sayle (Wyclif Soc., London, 1887), p. 8).

This, as we shall see later, is almost exactly the doctrine of Luther on the subject. Cf. the comment of R. W. and A. J. Carlyle:

'As we have just said, it seems to us that his conception of "dominium" had little real significance, at least in political theory, and there is nothing new in his conception of the source of political authority. He evidently accepted the normal principle of the Middle Ages, that political authority was derived ultimately from God, but immediately from the community. When, however, we turn to his conception of the nature of this authority we find that Wycliffe reasserted that conception of the duty of absolute obedience to the

(3) For, if reason be distrusted, we are left, as has been said, to revelation for a knowledge of God's will. But revelation is contained chiefly in Scripture, and already Wycliffe and Huss were questioning the exclusive right of the hierarchical Church to interpret the Bible. Their insistence upon making Scripture available to the laity already implies, if it does not assert, the principle of private judgement, which still further undermines the medieval notion of the Church as a corporation with rights of its own, not shared by secular society. The underlying implications here will be brought out by Luther in his *Appeal to the Christian Nobility of the German Nation.*[1]

(4) Here we observe a contact with the individualism which has so often been remarked as a force at this time making inroads upon medieval collectivism. The growth of Nominalism in philosophy, with its tendency to abolish all categories save that of the unique, here joined hands with the interest in human personality manifested by humanists, as what is conventionally called the Renaissance took form and shape.[2] Checked in political efflorescence by the contemporary enthusiasm for despotism, already noted, the individualistic spirit took refuge in religion, as in a citadel. Already, in the *devotio moderna* of the Low Countries it can be noticed: the *Imitation of Christ* (if it is rightly associated with this school)[3]

prince, and of the wickedness of resistance, which, as we have often pointed out, was dogmatically stated by Gregory the Great, but had practically disappeared in the Middle Ages, being asserted only by a few writers like Gregory of Catino in the eleventh century. Wycliffe in the "De officio Regis" states this dogmatically and without qualification. He held, no doubt, that the prince ought to obey the law, but, like many of the Civilians, when they interpreted the "Digna vox" of "Cod." i. 14. 4, he thought that the obedience of the prince should be voluntary and was not compulsory' (*A History of Mediaeval Political Theory in the West*, vol. vi (London and Edinburgh, 1936), p. 62).

[1] 'The reason is that the social corpus of Christendom includes secular government as one of its component functions. This government is spiritual in status, although it discharges a secular duty. It should operate, freely and unhindered, upon all members of the entire corpus, should punish and compel where guilt deserves or necessity requires, in spite of pope, bishops and priests; and whether they denounce or excommunicate to their heart's desire' ('An Appeal to the Ruling Class of German Nationality', E. T. Bertram Lee Woolf, *Reformation Writings of Martin Luther*, vol. i (London, 1952), p. 117).

[2] For a review of modern interpretations of the Renaissance, see Wallace K. Ferguson, *The Renaissance in Historical Thought* (Cambridge, Mass., 1948).

[3] For a discussion of the present stage of this long-standing dispute, see E. F. Jacob, *Essays in the Conciliar Epoch* (2nd edit., Manchester, 1953), chaps. vii and viii and notes on pp. 248-250.

CHRISTIANITY AND THE STATE

is a book which, for all its beauty, almost ignores the corporate aspect of Christianity. By the end of the fifteenth century individualist religion had become a force to be reckoned with. As Lucien Febvre has pointed out, the real force behind the Reformation came from men, largely of the newly educated and influential bourgeois class, who sought a more adequate personal religion than that offered by a Church in its popular aspects singularly out of touch with the deeper needs of the contemporary soul.[1]

If we consider together all these phenomena, do we not seem to see a picture which largely explains the great revolution in the relations of Church and State about to be accomplished in the sixteenth century and already gathering momentum? On the one hand is an increasing tendency to a form of religion which has little use for reason, demands personal experience and is increasingly impatient of ecclesiastical control. On the other hand is seen a growing dislike of ecclesiastical pretensions to independence from, and yet control of, civil society, a dislike based partly upon experience of clerical shortcomings in exercising the role claimed for the Church, partly upon a nascent *étatisme*, a mystique of political society finding expression in that revival and expansion of the theory of the divine right of kings, traced by J. N. Figgis in one of his best known books.[2] And this last movement is already showing signs of a wish to divorce politics from ethics in a way surprisingly out of harmony with the exalted claims being made for the Divine origin of civil power.

Yet at the same time the tendencies of the age were proving fatal to any reform of the Church upon traditional lines. Figgis

[1] 'Désaccord. Entre les aspirations d'une bourgeoisie travailleuse, avide d'accorder son action et sa foi, et les satisfactions, tantôt dérisoires, tantôt insuffisantes et mal adaptées qui lui proposait une Église anachronique, une abîme se creusait davantage chaque jour. Ceci, d'autant plus que le clergé, que les théologiens surtout, fort peu mêlés à la vie, ignorants des choses de leur temps et d'ailleurs médiocrement soucieux de les connaître, continuaient à vivre entre eux, en vase clos, les yeux fermés à toute réalité: dans leur dédain aristocratique des gens du siècle ne se figuraient-ils point toujours que les religieux c'étaient eux, et eux seuls?' (Lucien Febvre, 'Une Question mal posée: les origines de la Réforme française et le problème général des causes de la Réforme', in *Revue historique*, vol. clxi, mai-août 1929, p. 43).

[2] J. N. Figgis, *The Divine Right of Kings* (2nd edit., Cambridge, 1914).

and others have remarked that the Conciliar Movement's attempt to constitutionalise the Papacy broke down partly owing to the general current of thought making away from limited sovereignty towards absolutism. Another factor in its general failure was undoubtedly the Conciliar Movement's inability, despite efforts like Nicholas of Cusa's *De concordantia catholica*, to evolve a full and satisfactory theology of the Church as an organism, as the Body of Christ. Although never lost, the doctrine of the Mystical Body had been obscured in the Middle Ages by the hierarchical sacerdotalism, which was partly the result of the Dark Ages' pedagogical function of the Church, and by the theocratic ideal which evolved from it.[1] Authoritarianism in the field of ecclesiastical politics, individualism in the field of devotion. It is an explosive juxtaposition. In such an atmosphere the very idea of the Church as a society, in any but a formal sense of the word, was in danger of being lost.

Yet, it is only as a visible organised body that the Church can hope to vindicate its rights as against a unitary conception of the State. Only as a society can it offer any competition to a secularised, all-embracing Leviathan, the *reductio ad absurdum* of which was one day to find a prophet in Thomas Hobbes. The new, and to a medieval mind revolutionary, ideas about the relations of Church and State which will meet us in the sixteenth century should not, I suggest, surprise us if we bear all these facts in mind. We must give full attention to these forces, as yet inchoate, which make their presence felt as the medieval spring turns to autumn with at best but an Indian summer in between. But that Indian summer,

---

[1] Recent study has much modified the older idea of the Conciliar Movement as essentially revolutionary. See Brian Tierney, 'A Conciliar Theory of the Thirteenth Century', in *The Catholic Historical Review*, vol. xxxvi (1951), pp. 415-440, and 'Ockham, the Conciliar Theory and the Canonists', the *Journal of the History of Ideas*, vol. xv (1954), pp. 40-70. Professor E. F. Jacob has pointed out the importance of the idea of the Mystical Body in the thought of Gerson, one of the greatest of the Conciliarists (*Essays in the Conciliar Epoch*, 2nd edit., chap. i, 'Conciliar Thought', and notes on pp. 240-241). Yet it remains true that St. Thomas Aquinas's *Summa Theologica* has no section on 'De Ecclesia' and that H.-X. Arquillière could accurately entitle his edition of James of Viterbo's *De Regimine Christiano* (written in 1301-2) 'Le Plus Ancien Traité de l'Église' (Paris, 1926). So much had theological ecclesiology been neglected in the heyday of medieval thought.

however brief and fragile, remains an inspiration to many, who believe that, with all its limitations, medieval thought has bequeathed a real legacy to later ages. Those ages, to judge by their history and by the signs of our own times, find no very secure barrier against intellectual and political bankruptcy in the resources they themselves have garnered.

CHAPTER VIII

REFORMATION ECCLESIOLOGY AND THE STATE

'The same day were all the fountains of the great deep broken up, and the windows of heaven were opened.'[1] The Biblical description of the beginning of the Flood comes forcibly to mind when we begin the study of the sixteenth century. Easy, and wrong, as it is to dramatise the past, yet there are nevertheless centuries of cataclysm, ages in which the institutions, the balanced systems and the assumptions of more stable times dissolve rapidly into a chaos, are attacked and defended on all sides and in the process damaged beyond repair. There are times in which new forces, or, more usually, new combinations of old forces, burst upon a society hitherto relatively static and make the shape of things to come problematic and incalculable.

Such an age was the sixteenth century. Not that later medieval society was really static, still less secure—as we saw in the last lecture. It was not even placid on the surface. But the shocks disturbing it were not yet the earthquake itself, of which they were premonitory rumblings. Then came the crisis. Within a comparatively short time, the last decade of the fifteenth century and the first twenty years of the sixteenth, the first explosion came. Not without reason is 1494, the year of Charles VIII of France's invasion of Italy, taken as a turning point. For it began the series of wars which developed into the great Valois-Hapsburg struggle by which Europe was divided and which determined its history for more than a century. Those wars in turn revealed the political schisms in what had been thought of as Christendom, political schisms whose effect upon one thinking mind can be measured by the sad sarcasm of the opening part of More's *Utopia*. Political schism was soon to be duplicated by a religious cleavage of much greater ultimate significance. Within twenty-three years of 1494 began Luther's revolt against the medieval church system, since

[1] Gen. vii. 11.

which Western Christianity has never again been a unity. Behind both, less noticed and less obvious, were going on at an increasing pace the economic changes which would replace the medieval structure of work and wealth by a new configuration, the economic pattern, or lack of pattern, of modern times. It would be foolish, as already said, to think of all this as an unpredictable cataclysm: the explosive forces had been maturing for at least two centuries. But, as with the explosion of 1914 (which may very well seem to future historians to present parallels to this), it was at this epoch that the hidden fires burst into active eruption.

From the angle of approach adopted to history in these lectures what is to be said of the period? Our terms of reference limit us to the relations of Church and State. Political events and theories, the theological controversies and the economic development of the century concern us, therefore, only to the extent to which they bear upon this theme. Yet, clearly, they do bear upon it in many ways. Let me suggest the significance of the political, the theological and the economic factors in turn.

(1) In politics, it is clear that the concentration upon statecraft as an art, characteristic of the age, was accompanied by a growing divorce between politics and theology. Machiavelli, the first to state this divorce explicitly, has often been regarded as its originator. In fact he was an observer rather than a pioneer, a symptom more than a cause. 'Machiavelli', says Professor J. W. Allen, 'had perceived and defined many of the leading characteristics of the States not only of his own time but those of the sixteenth century as a whole. We might go further and say boldly of the modern State, meaning by that of States ever since. He had perceived much of what, under the given conditions, needs must, if not exist, at least be desired and insisted on and striven after.[1] The same author later defines what he means by this statement.

'Just as Renaissance Italy had detached the statue from the great architectural background which gave it symbolic meaning and

---

[1] J. W. Allen, *A History of Political Thought in the Sixteenth Century* (London, 1928), p. 483.

set it up on a pedestal to stand by itself as the expression of, or comment on, a mere visible thing, so Machiavelli detached the State from the Church, making it an organization of force for the attainment of merely earthly ends.'[1]

Yet, as Allen points out, in so doing Machiavelli to a great extent isolated himself from the political thought of the time, which in general proceeded upon traditional lines, not realising the changing conditions around it. Practice outstripped theory, and it was only gradually that current views of the relations between religion and the civil power adapted themselves to the newer conception of the State, even though the first overt breach with tradition had been made.

(2) The theologians of the century were no less slow in this respect than the political thinkers. From the very moment of the outbreak of the Reformation they were faced, it is true, with one drastic change in their background. The notion of one un-questioned visible Church had crumbled, and theological thinking about the relations of Church and State was soon affected by the fact. But the divorce between religion and statecraft, so brutally assumed by Machiavelli, they for long ignored. No idea of a purely secular State could yet be present to them: the assumption of a close unity between religion and secular life still remained a postulate of theology.

(3) In the economic sphere, too, it was long before any idea gained ground that man's daily bread and his ways of winning it can be outside the theologian's purview. And, in spite of a con-sciousness of economic change, which was outstripping existing notions of the moral theology which applied to economics, theological thought was barely affected by what was happening. For this reason, important as it is, the economic history of the period affects our study only to the extent that it often throws light upon developments otherwise obscure. It was not to any great extent a matter of contemporary debate.

In all these fields, then, we observe a time-lag of thought, slow to accommodate itself to new conditions. Hence, in our own

[1] Allen, p. 484.

field of study, we shall not be surprised to find a curious amalgam of medieval and post-medieval ideas. The *caveat* is perhaps needed more by theologians than by historians. The latter are, or should be, by now fully aware of the dangers of thinking cataclysmically, even about a cataclysmic age. No historical change is really clear cut or abrupt: events and dates never really break the line of historical development. The theologian, however, dealing as he does with ideas, is apt to assume that a particular book or sermon marks a real break in continuity, can be taken as a turning point.[1] In fact the sixteenth century was very much the child of the fifteenth: its originality is often over-estimated.

Bearing all this in mind, let us begin, as we are bound to do, with Luther, the pioneer, and in some ways most characteristic, Protestant Reformer, in our survey of the impact of Reformation theology upon the relations of Christianity with the State. Fully to discuss the ecclesiological and political thought of that remarkable man would demand a complete *exposé* of his highly individual theology—an impossible task in this setting. Nevertheless we can understand its characteristics sufficiently for our purpose if we bear in mind two capital points in his outlook:

(1) His predominant interest was in soteriology, in the problem of human reconciliation with God, and so in the individual soul. He was by no means indifferent to the fact of the Church, nor was he without concern for communal life. But the centre of theology was for him the soul's relation to God. Saving faith, the state of mind implanted by God into His chosen ones, by which man enters God's favour and is removed from His wrath, is, as Luther so often insisted, in his view the core of the Gospel, which by synecdoche can be called the Gospel itself, the principle in the light of which everything else in religion is to be understood. Though the reception of saving faith is effected partly by external means (chiefly the Church's preaching of God's Word), yet essentially it comes from God's direct gift. It follows that in

[1] True, the study of *théologie positive*, the scientific history of dogma, should correct this failing. Nevertheless, professional theologians sometimes treat this part of their discipline too lightly, or pursue it with a *parti pris* more appropriate to apologetics.

Luther's thought the visible Church occupies a secondary, even if important, place. He thinks of it, not as the historical ontological link between Christ's work of salvation and the Christian, but rather as a means used by God from age to age for His purpose of salvation. Like all other such means, it can fail through human frailty and, according to Luther, did so fail during the long period before his own day in which the Papacy succeeded in imposing upon it a 'Babylonish captivity' by means of which the true Gospel was obscured. Luther is prepared to admit a discontinuity in the Church's historic life, and holds (as his teaching on the ministry makes clear)[1] that any group of true Christians, who hold the genuine Gospel, can, as it were, create a cell of the Church at any time and place: there is no necessity for them to derive their ministry and authority from the historic Church in its hierarchical form. For to Luther the ministry is essentially a body of delegates, set apart to perform on behalf of the local community the priestly functions possessed by every Christian in virtue of baptism.[2] The importance of this view in the political sphere lies in the fact that the clergy can never be a 'spiritual estate'—a privileged body independent of the laity or of the State.[3]

(2) Although a rebel against the medieval depreciation of everyday life in comparison with ascetic renunciation of the world, Luther nevertheless drew a sharp distinction of another kind between religious and secular affairs. Christian liberty, the freedom

[1] 'Und das ichs noch klerer sag, Wen ein heufflin fromer Christen leyen wurden gefangen unnd in ein wusterey gesetz, die nit bey sich hetten einen geweyheten priester von einen Bischoff, unnd wurden alda der sachen eynisz, erweleten eynen unter yhn, er were ehlich odder nit, und befilhen ym das ampt zu teuffen, mesz halten, absolvieren und predigenn, der wer warhafftig ein priester, als ob yhn alle Bischoffe unnd Bepste hetten geweyhet. Daher kumpts, das in der not ein yglicher teuffen und absolvieren kan, das nit muglich were, wen wir nit alle priester weren' (An den christlichen Adel deutscher Nation, W.E. vi. 407-408).

[2] 'Drumb ist des Bischoffs weyhen nicht anders, den als wen er an stat und person der gantzen samlung eynen auss dem hauffen nehme, die alle gleiche gewalt haben, und yhm befilh, die selben gewalt fur die andern ausztzurichten' (ibid. W.E. vi. 407).

[3] 'Dan alle Christen sein warhafftig geystlichs stands, unnd ist unter yhn kein unterscheyd, denn des ampts halben allein' (ibid. W.E. vi. 407).

E.T. of these passages in Bertram Lee Woolf, Reformation Writings of Martin Luther, vol. i (London, 1952), pp. 113-114. Cf. B. J. Kidd, Documents illustrative of the Continental Reformation (Oxford, 1911), n. 35, pp. 63-64.

which springs from right relationship to God, freed, he held, the believer from all deep concern with mundane matters, in much the same way as the scholar, immersed in his own kingdom of the mind, has little time to spare for worldly interests. Hence, in a completely Christian world, there would be no need for political organisation at all. In particular, positive law is not needed by the true Christian, who has the law of God and of nature written in his heart. As he says, 'A good tree has no need of teaching or of codes of law in order to bear good fruits: it brings forth fruit according to its kind by its nature, without teaching or code. And it would be the act of a madman to make a book full of laws and jurisprudence for the apple tree to teach it to bring forth apples and not medlars.'[1] Luther took very literally the Apostolic statement that 'the law is not made for a righteous man, but for the lawless and disobedient'.[2]

From these two convictions spring many of Luther's ideas upon the right relation of Church and State. Since for him the Church is primarily a society of believers the outward organisation of which (providing that its faith and worship are true to the Word of God) is relatively unimportant, it can never be, and should not attempt to be, a competitor of the State. It is not in any sense a kingdom of this world. In particular the clergy (who, as we have seen, are appointees of the whole body, not a permanent caste) have no right to privilege or to immunity from State control. He takes over whole-heartedly the view of Marsilius of Padua that the clergy are but one specialised section of society, without coercive powers over it, and so knocks away the very foundations of any doctrine of priestly theocracy.

We might, however, suppose that the other aspect of his teaching mentioned, his otherworldliness, would lead him to attach little importance to the State. But here we must take into account

---

[1] 'Eyn gůtter baum darff kehner leere noch rechts, des er gůtter frůcht trage, sondern seyn natur gibts, das er on alles recht und lere tregt, wie seyn art ist. Denn es sollt myr gar eyn nerrischer mensch seyn, der eym apffel baum eyn buch machte voll gesetz und rechts, wie er sollt epffel und nicht dornen tragen, szo er dasselb besser von eigener art thut, denn ers mit allen bůchern beschreyben und gepieten kan' (*Von weltlicher Oberkeit,* W.E. xi. 250).
[2] I Tim. i. 9.

Luther's strong practical sense. In an ideal Christian world the State would indeed in his view be unnecessary; just as to the Marxist it would be unnecessary in a classless society. But we do not live in such an ideal world. So in this age the State is as necessary in Luther's eyes as it is to the Marxist in a world emerging from capitalism. 'The world and greater number of men', he says (with especial justification in the circumstances of the sixteenth century), 'are and always will be unchristian, even if they are all baptized and called Christians.'[1] Hence there is plenty of work for the State to do, since it exists by God's ordinance especially to restrain and punish the lawless.

We touch here upon a thought characteristic of much Reformation teaching about the State—a curious one in many ways. The Reformers tended to think of the State's function as first and foremost negative. It exists primarily to repress active wickedness, only secondarily, if at all, to promote virtue. It would seem that the attitude derives, partly at least, from another very literal following of St. Paul, who had described the civil ruler as 'the minister of God, a revenger to execute wrath upon him that doeth evil'.[2] One can trace in it also the influence of the idea which inspired Machiavelli—namely, that men are incurably depraved and can be kept from doing harm to themselves and others only by a stern rule of law.[3] No doubt the Reformers' doctrine of total depravity, a reaction from the optimistic and sometimes semi-Pelagian estimate of human nature adopted by later medieval

[1] 'Das wirstu aber nymer mehr thun, denn die wellt und die menge ist und bleybt unchristen, ob sie gleych alle getaufft und Christen heyssen' (*Von weltlicher Oberkeit*, W.E. xi. 251). [2] Rom. xiii. 4.

[3] 'Como dimostrano tutti coloro che ragionano del vivere civile, e come ne è piene di esempli ogni istoria, è necessario a chi dispone una republica, ed ordina leggi in quella, presuppore tutti gli uomini rei, e che li abbiano sempre a usare le malignità dello animo loro, qualunque volta ne abbiano occasione' (*Discorsi*, I. iii. 1).

'La quale cosa fa testimonianza a quello che di sopra ho detto, che gli uomini non operono mai nulla bene, se non per necessità; ma, dove la elezione abonda, e che vi si può usare licenza, si riempie subito ogni cosa di confusione e di disordine. Pero si dice che la fame et la povertà fa gli uomini industriosi, e le leggi gli fanno buoni' (*Discorsi*, I. iii. 3).

On the sense to be attributed to these statements, see Leslie J. Walker, S.J., *The Discourses of Niccolò Machiavelli*, vol. i (London, 1950), Introd. xiii, 'The Alleged Depravity of Mankind', pp. 128-134, and H. Butterfield, *The Statecraft of Machiavelli* (London, 1940), pp. 110 *sqq.*

theology of the Scotist tradition, had something to do with this.[1] Whatever the reason, the Reformers, from Luther onward, commonly saw in the State's duty of awarding punishment its chief *raison d'être*. Never is it more truly itself, never does it more perfectly fulfil the purpose for which God has ordained it, than when inflicting punishment and using force. So Luther could even say: 'It is God, not man, who hangs and breaks on the wheel, decapitates and flogs: it is God who wages war'.[2] He insists strongly upon this as the God-given vocation of those to whom the secular arm is committed: in exercising it they are dispensed from the moral Christian law of mercy.[3] Precisely because it acts in a sphere sharply distinguished from that of religion, the State is primarily a system of force, force which has Divine sanction and blessing. Even Calvin, who has a much more balanced and positive idea of the State's function, urges Christian rulers, if they wish to obey God and to be approved by Him, to attend to the 'ministry' of executing divine vengeance: he cites the example of the normally meek Moses, who once slew three thousand sinners in one day, and of David, who, with his last breath, left the execution of Joab and Shimei as a legacy of duty to Solomon, his

[1] That doctrine referred primarily to the total inability of fallen human nature to do works intrinsically pleasing to God and deserving of salvation. The Reformers admitted a certain degree of natural virtue, even in fallen man, and were not wholly cynical about human nature apart from grace. But clearly a conviction of the worthlessness of human effort *sub specie aeternitatis* would conduce to a pessimistic view of society.

[2] 'Darumb ehret auch Gott das schwerd also hoch, das ers seine eigen ordnunge heist, und wil nicht, das man sagen odder wehren solle, menschen habens erfunden odder eingeseszt. Denn die hand, die solch schwerd fueret und wuerget, ist auch als denn nicht mehr menschen hand sondern Gottes hand, und nicht der mensch sondern Gott henget, redert, entheubt, wurget und kniget. Es sind alles seine werck und seine gerichte' (*Ob Kriegsleute*, W.E. xix. 626).
Cf. Pierre Mesnard, *L'Essor de la philosophie politique au XVIe siècle* (new edit., Paris, 1951), p. 231. 'Le thème du prince-bourreau, repris sur tous les tons et à tous les instants, est capable de s'enfler jusqu'à recouvrir toute autre voix d'un fracas d'apocalypse.'

[3] 'Aber das weltliche reich, wilchs ist nichts denn Goettlichs zorns diener uber die boesen und eyn rechter vorlaufft der hellen und ewiges todtes, soll nicht barmhertzig, sondern strenge, ernst und zornig seyn ynn seynem ampt und werck. Denn syne handzeueg ist nicht eyn rosenkrantz odder eyn bluemlein von der liebe, sondern eyn blos schwerd' (*Ein Sendbrief von dem harten Büchlein wider die Bauern*, 1525, W.E. xviii. 389).
'Szo musz auch das alles Gottis dienst seyn, das der gewallt nott ist, das schwerd zue fueren. Es musz yhe seyn der die boeszen sehet, verklagt, wuerget unnd umbringt, die guten schueszt, entschuldigt, verantworttet und erredtet' (*Von weltlicher Oberkeit*, W.E. xi. 260-261).

son.[1] The same obsession with legal violence has left a curious echo even in the Book of Common Prayer, where, in the Prayer for the Church Militant, the first duty of the king's ministers in doing justice is assumed to be 'the punishment of wickedness and vice', the maintenance of God's true religion and virtue coming second.

We must probably see in this extraordinary attitude a tendency common to the sixteenth-century mind, not something peculiar to Protestantism, though it is there given most explicit expression. It was this century, after all, which brought to a fine art the technique of punishment, as is to be seen in the perfection of executions as public spectacles, with their macabre apparatus of scaffolds, dying speeches, masked executioners and the like. The phenomenon extends in varying form from the beheadings and hangings (with drawing and quartering) of medieval England to the *autos-de-fé* of Spain. The age developed a *mystique* of blood rather like that prevailing in many parts of the world today, though more picturesque and less crude, if equally repulsive. Psychologists could perhaps throw some light upon it.[2] Here attention is drawn to it only to bring out the extent to which Reformation ideas, in setting the State free from the close control of the Church, could yet (at least in Lutheran form) fall very far short of ascribing to the State any very exalted role. Indeed, Luther roundly asserted once that most rulers were fools and knaves, even though, for the sake of God's ordinance, they had to be obeyed by Christians.[3] We have

---

[1] 'Non frustra gladium gerunt, inquit Paulus: nam Dei ministri sunt ad iram, ultores male agentibus. Itaque, si nihil Domino sua obedientia fore acceptius norunt principes aliique praefecti, in hoc ministerium incumbant, si quidem suam Deo pietatem, iustitiam, integritatem approbare student. Hoc scilicet affectu agebatur Moses, quum se destinatum Domini virtute populi sui liberatorem cognoscens Aegyptio manus intulit. Deinde quum, caesis uno die tribus hominum milibus, in populi sacrilegium vindicavit. David quoque, quum sub vitae suae finem Solomoni filio praecepit de occidendo Ioab et Semei' (*Institutes* (ed. 1559), IV. xx. 10).
Cf. Luther. 'Denn es sind Gottis stockmeyster und hencker, und seyn gotlicher zorn gebraucht yhr, zu straffen die boszen und euszerlichen fride zu halten. Es ist eyn grosser herr unser Gott, Darumb musz er auch solch edelle, hochgeporne, reyche hencker und bottel haben unnd will das sie reychthum, ehre unnd furcht von yederman die geusse und die menge haben sollen' (*Von weltlicher Oberkeit*, W.E. xi. 268).
[2] The violent and tortured art of northern painters of the period, such as Grünwald, Bosch, Dürer and Holbein, seems to illustrate this frame of mind.
[3] 'Und solt wissen, das von anbegynn der welt gar eyn seltsam vogel is umb eyn klügen fursten, noch viel seltsamer umb eyn frumen fursten. Sie sind gemynlich die

not yet reached the nineteenth-century metaphysical theory of the State, which all but deified it.

This comes out all the more strongly when we come to ask the question whether, in Luther's view, the State has any concern with religion at all. For there exists a certain duality in his thought. He had been nurtured in the great medieval tradition, according to which a complete separation between things secular and spiritual was unthinkable. Hence he is willing to ascribe to princes considerable powers in religious matters. It suffices to quote the classic passages from his historic appeal *To the Christian Nobility of the German Nation respecting the Reformation of the Christian State.*

'Those who exercise secular authority have been baptized like the rest of us, and have the same faith and the same gospel; therefore we must admit that they are priests and bishops. They discharge their office as an office of the Christian community, and for the benefit of that community.'

'Therefore, I maintain, that since the secular authorities are ordained by God to punish evil-doers and to protect the law-abiding, so we ought to leave them free to do their work without let or hindrance everywhere in Christian countries, and without partiality, whether for pope, bishops, pastors, monks, nuns or anyone else.'[1]

We may, if we like, dismiss this as a doctrine of opportunism. Luther knew well that the Princes of the Empire alone could effect the work of reformation he desired. But this seems unfair. In fact the idea fits in with the whole of his theology, and derives, as we have seen, from what may be called the Marsilian theory of Church and State.

And we must realise that, on the other hand, Luther allows the State no share in what he regards as the essential centre of religious

grosten narren odder die ergisten buben auff erden' (*Von weltlicher Oberkeit*, W.E. xi. 267-268).

[1] E.T. from Bertram Lee Woolf, i. 114 and 116.

'Die weyl dan nu die weltlich gewalt ist gleich mit uns getaufft, hat den selben glauben unnd Evengeln, mussen wir sie lassen priester und Bischoff sein, und ur ampt zelen als ein ampt, das da gehore und nutzlich sey der Christlichen gemeyne.'

'Drumb sag ich, die weil weltlich gewalt von got geordnet ist, die boszen zustraffen und die frumen zuschutzen, szo sol man yhr ampt lassen frey gehn unvorhyndert durch die gantzen corper der Christenheit, niemants angesehen, sie treff Bapst, Bischoff, pfaffen, munch, Nonne, odder was est ist.' (*An den christ. Adel deutscher Nation*, W.E. vi. 408 and 409)

life, the domain of the human soul. Over this, as he says, 'God neither can nor will allow that anyone rule but Himself only'.[1] In a famous passage of his *Von weltlicher Oberkeit*, he counsels passive resistance (which otherwise he does not approve) if a prince should attempt to take away the soul's means of union with God, faith and Scripture.

'Dear Lord (you shall say) I am bound to obey you with my body and my goods; command me within the measure of your earthly authority and I will obey you. But if you will take away my faith and my Scriptures, I will not obey you any further, for in this you are a tyrant and go beyond your rights.'[2]

If we remember the Lutheran conception of religion as primarily an inward matter, we shall not perhaps think that his increasing advocacy, as time went on, of the State's duty of forcible interference in ecclesiastical affairs marks such a change of attitude as such authors as Pierre Mesnard have represented it. As Holl has pointed out, Luther's movement away from his earlier tolerant attitude (fairly consistent from 1520 to 1525, during which time he deprecated the forcible suppression of heresy) was due largely to his growing conviction that the Catholic Mass was a blasphemy and insult to God which would draw down calamities upon any land in which it was celebrated: it was therefore the duty of a Christian prince, for temporal no less than spiritual reasons, to suppress it.[3] There is a curious analogy here with the attitude of the Christian Fathers which we noted earlier, who regarded pagan sacrifices as dangerous practices

---

[1] 'Denn uber die seele kan und will Gott niemant lassen regirn denn sich selbs alleyne' (*Von weltlicher Oberkeit*, W.E. xi. 262).

[2] 'Wenn nu deyn furst oder welltlicher herr dyr gepeut, mit dem Bapst zů hallten, sonst oder so zu glewben, oder gepeutt dyr buecher von dur zu thun, solltu also sagen: "Es gepuertt Lucifer nicht, neben Gott zů sitzen. Lieber herr, ich bynn euch schuldig zů gehorchen mit leyb unnd gůtt, gepietet myr nach ewr gewalt masz auff erden, so will ich folgen. Heysst yhr aber mich glewben unnd buecher von myr thun, so will ich nicht gehorchen. Denn da seyt yhr eyn tyrann unnd grewfft zů hoch, gepietet, da yhr widder recht noch macht habt u." Nympt er dyr drueber deyn gůtt unnd strafft solchen unge-horsam, selig bistu unnd danck Gott, das du wirdig bist umb gotlichs wort willen zů leyden, lass yhn nur toben den narren. Er wirtt seynen richter wol finden' (*Von weltlicher Oberkeit*, W.E. xi. 267).

[3] Mesnard, pp. 213-214. Cf. Karl Holl, *Aufsätze zur Kirchengeschichte*, vol. i, 'Luther' (Tübingen, 1927), p. 355.

which it was the bounden duty of the Christian State to extirpate. But one may doubt whether Luther, any more than they, thought that he was approving of the violation of conscience by the civil power. They recked little of the right of the individual to error: Luther thought all outward observances of religion secondary matters, in dictating about which the State is not really invading the sphere of the soul, the one part of man to which its power does not extend. That others did not accept his major premise meant no more to him than to other doctrinaire thinkers.

Whatever the reason, Luther certainly acquiesced more and more, as his life went on, in State control of religion, largely because he saw the social and political disorders to which religious disputes of the day were giving rise, disorders only to be pacified by the State's strong arm. The rise of the Anabaptist enthusiasm and the horrible episodes of the rising in Münster in 1534–35: the increasing Catholic armed resistance to the Reformation, all played their part. On Luther's own presuppositions it was the State's duty to intervene if it was to fulfil its God-given function of preserving order. It was not his intention to subject Church to State. On the contrary, he had first of all appealed to the State to rescue the Church from papal tyranny, as he conceived it, and leave it free to live its own life. It may well be that Charles Andler's explanation of Luther's attitude is right, that he was dominated in his thought by eschatology and, expecting a speedy end to this world, he looked no further than the immediate destruction of the abuses he so much detested by the one power capable of swift action, namely the temporal arm.[1] Nevertheless, by so acting he had unintentionally riveted upon Lutheranism that 'Erastian' attitude which has dogged its footsteps ever since. Imbart de la Tour summed up the result in his centenary article on Luther

---

[1] 'Toute la doctrine de Luther est eschatologique. Il s'attend à la fin du monde proche. et que présage déjà la présente dissolution. Le grand conflit de la Foi contre l'Incroyance, décrit par saint Augustin dans la Cité de Dieu, va s'engager à fond par le déchaînement du démon délié de ses liens. Ce sera pour demain sans doute, Luther le croit avec saint Paul, La Réforme universelle, dont la sienne n'est qu'une humble préparation destinée à nous garer de Satan, ramènera seule l'unité: elle ne viendra qu'avec cette fin du monde' (Charles Andler, 'L'Esprit conservateur et l'esprit révolutionnaire dans le luthéranisme' in Revue de métaphysique et de morale, xxv (1918), p. 943).

in the *Revue de métaphysique et de morale* in these words: 'It was the idea of an international church which was collapsing. An aggregate of local churches, without any other bond between them than their common confession of faith, handed over to the oversight and will of the princes, closely incorporated in the State, made one of the cogs in its machine, such is to be the new Christianity of Germany. Let us wait less than a century. We shall see then the logical outcome in the famous formula that the prince's religion is that of his subjects, that belief is determined by territory. The triumph of the national principle is complete and, a striking contrast, German Christianity, which claimed to free the Christian religion from paganism, ends in a complete return to the basis of primitive religion, the close union of priesthood and worship alike with the State.'[1]

The judgement, if perhaps somewhat coloured by its date of publication, 1918, is nevertheless difficult to gainsay.

It was not Luther's intention that this should happen. But such was the inevitable result of his ideas in the peculiar circumstances of his day. He was no secularist. It would, indeed, have been better had he possessed more worldly wisdom and acquaintance with the statecraft upon which he looked down with the *hauteur* of a professional theologian. If the history of Calvinism shows the Nemesis of ecclesiasticism which meddles overmuch with politics, Lutheran history by contrast is a warning of the danger of founding religion too much on personal pietism, on an outlook which renounces the world and accepts too much *au pied de la lettre* the statement that Christ's kingdom is not of this world. For Luther canonised still more the irresponsibility of the State in the wide sphere he allowed it by steadfastly denying any right of rebellion

---

[1] 'C'était aussi l'idée d'une Église internationale qui s'écroulait. Un agrégat d'Églises locales, sans autre lien entre elles que leur confession de foi, livrées à la surveillance et à la volonté des princes, encadrées fortement dans l'État, devenues un de ses rouages, tel sera le nouveau christianisme de l'Allemagne. Attendons moins d'un siècle. Nous en verrons l'aboutissant logique dans la fameuse formule que la religion du prince est celle de ses sujets, que la croyance est déterminée par le territoire. Le triomphe du principe national est complet; et, contraste saisissant! le christianisme allemand qui prétendait affranchir du paganisme la religion chrétienne, finit par le retour même au principe des religions antiques: l'union étroite du sacerdoce comme du culte à la cité.' (P. Imbart de la Tour, 'Pourquoi Luther n'a-t-il créé qu'un christianisme allemand?' in *Revue de métaphysique et de morale*, xxv (1918), p. 610.)

to Christian men. Only passive resistance is justified even when the State invades the realm of conscience. There is a nobility in his exclamation, *Leyden, leyden, Creutz Creutz is der Christen recht, des und keyn anders*.[1] But such an attitude leads neither to political freedom nor to the freedom of the Church, if it is interpreted as Luther interpreted it.

That subjection of Church to State was not a necessary outcome of Reformation theology is apparent when we turn to the other great Protestant system, that of Calvin. Here we note at once two factors which combine to differentiate sharply the Calvinist polity from the Lutheran, one political and the other theological. First and foremost there is a striking difference of environment. Lutheranism began in Saxony, a typical princely state of the Empire, and, though it spread to self-governing cities, it retained always something of the imprint of its first surroundings. Calvinism, on the other hand, besides being French in origin, developed in the midst of the burgher community in Switzerland, the land of freedom, where republican traditions were strong. Hence the Christian community it envisaged consisted, not of subjects of a monarch, but of men of whom a considerable proportion had experience of self-determination. It was not the first form of Swiss Protestantism. Zwingli had earlier established the Reformation in Zürich and so given an impetus to religious change in the neighbouring cities. And it is interesting to notice that, whilst he went beyond Luther in allowing the State to control religion, even to the extent of making his town councils the censors of the doctrine preached, he nevertheless gave to his parish congregations the theoretical right (not realised in practice) to determine their own church life. Here one can see already the germ from which Calvin would develop a new theory of ecclesiastical independence.[2]

The second and theological reason for the divergent develop-

[1] *Ermahnung zum Frieden auf die zwölf Artikel der Bauerschaft in Schwaben, 1525,* W.E. xviii. 310.

[2] The following quotation indicates the completeness of Zwingli's identification of civil life and religion in its outward manifestations.

'Quid ergo . . . distat ecclesiae Christiane vita attinet quae videmus a civitatis vita? Nihil penitus: rem utraque requirit quod altera. Dico autem de exterioribus vitae con-

ment of Calvinism and Lutheranism in regard to Church-State relations lies in Calvin's conviction that the supreme principle in theology is the will of God. What God has commanded must by all means be done, down to the least detail. Luther would not have disagreed, but he would not have laid the same stress as Calvin upon external Divine positive law. Calvin rejects the Lutheran notion that no law is needed by the truly religious man.[1] Even those endowed with saving faith need a law to bring home to them God's positive demands. And that law must be enforced by discipline. Hence to Calvin the State is more than just a police-man set up by God to control the criminal class of non-Christians or nominal Christians, as Luther tended to think; it is a society planned by God to promote and enforce the Christian religion. Yet it is not for the State, as such, to say what *is* the Christian religion. Calvin draws, though in a different way, as sharp a dis-tinction between the spiritual and temporal powers as any medieval Catholic. To quote his own words: 'There are, as it were, two worlds in man, which can be governed by different kings and by diverse laws'.[2]

Over man on his spiritual side rules the spiritual power—not, according to Calvin, tyrannically, for he agrees with Luther that the conscience is not subject to any external authority.[3] The

suetudinibus et communicationibus. . . . Sed quod ad interiorem hominem adtinet, immensum est discrimen.'

See on this Jakob Kreutzer, *Zwinglis Lehre von der Obrigkeit* (Kirchenrechtliche Abhand-lungen hrsg. von Ulrich Stutz, Heft 57, Stuttgart, 1909), pp. 32-33.

[1] Indeed he insists, as against the Antinomians, who were carrying Luther's principle of Christian freedom from law to extreme conclusions, that the moral precepts of the Mosaic Law still bind Christians, since God has not ordained different rules of life for different ages of the world but a law which is *una . . . perpetua et inflexibilis vivendi (Inst.* (edit. 1559), II. vii. 13).

[2] 'Primum animadvertamus duplex esse in homine regimen: alterum spirituale, quo conscientia ad pietatem et ad cultum Dei instituitur: alterum politicum, quo ad humanitatis et civilitatis officia, quae inter homines servanda sunt, homo eruditur. Vulgo appellari solent iurisdictio spiritualis et temporalis, non impropriis nominibus. . . . Alterum vocare nobis liceat regnum spirituale, alterum regnum politicum. Haec autem duo, ut partiti sumus, seorsum singula dispicienda semper sunt; et, dum alterum consideratur, avocandi avertendique ab alterius cogitatione animi. Sunt enim in homine veluti mundi duo, quibus et varii reges et variae leges praeesse possunt' (*Inst.* (ed. 1559), III. xix. 15).

[3] 'Iam vero quum hac libertatis praerogativa, qualem antea descripsimus, donatae fideles conscientiae id Christi beneficio, consequutae sint, ne ullis observationum laqueis in iis rebus implicentur, in quibus eas esse liberas Dominus voluit, omnium hominum

CHRISTIANITY AND THE STATE

spiritual power can but confront man with the Word of God by which he must judge himself. But not all men *will* judge themselves. There are always rebellious souls and Calvin in fact found Geneva full of them. Such rebels must be constrained by spiritual censures, excommunication and the like, lest they corrupt others. So, by a less direct route than the Catholic argument, we return to the idea of a Church possessing coercive power.

As in the medieval Catholic system, the spiritual power needs in carrying out its coercive functions the support of the State, which, however, cannot control the Church. For this principle Calvin fought a long battle in Geneva to force the civic authorities to respect the ecclesiastical power's right to excommunicate without the permission of the State. It is easy to see here a revival of the idea of the clergy as a separate, privileged estate. This nevertheless would be a mistake, for such a notion overlooks the fact that in the Calvinist church polity discipline was administered not by the ministers alone but by a Consistory including representatives of the laity. De Lagarde is undoubtedly right in regarding Calvin as in the true line of Reformation thought, which treats Church and State as one single community organised in two different ways.

'In fact the wish to separate the two *administrations* was in itself the sign that the confusion brought about by the Reformation between the two *societies* was accepted.'[1]

According to Calvinism, concludes the same author, 'the Church is not an independent society: it is a function of the Christian State, which operates under its inspection and direction'. 'Church and State should form but one sole and identical entity in their common submission to the exclusive sovereignty of God.'[2]

potestate exemptas esse constituimus' (*Inst.* (ed. 1559), III. xix. 14) (The reference is primarily to freedom from religious rites and duties of the kind imposed upon the faithful by the medieval Church.)

[1] 'En fait, le désir de séparer les deux *administrations* était le signe même que l'on acceptait la confusion créée par la Réforme entre les deux sociétés temporelle et spirituelle' (Georges de Lagarde, *Recherches sur l'esprit politique de la Réforme* (Paris, 1926), p. 353).

[2] 'L'Église calviniste a un statut propre, mais elle se constitue dans le cadre de l'État. L'Église n'est pas une société indépendante, elle est une fonction de l'État chrétien, qui s'exerce sous son contrôle et sous sa direction.' 'L'Église et l'État ne devaient former qu'un seul et même être dans leur soumission commune à la souveraineté exclusive de Dieu.' (De Lagarde, p. 358.)

In short, Calvinism differs from the Lutheran system solely in the greater degree of influence it gives to the Christian community as organised for worship and spiritual life, and to the more democratic form of government the community so organised enjoys in deciding matters of faith and practice. To quote de Lagarde once again: 'By modifying the meaning of the principle of distinction between the two powers the Reformation had desired that all outward Christian life should be organised within the framework of a single social order. The State had subjected to its sovereignty the divine law and the spiritual power. With Calvin we witness the turning of the tables by the spiritual power upon the temporal which had tried to enslave it. In outward matters the State remains absolute sovereign, but the spiritual life which it had tried to bring within its own sphere now in turn dominates it. It is the traditional victory of the vanquished. The State loses little by little its own character. It takes on a clerical spirit. It preaches instead of ruling. The first Reformers had tried to laicize the Church. Calvin had succeeded in clericalizing the State.'[1]

It should, however, be remembered that Calvinism, though it originated in a city-state, proved in the long run to be adaptable to other backgrounds. Indeed, unlike Lutheranism which made little progress outside Germany and the kindred Scandinavian countries, the Calvinist version of Protestantism spread widely in very varied *milieux*. In France, in Holland, and in Scotland strong Calvinist churches were established, which in the latter two countries became the national religion. In England it was an open question down to 1660 whether Calvinism would not capture the nation. In Germany itself Calvinism made considerable inroads at the expense of the earlier established Lutheran religion and remains

[1] 'En modifiant le sens du principe de distinction des deux puissances, la Réforme avait voulu que toute la vie chrétienne extérieure fût organisée dans les cadres d'un ordre social unique. L'État avait réduit à sa souveraineté le droit sacré et l'organisation spirituelle. Avec Calvin nous assistons à la revanche du spirituel sur le temporel qui l'a voulu asservir. L'État extérieurement reste le souverain absolu, mais la vie spirituelle qu'il a voulu ramener dans sa compétence, le domine à son tour. Éternelle victoire du vaincu. L'État perd peu à peu sa physionomie propre. Il se fait une âme de clerc. Il prêche au lieu de gouverner. Les premiers réformateurs avait voulu laïciser l'Église. Calvin avait réussi à cléricaliser l'État' (de Lagarde, p. 374).

to this day a strong factor in German Protestantism. In Central and Eastern Europe, though dislodged later by the Counter-Reformation, Calvinism established itself during the sixteenth century. For these successes, which contrast with the limited viability of the Lutheran Reformation, reason may be found in the greater precision of Calvinist doctrine and the more organised character of its church polity, as well as in the educational work of Geneva, which became a training centre for Calvinist missionaries and a source of inspiration to Calvinists everywhere. Yet it is important for our purposes to notice that one factor in Calvinist success was the adaptability the creed displayed in its attitude to politics. At first sight Calvin's principles upon this subject seem moulded by the peculiar circumstances of Geneva: hardly anywhere else, it would seem, could the distinction, and yet the close union, of Church and State be expressed with the precision possible in a self-governing city-state. Yet, when Calvinism penetrated the larger nation-states of Europe it found it possible to express its characteristics upon a larger stage almost as well as upon the narrower platform of Genevese politics. Holland and Scotland are notable examples of success, although in both cases the result was not attained without conflict. In England, Calvinistic Puritanism brought about a successful revolution in the seventeenth century, only to collapse before the more characteristically English religious movements of Anglicanism and Independency. In France a bitter struggle with the Crown and the Catholic tradition ended in the defeat and suppression of the Calvinistic elements. Success or failure were due partly to the strength or weakness of opposition, partly to the degree to which Calvinism corresponded to national traditions. What, however, is significant is its ability in every instance to put up a stern fight for supremacy, and this, as has been suggested, can be attributed no less to the adaptability of the movement than to its close-knit creed and organisation.

A glance at the history of Calvinism in Calvin's native land will make this point clearer. The Huguenot problem, which dominated French politics from the mid-sixteenth century to the days of

Richelieu, cannot be understood except in the light of French constitutional development. Whilst it is easy to over-estimate the degree of centralisation achieved by the French monarchy by the time of the Reformation, it is a well-known fact that, when Calvinism appeared, a struggle was developing between the centripetal and centrifugal tendencies which had both been prominent in medieval France. Professor J. W. Allen lays stress upon the latter: 'At the commencement of the sixteenth century France, though far more settled than Germany, was yet, in many respects, chaotic. In every part of its territory, the action of the central government was limited or obstructed by clerical, noble, provincial and communal privilege or custom. All powers were already claimed for the King; but his recognized positive rights varied from province to province. The centralised machinery of administration, so far as it existed, was at once extremely insufficient and very imperfectly controlled. Law varied from province to province and even from town to town. Though France was very conscious of its Frenchness, yet popular sentiment was very largely local rather than national. All through the century men talk of going out of Guienne into France.'[1]

This is clearly an exaggerated picture. The local differences enumerated lasted until the Revolution without noticeably diminishing the absolutism of the French Crown, whilst even today Cornishmen, in a state unified much earlier than France, speak of a journey to Plymouth as one into England. Nevertheless the judgement contains a truth, because it reminds us of the enduring strength of traditions of local and personal independence in France of the sixteenth century. And it was to these traditions that Calvinism, which made most headway among the nobility and bourgeois of the always independently minded South, attached itself by force of circumstances. No doubt the Huguenots would have liked to capture the central government: yet their final champion, Henry of Navarre, could do so only at the price of abandoning his Protestantism. France as a nation remained Catholic and therefore Calvinism was always a minority movement, albeit a minority

[1] Allen, *Political Thought in the Sixteenth Century*, p. 271.

movement which was anchored firmly in one tradition of French political life.

Such a situation inevitably modified the classic Calvinist view of Church-State relations. Only in local institutions, in those parts of the French realm where it prevailed, could Calvinism even partly imitate the Genevan model. With the central government its relations were bound to be hostile. It is not therefore surprising to find French Calvinism developing a theory of lawful resistance to oppressive government controlled by persecutors: it was a choice between that and extinction, since Calvin, like Luther, had preached a doctrine of non-resistance.[1] Force of circumstances compelled the modification of this dogma, and the change can be seen in Calvin's disciple, Beza. In 1554 Beza had written on the authority of magistrates, maintaining especially the right of the civil power to punish heresy and intending especially to justify the execution of Servetus at Geneva in 1553 by the Genevan magistrates upon Calvin's insistence. In this he had repeated Calvin's doctrine of the divine authority even of evil rulers.[2] By 1576, a work, almost certainly by the same author, teaches a very different doctrine. The *Du droit des magistrats sur leurs sujets*[3] maintains that the power of the civil magistrate comes ultimately from the people, and that they are bound to the fundamental laws of their realms by a social contract with their people, the violation of which takes away their right to obedience. Not that private individuals have a right to rebel, but the subordinate civil authorities possess a right and duty to oppose and, if necessary, to depose a tyrant. The application of this to French circumstances is obvious. The inferior magistrates are identified with the nobility, many of whom were the props of Calvinism, occupying much the same position as the Lords of the Congregation in Scotland, and to

[1] 'Verum in eo probando insistamus magis, quod non ita facile in hominum mentes cadit: in homine deterrimo honoreque omni indignissimo, penes quem modo sit publica potestas, praeclaram illam et divinam potestatem residere, quam Dominus iustitiae ac iudicii sui ministris verbo suo detulit: proinde a subditis eadem in reverentia et dignatione habendum, quantum ad publicam obedientiam attinet, qua optimum legem, si daretur, habituri essent' (*Inst.* (ed. 1559), IV. xx. 25).

[2] Mesnard, *L'Essor de la philosophie politique*, p. 310.

[3] See on this, Mesnard, pp. 315 *sqq.*, Allen, pp. 314 *sqq.*

them is given the right of deposing a persecuting monarch. Nor is the doctrine one of majorities: in true medieval fashion the *sanior pars* of the people, whether greater or less than the unthinking remainder, is the ultimate deciding authority, acting through the inferior magistrates who share its view.

In one sense Beza had not gone very much further than Calvin himself in enunciating this doctrine of the privileges of subordinate magistrates. His master had not only insisted that the ultimate reward of patience under tyranny was the probability that God, as He had so often done, would raise up a providential man, like Moses or the Judges, to rescue the people from tyrants.[1] He had also recognised that some constitutions gave power to inferior magistrates, such as the Spartan ephors, to control monarchs.[2] But Beza goes much further in his view that government rests upon contract, a position Calvin had never taken up, but had implicitly denied in his insistence that the powers that be, whatever their nature, character or origin, were ordained of God.[3] He had set his face firmly against the Anabaptists who, 'when they hear liberty promised in the Gospel, which recognises no king among men and no magistrate, but looks towards Christ alone, think that they can receive no fruit of their liberty so long as they see any power raised up above themselves',[4] and for this

[1] *Inst.* (ed. 1559), IV. xx. 30. Such exceptional figures are, so to say, dispensed from the ordinary rule requiring obedience to the powers that be. 'Priores enim illi quando ad edenda talia facinora legitima Dei vocatione accersiti erant, in reges arma sumendo minime violabant eam, quae divina ordinatione regibus indita est, maiestatem.'

[2] 'De privatis hominibus semper loquor. Nam siqui nunc sint populares magistratus ad moderandam Regum libidinem constituti (quales olim erant, qui Lacedaemoniis Regibus oppositi erant Ephori: aut Romanis Consulibus Tribuni plebis: aut Atheniensium senatui Demarchi: et qua etiam forte potestate, ut nunc res habent, funguntur in singulis regnis tres ordines, quum primarios conventus peragunt) adeo illos ferocienti Regum licentiae pro officio intercedere non veto, ut si Regibus impotenter grassantibus et humili plebeculae insultantibus conniveant, eorum dissimulationem nefaria perfidia non carere affirmem: quia populi libertatem, cuius se Dei ordinatione tutores positos norunt, fraudulenter produnt' (*Inst.* (ed. 1559), IV. xx. 31).

[3] 'Praeterea inter ipsos magistratus, tametsi variae sunt formae, nullum tamen discrimen hac in parte est, quin pro Dei ordinibus suscipiendae a nobis omnes sint' (*Inst.* (ed. 1559), IV. xx. 7).

[4] 'Illi enim, quum in Evangelio promitti libertatem audiunt, quae nullum inter homines regem, nullumque magistratum agnoscat, sed in Christum unum intueatur: nullum libertatis suae fructum capere se posse putant, quandiu aliquam supra se eminere potestatem vident. Itaque nihil fore salvum existimant, nisi totus in novam faciem orbis reformetur:

very reason was unwilling to concede anything to those who would detract from the divine right of rulers. To one who was in his later life the uncrowned king of Geneva such an attitude was easy and possible: to his followers threatened with pains, penalties and extinction by the monarchy of France it was not.

Circumstances alter cases and so it came about that Calvinism by the late sixteenth century and later came to be regarded as a challenge to absolutism, so that Sir Robert Filmer could say, after referring to the 'perilous conclusion . . . that the people or multitude have power to punish or deprive the Prince if he transgress the laws of the kingdom', 'Cardinal Bellarmine and Mr. Calvin both look asquint this way'.[1] It was the struggle of Calvinism against persecution, especially in France, which had wrought the transformation.

It would be superfluous to trace the details of the Huguenot thesis of the right of resistance through the many writers and pamphleteers who expressed it in different forms. Their writings have been more than once explored and summarised and their doctrines, together with those of their opponents and critics, were given classic exposition by Figgis in his *From Gerson to Grotius*.[2] It is, however, worth while bearing in mind that opportunism entered into sixteenth-century political theory as well as abstract principle, and that in consequence one cannot talk too simply of Huguenot or Catholic political theory, nor even of any one theory of the *politiques*, those thinkers whose one chief interest was less religious than secular, the promotion of the authority of the State against the fanatical religionists who from both sides were, in their opinion, destroying France itself. In all camps the need of the moment caused variations in teaching. Thus, to quote Mr. J. W. Gough: 'The religious struggles in France in the second half of the sixteenth century gave rise to the most prolific crop of writings of

ubi nec iudicia sint, nec leges, nec magistratus, et si quid simile est quod officere suae libertati opinantur' (*Inst.* (ed. 1559), IV. xx. 1).

[1] *Patriarcha and other Political Works of Sir Robert Filmer*, ed. Peter Laslett (Oxford, 1949), pp. 53-54.

[2] J. N. Figgis, *Studies of Political Thought from Gerson to Grotius: 1414-1625* (2nd edit., Cambridge, 1916).

this school [that of the social contract], and also showed how completely opportunist they all were, whether Protestant or Catholic. Under the later Valois kings, and especially after the Massacre of St. Bartholomew, the Huguenots in France were in rebellion against the government that persecuted them, and their pamphlets attacked the monarchy. But when their leader, Henry of Navarre, became heir to the throne, their hopes became centred in the Salic Law, while the Catholics took up the weapons the Huguenots had discarded, and proclaimed the incapacity of a heretic king to rule.'[1]

In spite of this, it is possible to see in later sixteenth-century political thought a line of demarcation, which does not follow denominational lines and yet is of vital importance in the general history of thought about Church and State. If we have been right in seeing Reformation theology, whether in Lutheran or Calvinist form, as essentially agreed in preaching an ultimate identity of Church and State, as in essence a return to the Byzantine tradition, we shall better understand the struggle in the later sixteenth century between two opposite notions of what ought to be the State's policy in religious matters. Too often this has been loosely described as a struggle between tolerance and intolerance, and so in appearance it was. Superficially the issue appears to be on the one hand the claim of Protestants in France or the Netherlands for freedom of worship or on the other a similar claim by Roman Catholics in England or parts of Germany to corresponding rights. Yet we need constantly to remind ourselves that there is no real parallel between these sixteenth-century disputes and those of the eighteenth and nineteenth centuries between Liberalism and authoritarianism. Only a few individuals, such as Castellion, pleaded the abstract rights of conscience and they were almost unanimously regarded as heretics and cranks. To say that neither Catholics nor Protestants then believed in toleration has become a truism: it is nevertheless a truism constantly forgotten by those devoid of the gift of thinking themselves back into the past, and therefore needs to be reiterated.

[1] J. W. Gough, *The Social Contract* (Oxford, 1936), p. 49.

What then was the real issue? It was, I believe, between those who believed in the necessary unity of Church and State, and those who were ceasing to do so. It was, moreover, complicated by the fact that most of those who were adopting the latter view, were coming to it not through conviction, but by force of circumstances and this made the contest more than ever a fight in the dark. We have seen that the deeper interpretation of the apparent difference separating Lutheranism and Calvinism in their attitude to the State suggests that both are really different forms of a theory of Church-State identity, both deriving on different lines from the medieval conviction of the unity of the Christian *respublica*. But any such theory depends for practical validity upon a wide measure of religious agreement within any given nation. If opinion is sharply divided and neither side has an overwhelming majority it becomes unreal and meaningless except as an ideal. This is precisely what happened in many places in the later stages of the Reformation. The Lutheran theory of Church and State could work in German states of relatively small size, where the religion of the prince was, or could easily be made, that of his subjects. Similarly, Calvinism could achieve its ideals in the city-state of Geneva. It was another question altogether in the Empire considered as a whole, and a much more acute problem still in the Kingdom of France, a unified state in which Huguenotism and Catholicism reached a stalemate. There the Huguenot refusal to acquiesce in the attempt of the French monarchy to suppress their religion drove the first deep breach into the theoretical structure of Calvinist polity, by causing Calvinists to preach a right of resistance to the State, a right which hitherto, like the Lutherans, they had denied. From what has been said earlier it can be seen that this really involved the abandonment of the classic idea of Church and State as two facets of one community.

In much the same way Catholicism (except in its Gallican form) was forced by circumstances to renounce a not dissimilar doctrine. It too inherited the medieval ideal of a unified *respublica christiana*. But the realisation that to stand out unequivocally for an absolute unity of Church and State might, especially in France, result in a state founded upon Protestantism, if the tide of war turned against the Catholics, led some of the more original Catholic thinkers to postulate a theory of Church and State as two different entities, two *societates perfectae*, each with its own rights and functions. In few cases, if any, was this theory carried to a completely logical conclusion, since most Catholic theorists felt bound to maintain the Church's ultimate right to censure and interfere with the State when this was necessary in the interests of souls. Thus, Bellarmine, whilst denying the extreme medieval papalist theory that secular authority, no less than spiritual, derives from the Pope, yet believed that in the last resort the Pope, by the use of indirect authority in temporal matters, can depose a king.[1] Only Mariana, to quote Professor J. W. Allen, 'conceived the State in no sense as theocratic', and thus 'with whatever inward qualifications, was accepting the national and secular State, resting on mere earthly needs and on the will to peace and security, as something complete in itself, potentially and logically independent of any Church'.[2] The idea was less novel to any thinker brought up like Mariana on scholastic teaching than Allen supposed, for Thomism had accepted and endorsed the Aristotelian view of the natural origins of the State and did not necessarily deny to pagan communities the rights of true states. Yet, in the context of sixteenth-century developments, the explicit reaffirmation of these ideas was significant for the future. It at least recognised that the ideal of a united Christian community was becoming more and more impossible to maintain.

No less significant was the Jesuit tendency to rest political authority upon popular consent. Here, too, they were not pioneers in Catholic thought, for St. Thomas Aquinas, Lord Acton's 'first Whig', had taught a theory of ultimate popular sovereignty, though not so explicitly as his sixteenth-century successors. But, once again, in the sixteenth-century context the affirmation acquired a new and prophetic significance. Catholicism perceived that it could not rest hopes of the future upon doctrines

---

[1] Allen, *Political Thought in the Sixteenth Century*, p. 358.
[2] Allen, pp. 365-366.

of the divine right of kings, doctrines which could both ignore the vital question of the king's orthodoxy and give him pretexts for controlling the Church.

In a curious way, these ideas of mutual independence of Church and State chimed in with the views of the *politiques*, of whom Jean Bodin is perhaps the most thoroughgoing. These men, concerned by the religious fanaticism which was tearing apart states by religious war, regarded religion as a secondary consideration for the State. Therefore they preached the absolute rights of secular sovereignty and the necessity of subordinating religious issues to national solidarity. This last principle, however, in the circumstances of the time, involved in practice religious toleration. It necessitated the idea of a State which would be neutral, or at least accommodating, in matters of religion, which would accept the idea, so abhorrent to many sixteenth-century minds, of a nation of mixed faith. To reconcile the mind to this idea cost an effort to anyone at the time, for on the one hand toleration was contrary to the medieval tradition which regarded heresy as a sin to be extirpated, and on the other it was by many taken as axiomatic that religious divisions weakened the State in the face of outside enemies and promoted internal order. But the alternatives, as experience showed, were continuing religious wars. As Professor Butterfield has put it: 'Parties like that of the Politiques in France might still acknowledge that persecution was the religious ideal and one religion alone the true one, but decided that persecution could not be carried out on the scale of a massacre, and said that the state must not be wrecked for the sake of religion. As the struggles proceeded the state found the opportunity to rise into the position of adjudicator, while the religious bodies tended to look like conflicting parties within the state; the secular government, instead of regarding itself as the servant of the one true faith, might even stand out as the guardian of the interests of society, imposing peace upon religious factions. In all these ways toleration emerges with the return of religious indifference. It comes as a secular ideal. It is the reassertion of the rights of society and the rights of this world against religions which by their warfare and by the absoluteness of their claims were acting in defiance of social consequences.'[1]

Now, unintentionally perhaps, though quite surely, the Jesuit theorists who promulgated a notion of two distinct societies of mankind, Church and State, were coming to a similar attitude from premisses not so diverse from those of the *politiques* as might be supposed. Attention has been called earlier to the Aristotelian background of their thought about the State, mediated through Thomism. It is interesting to notice that Bodin, the king of *politiques*, was broadly Aristotelian in outlook, even though he regarded the Stagirite as an opponent and attacked his views in detail.[2] That is to say, Bodin conceives the State as a natural and necessary feature of human life and studies it upon historical lines. Political science is for him, as for Aristotle and Machiavelli, an inductive study with its own rules, not a department of theology. And his main doctrine is, as has been said by Mesnard, an affirmation of 'the value and power of order'.[3]

Here then we see both religious and secular approaches to the problems raised by the Reformation controversies moving slowly and as yet unconsciously towards the solution of the problem of religion and civil society to be canonised in the nineteenth century in Cavour's slogan of 'a free Church in a free State'. However much opposed by the Ultramontanes of Cavour's day his principle owes something historically to the sixteenth-century Jesuits as well as to the *politiques*. A new phase in the old problem is beginning to open and, since I have deliberately restricted the scope of this examination of Church and State relations to early and medieval times, I may here take leave of my subject. The conception of an identity of Christian Church and Christian State, originating, as we have seen, from the moment of Constantine's conversion, though with earlier adumbrations, was slow in dying, and indeed is not yet dead. In England, it was maintained against both Puritan and Separatist until it broke down in the Civil War.

[1] H. Butterfield, *The Whig Interpretation of History* (London, 1931), pp. 83-84.
[2] Allen, *Political Thought in the Sixteenth Century*, p. 403.
[3] 'Elle consiste avant tout à affirmer la valeur et la puissance de l'ordre' (Mesnard, *L'Essor de la philosophie politique*, p. 546).

There at the close of the sixteenth century it was given classic, but already outmoded, expression by Hooker. The *Ecclesiastical Polity* is the swan song of a great ideal. In the nineteenth century it was still defended in modified form by Gladstone, who lived to give the lie to it in his later policy. It still finds patrons in thinkers of our own day. But it could not succeed in practice in the post-Reformation world, driven by sheer pressure of events to accept the notion of states as secular entities and of churches as voluntary associations within them. How far that conception is still crumbling beneath the pressure upon societies, external and internal, which has led to modern totalitarianism is a matter beyond my aim, and would require treatment at length. But it is clearly at this point that what I have intended to be primarily an historical survey of the relations of Church and State in the first millennium and a half of Christianity comes most closely into context with modern problems.

EPILOGUE

It is not my intention to draw a moral from the tale I have tried to tell. To do so would be to run the risk of introducing a distorting element into what has striven to be as objective a treatment of the theme as possible. But it would perhaps be insanely purist to close this series of lectures without any word of what seems to emerge from the long historical pilgrimage in which you have so patiently joined with me. Let this, then, be said shortly. As I tried to study a subject of undoubted fascination and complexity, it has been borne in upon me more and more that the real problem of Church and State arises from one fact. Christianity is a religion not easily fitted into the categories of natural human life. The secularist would say that this is because it is unnatural, a dream out of relation to the realities of human life. The Christian would reply that the reason is that Christianity is supernatural, so that the real recalcitrance comes, not from nature, but from fallen human nature which has lost the supernatural element given it at its creation. Ideally grace builds upon nature and does not destroy it. Upon fallen nature its action is bound to be partly surgical and therefore disturbing. But, in so doing, the Christian would feel bound to add that his faith has never professed to fulfil itself in this world alone, because it contains an eschatological element, essential to it and singularly resistant to attempts to explain it away. 'My kingdom is not of this world'[1] is a text which (in the manner of Johannine texts) seems more and more profound the more it is meditated. So Augustine, the greatest Christian philosopher of history, found his *City of God* inevitably leading up to the eschatological section which ends the book—inevitably, because the story is without a real *dénouement* in this world. May it not be that the many minds which have sought in vain a tidy formula for the ideal relations of Church and State in a sinful world have failed because their task was like that of mixing oil and water or yoking together incompatible animals of the plough? Certainly no attempt here examined seems to be perfectly self-consistent or

[1] John xviii. 36.

171

stands up fully to the logic of facts. Is it possible that men have sought a synthesis where they could expect to find only a *modus vivendi*?

In any case, the latter is all that, in my opinion, anyone may expect to find in the days that are coming, for I cannot regard the revived interest shown today in theocratic systems of the past—especially in those which postulate an identity of Church and State—as anything more than an illustration of the truth that men cling closest to that which is perishing—sometimes to the shadow of that which has already perished. The problem before Christianity in any foreseeable future is not that of adjustment to the State, but one of survival in the face of a State with ever-increasing claims and ambitions—until at last Leviathan collapses under his own weight. Nevertheless, I make bold to suppose that a study of past efforts to correlate natural and supernatural human society may not be without its uses in facing this problem also.

INDEX

Aaron, 9
Acacius, Patriarch of Constantinople, 75
Acton, Lord, 167
Adoptianist heresy, 93, 94
Alans, 84
Alaric, King of the Visigoths, 84, 87
Albert, Archduke of Austria, 132
Alcuin, 94
Alexander, Bishop of Alexandria, 52
Alexander the Great, 63
Alexander III, Pope, 124
Alexander VI, Pope, 130
Alexander Balas, 13
Alexander Jannaeus, 13
Alföldi, Andrew, 47, 51
Allen, Professor J.W., 144-145, 161, 167
Altar of Victory, the, 59
Amann, Émile, 96
Ambrose, St., 50
Anabaptists, 154, 163
Anagni, 131
Anastasius the Librarian, 94
Andler, Charles, 154
'Anonymous of York', 134
Ansegisus, Abbot of St.Wandrille, 93
Antichrist, 19
Antiochus Epiphanes, 12, 33
Anulinus, Proconsul of Africa, 54
Apocalypticism, 20-21, 36-40, 154
Apologists, 36, 37, 38
Appeal to the Christian Nobility of the German Nation . . . (Luther), 139, 152
Appellants, 27
Aquileia, province of, 90
Aragon, 103, 104
Arian church, the, 88
Arian controversy, 57, 58, 60, 86
Arianism, 48, 57, 58, 60, 86, 87, 88, 89; Germanic Arianism, 86, 97, 106
Aristotle, 167, 169
Arius, 57
Arles, Council of, 47, 55, 56
Arles, Province of, 89
Arquillière, H.-X., 113, 118, 119, 124
Artemis of the Ephesians, 23
Athanasius, St., 53, 57, 59, 61

Athaulf, King of the Visigoths, 84, 86
Athens, 3
Augustine, St., 19, 34, 55, 124, 171
Augustus, 35, 43, 63
Avignon Papacy, 133

Bancroft, Richard, Archbishop of Canterbury, 27
Barak, 9
Barry, Dr. Alfred, 6
Basil, St., 61
Batiffol, Mgr. Pierre, 52
Bellarmine, Cardinal, 131, 164, 167
Bernard, St., 120
Bevan, Sir Edwyn, 14
Beza, Theodore, 162, 163; Du droit des magistrats sur leurs sujets, 162
Bishops, 25, 47, 51, 53-56, 60, 61-62, 69, 75, 88-94, 107-109, 112, 113-114, 117, 125-126
Bithynia, 30
Bloch, Marc, 102
Bodin, Jean, 168, 169
Böhmer, Heinrich, 134
Boissier, Gaston, 49
Bologna, 127
Boniface VIII, Pope, 72, 130, 131, 132
Borgia, Cesare, 130
Borino, G. B., 112, 113
Boswell, James, 59
Britain, 33
Brooke, Professor Z. N., 113, 134
Bruno of Toul, see under Leo IX, Pope
Brutus, 60
Burckhardt, Jacob, 45
Burgundy, 89
Burney, C. F., 6
Butterfield, Professor Herbert, 168
Byrd, William, 27
Byzantium, 66-80, 95, 97, 117; Byzantine ecclesiastical policy, 96, 97; Byzantine tradition of Church and State, 165

Caecilian, Bishop of Carthage, 54
Caesaro-papism, 59, 72, 73, 76
Calixtus II, Pope, 113

Calvin, John, 150, 156, 157, 158, 159, 160, 162, 163, 164
Calvinism, 155, 156, 157, 158, 159, 160, 161, 162, 164, 166; in France, 156, 161, 162
Calvinists, 45, 166
Cartagena, 91
Caspar, Erich, 45, 113
Castellion, Sébastien, 165
Catechetical School of Alexandria, 28
Cato, 3
Cavour, Count C. B., 169
Chalcedon, Council of, 61, 73
Charlemagne, Emperor, 74, 93, 94, 95, 96, 97, 99
Charles II (the Bald), Emperor, 102
Charles VIII, King of France, 143
Chasidim, 13
Chrysopolis, Battle of, 44
Civil Law, Roman, 127
Civilitas, 85
Clayton, Professor I. W., 30 n.
Clement of Alexandria, 37
Clovis, King of the Franks, 49, 87, 90
Coërcitio, 31
Commodus, Emperor, 28, 82
Conciliar Movement, 141
Consilium de emendanda ecclesia, 128
Constans II, Emperor, 73
Constantine the Great, 41, 42, 43-58, 59, 64, 70, 76, 79, 82, 93, 98, 99, 122, 169
Constantine V, Emperor, 75
Constantinople, see under Byzantium
Constantinople, Second Council of, 73
Constantius Chlorus I, Emperor, 43
Constantius II, Emperor, 58, 61, 72
Counter-Reformation, the, 160
Cromwell, Thomas, 135

Dante, 122, 133
David, 10, 70, 150
Deborah, 9
Decius, Emperor, 27, 41, 47, 48
De concordantia catholica (Nicholas of Cusa), 141

Defensor Pacis, 135
De monarchia (Dante), 133
De unitate ecclesiae conservanda, 115
Devotio moderna, 139
Dictatus Papae, 112, 113
Diocletian, Emperor, 43, 52; Diocletian's persecution, 41
Diodorus Siculus, 4
Divine kingship, 3-5, 6-7, 34, 60, 70-71
Donatism, 48, 54, 55, 56, 58, 61, 62
Double Procession of the Holy Spirit, quarrel about, 95
Du droit des magistrats sur leurs sujets (Beza), 162
Durham, Palatinate of, 108
Dvornik, F., 78

Eborius, Bishop of York, 47
Ecclesiastical Polity (Hooker), 170
Ecthesis, Heraclius's, 73
Edict of Milan, 50
Edict of Union, see under Henoticon
Eigenkirchen, 105, 106
England, 159, 160, 161
Ephesus, 23; Council of, 61
Epicureanism, 35
Epistle to Diognetus, 36
Erasmus, 67
Etatin, Nigeria, 5
Europe, Central and Eastern, 160
Eusebius of Caesarea, 44, 45, 53, 59
Eusebius of Nicomedia, 53
Evans-Pritchard, Professor E. E., 5
Ezekiel, 11

Febvre, Lucien, 140
Felix, Bishop of Aptunga, 54
Felix, Bishop of Urgel, 94
Feudalism, effects of, upon the Church, 99-109
Figgis, J. N., 140, 164
Filmer, Sir Robert, 164
Fliche, A., 111
Fliche et Martin, Histoire de l'Église, 105
Flood, the, 143
Foederati, 84
Fourth Crusade, 125

France, 83, 90, 93, 107, 126, 159, 160, 161, 162, 164, 165, 166, 168; Merovingian, 99; French authorities, 130; French monarchy, 161, 166
Frankfort, Council of, 93, 95
Frankfort, Professor and Mrs. Henri, 2, 7 n.
Frankish Church, 90, 93, 96
Franks, the, 83, 86, 94, Catholic, 90
Frazer, Sir James, 3, 4
Frederick I (Barbarossa), Emperor, 114, 124
Frederick II, Emperor, 114, 123, 125, 132
Frederick William III, King of Prussia, 45, 46
'Free church in a free State', 169
Freeman, E. A., 82
Fustel de Coulanges, N. D., 23 n., 24 n.

Galerius, Emperor, 43, 47
Gaul, 85; Visigoths in, 84; Visigothic kingdom of Southern Gaul, 83, 89
Gelasius I, Pope, 115
Génestal, R., 126
Geneva, 158, 160, 162, 164, 166
Gerbert of Aurillac, see under Silvester II, Pope
Germanus, Patriarch of Constantinople, 75
Germany, 81, 82, 155, 159
Gibbon, Edward, 45, 52, 68, 80, 81, 82, 84
Gierke, Otto, 128
Giles of Rome, 132
Gladstone, W. E., 170
Gobineau, Count J. A. de, 82
Goering, Hermann, 25
Goths, 81, 83, 84, 87, 88; Spanish Goths, 90
Gough, J. W., 164
Gratian, Canonist, 127
Great Interregnum, the, 129
Gregory I (the Great), Pope, 91
Gregory VII, St., Pope, 72, 110, 111, 112, 113, 115, 118, 123, 124
Gregory IX, 125
Gregory of Tours, St., 49, 52, 82
Guntram, King of Burgundy, 91

Hadrian I, Pope, 95
Hallam, Henry, 104
Hampton Court Conference, 53
Hardy, E. G., 31
Harnack, Adolf von, 45, 47 n.
Hartmann, Ludo Moritz, 69
Hasmonean family, 12-13, 14, 109
Heliogabalus, Emperor, 82
Henoticon, of Zeno, 72, 75
Henry III, Emperor, 111
Henry IV, Emperor, 110, 111, 113; at Canossa, 124
Henry IV (of Navarre), King of France, 45, 46, 161, 165
Henry V, Emperor, 113, 114
Henry VIII, King of England, 129, 135
Heraclius, Emperor, 73, 78, 79
Hermas, 37
Herod the Great, 13
Herods, Idumean, 13
Hezekiah, 11
Hildebrand, see under Gregory VII, St., Pope
Hildebrandine movements, 109
Hinduism, 33, 35
Hobbes, Thomas, 80, 141
Hohenstaufen, House of, 122
Holl, Karl, 153
Holland, 139, 159, 160, 165
Holy Roman Empire, 121
Honorius, Emperor, 98
Hooker, Richard, 170
Horus, 3
Hosius, Bishop of Cordova, 53
Hospitalitas, 85
Huguenot political theory, 164
Huguenotism, 166
Huguenots, 160, 161, 165
Huizinga, J., 120
Humbert, Cardinal, 110, 111
Huss, John, 139

Iconoclasm, 74, 75, 94, 95
Iconoclastic controversy, 74, 93
Identity of Church and State, 1-5, 12-13, 22-24, 57-59, 62-64, 78-80, 88-98, 115-116, 135-136, 154-155, 165-170

Ignatius, Bishop of Antioch, 28
Imbart de la Tour, P., 154
Imitation of Christ (à Kempis), 139
Innocent III, Pope, 72, 125
Innocent IV, Pope, 122, 124, 125
Isidore of Seville, St., 91
Islam, 69, 77
Italy, 99, 137; Ostrogoths in, 83
Iustitia, 123

Jacobs, Joseph, 10
James I, King of England, 53; *True Law of Free Monarchies*, 132
James of Viterbo, 132
Japan, 25 n.
Jesuits, 167, 169
John of Paris, 132
John Chrysostom, St., 61
Jonathan, High Priest, 12
Josephus, 8, 9, 13, 14
Josiah, 11
Judas Maccabeus, 12, 15
Judges, the, 9, 163
Julian, Emperor, 58
Justinian, Emperor, 75, 79, 87

Kern, Fritz, 104
Kingsley, Charles, 82
Knox, Dr.Wilfred, 17

Lactantius, 39, 43, 44
Lagarde, Georges de, 136, 158, 159
Landeskirchen, 88, 90, 97, 99
Last, Professor Hugh, 32, 33 n.
Lateran Basilica, the, 51
Lay control of religion, 10-11, 52-59, 72-75, 88-96, 105-109, 135-136, 148, 152-155, 168-169
Leo IV (the Isaurian), Emperor, 75
Leo VI, Emperor, 74
Leo IX, Pope, 109
Lewis the Bavarian, Emperor, 133, 134
Liber Gomorrhianus (St. Peter Damian), 109
Liberalism, 165
Libri Carolini, 94, 96
Licinius, Emperor, 43, 50
Lightfoot, Bishop J. B., 121

Loewe, Dr. Herbert, 18 and n.
Lombards, 86, 91
Lombardy, 89, 99; bishops of, 89
Lot, Ferdinand, 41
Louis I (the Pious), Emperor, 93
Low Countries, *see under* Holland
Lucretius, 120
Luther, Martin, 129, 135, 143, 146, 147, 148, 149, 150, 151, 152, 153, 154, 155, 156, 157, 162; *Appeal to the Christian Nobility of the German Nation*, 139, 152; *Von weltlicher Oberkeit*, 153
Lutheran policy, 156
Lutheran Reformation, 160
Lutheranism, 156, 157, 159, 166
Lutherans, the, 45

Maccabean rebellion, the, 14, 33
Machiavelli, N., 144, 145, 149, 169
Magyars, 99
Manichaeism, 32
Marcia, 28
Marie-Antoinette, Queen, 67
Marinus, Bishop of Arles, 55
Maritain, Jacques, 131
Marsilian theory of Church and State, 152
Marsilius of Padua, 133, 135, 136, 148; *Defensor Pacis*, 135
Martyrdom of Polycarp, 22
Marxists, 149
Maternus, Bishop of Cologne, 55
Mattathias, 12
Maurienne, bishopric of, founded, 91
Maxentius, 43, 44, 47, 48
Maximin Daia, 43
'Melchites', 63
Melchizedek, 71
Merrill, E. T., 22 n.
Mesnard, Pierre, 153, 169
Messiah, the, 16-17, 20, 21, 35
Messianism, 12, 14, 16-17, 20-21, 35
Miltiades, Pope, 54, 60
Milvian Bridge, battle of the, 44, 49
Mishnah, The, 19 n.
Momigliano, A., 29 n.
Mommsen, Theodor, 31 and n.
Monophysitism, 63, 73, 74, 77

Monothelism, 73
More, Sir Thomas, 129; *Utopia*, 143
Moses, 8, 9, 150, 163
Muhammadan invasions, 77
Münster, 154

Naples, kingdom of, 123
Napoleon I, Emperor, 45, 46
Nero, Emperor, 29, 30, 82
Nestorianism, 63, 73
Nestorians, 68
Nestorius, 73
Netherlands, *see under* Holland
Newman, J. H., 37
Nicaea, 56, 93; Council of, 53, 57;
    Second Council of, 94, 95
Nicene faith, 87
Nicholas II, Pope, 112
Nicholas Mysticus, Patriarch of Con-
    stantinople, 75
Nicholas of Cusa, *De concordantia cath-
    olica*, 141
Nicomedia, 43
Nogaret, Guillaume de, 131
Nominalism, 139

Obedience, duty of, 16-20, 35-36, 38-
    40, 59-60, 73-75, 103-104, 127-129,
    138-139, 139 n., 152-153, 155-156,
    162-165
Occamism, 137
Ockham, William of, 134, 135
Odin, 81, 86
Oesterley, W. O. E., 10 n., 12 n., 17 n.
Optatus, St., of Mileris, 58
Orléans, 90
Orosius, 84, 87
Ostrogoths, 83
Otto III, Emperor, 110
Oxenstierna, Count Axel, 49

Pakistan, 16
Papacy, 12, 47, 54-55, 72, 74, 88, 93,
    95, 109-115, 121-125, 140-141, 147,
    167
Paschal II, Pope, 114, 125
Patronatus, 101
Paul, St., 19, 24, 29; the *Epistle to the
    Romans*, 19

Pax Romana, 39
Pelagianism, 149
Persecution, 22-35, 48, 51, 57-59, 73-
    74, 87, 122-125, 153-155, 162, 165
Peter, St., 19
Peter Damian, St., 110, 111; *Liber
    Gomorrhianus*, 109
Petrarch, 67
Pharaohs of Egypt, the, 3, 4, 7
Pharisees, 15, 17
Philip IV (the Fair), King of France,
    130, 131, 132
Pilate, Pontius, 29
Pirenne, H., 66
Pliny, 30, 32, 33
Pole, Cardinal Reginald, 128
Politiques, 168, 169
Polycarp, Bishop of Smyrna and
    martyr, 25
Pontifex maximus, 48, 59
Powicke, Sir Maurice, 103
Predestinarianism, 137
Procopius, 75
Puritanism, 160
Pusey, E. B., *Eirenicon*, 37

Ravenna, Archbishop of, 90
Rē, 3
Regalia, Imperial, 125
Regnum, 115, 118, 127
Reticius, Bishop of Autun, 55
Richelieu, Cardinal, 161
Roman Catholicism in England, per-
    secution of, 26-27
Romanitas, 35
Rousseau, J.-J., 79, 136
Russia, 26

Sacerdotium, 115, 118, 127
Sadducees, 15, 17
Saisset, Bernard, Bishop of Pamiers,
    130
Salvian of Marseilles, 82
Samuel, 9, 10
Sanior pars, 163
Saul, 10
Saxony, 156
Scandinavia, 99, 159
Schwartz, Eduard, 45, 47, 54

Scotist tradition, 150
Scotland, 159, 160, 162
Seeck, Otto, 54
Servetus, 162
Shamanism, 8
Shilluk, the, 5
Sidonius Apollinaris, 83
Silvester II, Pope, 110
Simon, High Priest, 13
Smith, A. L., 122, 124
Smyrna, 25
Snaith, Norman H., 7 n.
Societates perfectae, 167
Solomon, 10, 13, 150
Sophia, St., mosaics at, 71
Spain, 90, 91; Adoptianist heresy in, 93; Goths in, 90; Visigothic Spain, 92
Spanish bishops, the, 93
Stilicho, 87
Stutz, Ulrich, 105, 106
Sueves, 84
Switzerland, 156

Tacitus, 29
Tallis, Thomas, 27
Tertullian, 20, 25, 27, 30, 35, 37, 38, 39, 40
Teutonic deities, 71; paganism, 97
Teutons, 98
Theocracy, 8-9, 14, 65-80, 99-119, 121-122, 130, 134, 156-159
Theodore of Mopsuestia, 73
Theodoric the Great, King of the Ostrogoths, 85, 87
Theodosius I, Emperor, 86
Theudebert I, King of Austrasia, 90
Thomas Aquinas, St., 167
Thomism, 167
Three Chapters, 73, 75

Toledo, Archbishop of, 91
Toledo, archbishopric of, founded, 91
Toledo, Councils of, 91, 92
Toynbee, Arnold, 37
Trajan, Emperor, 30, 32
True Law of Free Monarchies (James I), 132
Turin, Bishop of, 91
Type, 73

Ullmann, Walter, 128
Ultramontanes, 169
Unam Sanctam, Bull, 131
Utopia (More), 143

Valens, Emperor, 61, 72
Vandals, 81, 83, 84, 87
Vigilius, Pope, 73
Vignaux, P., 136
Visigothic kingdom, 89
Visigoths, 83, 84, 87; Spanish, 91, 92
Vitale, San, at Ravenna, mosaics at, 71
Voigt, Karl, 88
Von weltlicher Oberkeit (Luther), 153

Williams, Dr. A. Lukyn, 6
Witenagemot, 75
Woodward, Sir Llewellyn, 63
Woolf, C. N. S., 98 n.
Worms, Concordat of, 113
Wycliffe, John, 138

Yahweh, 12 n.
York, 43, 47, 134

Zealotry, 15
Zeno, Emperor, 72-73, 75
Zerubbabel, 11
Zoë, 74
Zürich, 156
Zwingli, Huldreich, 156